GURRUMUL

GURRUMUL

HIS LIFE AND MUSIC

Robert Hillman

ABC
Books

When Gurrumul asked how he looked in this photo shoot, Michael described his shirt as black with a strong collar, and Gurrumul exclaimed 'Ahhh black's my grandmother's colour', and when he was told he had a gold suit, he said 'Ahhh Gumatj' his clan's colour of fire. It was truly a modern representation of traditional dress.

This book is for my family,
for the Yolŋu people of my home,
and for the people who love my music.
Thank you walal *(everyone).*

Gurrumul

OF ELCHO

UP CLOSE

3
OF FAME

ON RECORD

Author's Note

I first glimpsed Geoffrey Gurrumul Yunupiŋu in the foyer of the ABC's Melbourne studios in 2008, not long after the release of his solo album *Gurrumul*. Technicians bustled around him, setting up mics, draping cables across the floor, fashioning an impromptu stage. I was leaving the studios after spruiking a book I'd written about an Afghani refugee, and the subject of the book was with me, full of curiosity about this quiet Indigenous man in a black leather jacket. 'Robert, who is this person?'

I paused before saying anything, unsure of my answer. 'It's Gurrumul, I think. He's a singer.'

My friend said: 'Oh, I heard this man on the radio!'

We went on our way, my friend pestering me for more details about Gurrumul's life — information I couldn't provide. 'Is he blind, as they say?' 'How old is he?' 'Where does he live?' 'What language does he speak?' And, oddly, 'Has he been to Afghanistan?' That last question was the only one I could answer with any confidence: 'I doubt it.'

If my friend were to ask me these same questions now, I would be able to reel off answers one after another. I learnt all that I know of Gurrumul by following him from concert to concert, into recording studios and all the way to Elcho Island. I interviewed friends and family, musicians, professional colleagues; I gathered yarns, anecdotes, a great many facts, a great many figures. And I expanded by many degrees of magnitude my understanding of Indigenous culture, without ever feeling that I'd grasped more than a handful of red earth from the mountain of lore and learning that rears above Gurrumul and his people. But what I did learn, I am grateful for. When I was first introduced to Gurrumul at a concert in Melbourne, I thought: 'Soon I'll know everything.' The 'everything' that I learnt deepened my understanding of his genius, yes, but in every important way he remains to me what he was on stage at that concert in Melbourne: a man of his people, the heir to an incomparably rich culture that, happily, he is prepared to share with the world.

When I told my Afghani friend that I was writing the story of Gurrumul and was about to travel to Elcho Island, he said: 'Robert, bring me back his music,' as if anyone who wished to listen to Gurrumul's albums would have to receive them from the hand of the man himself. I did what my friend asked of me, and returned with an album for him. He telephoned me when he'd listened to it all the way through and said it was 'the most beautiful of all music'. The journey I have prepared for readers of this book will, I hope, deepen their appreciation of Gurrumul's brilliance. But I must confess, even the most conscientious reader is going to come by the most vital knowledge he or she will ever possess about Gurrumul by taking his superb solo albums, *Gurrumul*, *Rrakala* and the album that accompanies this book, sliding them into a CD player and listening. That's how I learnt about Gurrumul, and that is how my friend arrived at his heartfelt review: 'The most beautiful of all music.'

Susan Gurruwiwi reviews an early draft of the manuscript.

A Note from Skinnyfish Music

MARK T GROSE

In the mid 1980s I was working as a teacher with a group of young Indigenous men in Derby in the Kimberley. These young men were completely taken by an Aboriginal band called Warumpi and particularly the song 'Black fella White fella'. Warumpi were their idols and by association Warumpi became my favourite as well. On one of my trips back to Geelong to see my mother, I was asked about a band called Yothu Yindi and how popular they were 'up north', I had to admit that I had never heard of Yothu Yindi and that Warumpi were all the rage in the Kimberley.

A year or two later, I had the opportunity to see Yothu Yindi perform live and thoroughly enjoyed what they were about but I still believed that Warumpi were the better band. At no time during that concert did I notice a blind musician in the band nor did I hear any exceptional musicianship but that was to be expected; I know nothing about music, I just know what I like.

In 1996 I found myself on Elcho Island and quickly learnt the history of its most famous musician George Rrurrambu. I was thrilled one day when he turned up at the office, and the legend I had heard about and the hero of the young men of Derby was standing right there in front of me. On a couple of occasions I saw in the distance a young man being escorted about and when people noticed I was looking at him, they would whisper to me 'that's Gurrumul, he was in Yothu Yindi'. I never got to meet Gurrumul until after Michael Hohnen had finished his music workshop, so for a couple of years I was intrigued by this musician that I never noticed at the Yothu Yindi concert in Geelong and I was intrigued by this Island that had produced the legendary George and the seemingly legendary Gurrumul. I went on to manage Saltwater and Gurrumul, and found out that when I was about 15, Gurrumul and I both lived in Geelong at the same time. Now we both live on Elcho Island.

The young baby that was in Geelong when I was 15, the musician that I did not notice at a concert, the mysterious figure I would see in the distance had an enormous impact on my life, changing it forever, leaving me eternally grateful that I had entered the Yolŋu world.

MICHAEL HOHNEN

I have lived in Australia's Top End and Yolŋu country for nearly 20 years. In making my life here, for myself and my own family, I have come to appreciate the unique and extraordinary lives of Aboriginal people in Australia — their stories, music, art and culture.

All the people I have met in the Territory's remote communities and outstations with their different languages and ways of seeing the world we live in, have so much to teach someone like me, from the city, and are inextricably linked with my relationship with Gurrumul. From the tiny outstations and communities; to the members of Manmoyi's country-rock band, Nabarlek; to the extroverted Gumatj trail blazer, George Rrurrumbu; the genius poetry, songs and mentorship of Tom E Lewis, June and Ali Mills; the Tiwis (old and young); the people of Port Keats; the island life of Minjilang; the women of Borrolloola; the families at Ngukurr and many, many more. I have embraced their world and been embraced by it — and it has changed my life.

With Mark Grose, my business partner, and my family's support, care and blessing I have had the opportunity to work, and make music with Gurrumul, this clever, sharp, funny, intuitive, sensitive, brutally honest and talented man. It has been a privilege and an honour to have been given his ongoing trust and to be part of his story and music — and to share the richness of the unique culture of our Indigenous peoples with audiences, small and large, all over the world.

Skinnyfish Music is a Darwin-based company which records and promotes the work of Indigenous musicians. The philosophy behind this business is to empower Indigenous Australians to generate and pursue their own creative and economic activity. Established in 1998 by Mark Grose (Managing Director) and Michael Hohnen (Creative Director), Skinnyfish Music works in partnership with artists and their communities to produce music by, about and for them, and to take their music to the wider world. The company's aim is to provide opportunities for and to nurture the talents of artists who hail from communities across Australia and the region from Timor to Tasmania, through recording, distribution, publishing and performance.

Acknowledgments

FROM THE AUTHOR

With demands on their time from a hundred people each day, Michael Hohnen and Mark Grose of Skinnyfish Music somehow found the leisure to answer my many, many questions and to contribute with such grace and patience to this book. Helen Littleton, of ABC Books, who commissioned Gurrumul's story, and Julia Collingwood who edited the manuscript, will, I hope, accept this acknowledgment in recognition of the intelligence and tact seen everywhere in their comments. John Greatorex allowed me to plunder his subtle and extensive understanding of the Yolŋu people, so often revealing the rough-hewn quality of my own observations. Michael Chugg, Craig Pilkington and Francis Diatschenko provided tales and anecdotes of working with Gurrumul and Yothu Yindi that I could not have found anywhere else. Ann Dillon read the developing manuscript and made suggestions that were always affectionately astute and to the point. The generous contribution of Michelle Dowden who helped me better understand Indigenous culture and the loving relationship of Gurrumul, Michael Hohnen and Mark Grose. Gurrumul's aunts, Dorothy Gurruwiwi, Ann Gurruwiwi and Susan Dhäŋgal Gurruwiwi, and his uncle, David Djuŋa Yunupiŋu, offered me insights into Yolŋu culture that will stay with me forever. Manuel Dhurrkay listened to pages of the work-in-progress on the verandah of his home in Galiwin'ku, and was kind enough to laugh at the right places. Penny Arrow, the Skinnyfish manager, was helpful in a dozen ways over the period of the book's composition. Julie Herd, who met Gurrumul on Elcho Island when he was still a baby, shared her memories and letters with me in a way that has enriched the story told here. And I must thank Gurrumul himself, such a private man, for accepting intrusions into his life, and for so fully embracing a project that must have seemed, at times, a little crazy in its determination to put a living man between the two covers of a book.

Robert Hillman

The Yolŋu alphabet

The song lyrics presented in this book are written in English and several Yolŋu languages. The Yolŋu alphabet has seven more characters than English. Yolŋu languages are written using the special characters Ä ä Ŋ ŋ N̲ n̲ T̲ t̲ D̲ d̲ L̲ l̲ and '. People interested in learning from Yolŋu, and from an ancient but also vibrant and modern culture can visit the Yolŋu Studies website: www.cdu.edu.au/yolngu/. On this website there is information on the academic program, current research, Yolŋu stories and images, and resources. The Yolŋu Studies team comprises a group of senior Yolŋu advisers from five major towns and homelands, and staff from Charles Darwin University. The Yolŋu advisers guide the program which began over seventeen years ago. In 2005, the Yolŋu Studies team were awarded the Prime Minister's Award for University Teacher of the Year.

FROM SKINNYFISH MUSIC

The journey to this point has been 15 years in the making — an amazing journey that has culminated *Gurrumul: His Life and Music*. Producing this book has been an extraordinary experience, it has opened our eyes to just how many wonderful people have been involved in our crazy journey. We started Skinnyfish Music with a business idea that appeared to be impossible, and for that reason we never dared do a business plan in case we came to the conclusion that we were both completely mad! The musicians in Saltwater and Nabarlek were the first to support us — the first to place their trust in us to help them realise a dream. They were instrumental in helping us realise *our* dream.

We owe a sincere debt of gratitude to so many: Duane Preston and Matty McHugh both Skinnyfish photographers whose love of working in the bush is clearly seen in their beautiful photos; Sam Karinikos for the greatest album cover photo ever; Julie Herd and Matthew McClelland who supplied personal photos and stories about their time at Galiwin'ku. To Brendan and Eliza Loechel for pointing us in the right direction towards some amazing photos. Merrkiyawuy Ganambarr and Witiyana Marika for sharing their memories of Gurrumul's time in Yothu Yindi. The wonderful Gurruwiwi sisters (Dorothy, Susan and Anne) who in their gracious style shared so many affectionate memories of their nephew right from the time he was a baby. David Djuŋa Yunupiŋu for his constant support and encouragement.

To John Greatorex and Michael Christie for their contribution to ensuring the correctness of the Yolŋu cultural content and who as always, go beyond the call of duty. To Carly Bancroft, Clancy Breasley and Penelope Arrow who have been instrumental in searching scanning and soliciting content for this book and chasing up every loose end. To Gillian Harrison for checking, inspecting and correcting much of what we do. Francis Diatschenko deserves a special mention for his patience and dedication to the task of performing with and caring for Gurrumul on tour. To Michael Chugg one of the music industry's heavy weights who has great affection for Gurrumul and who did not hesitate in making a contribution. To all the photographers who have given their permission for us to use their fantastic shots.

A special thanks to all who have supported Gurrumul as fans, reviewers and radio hosts, espececially Bruce Elder and Deb Cameron whose support ignited the Gurrumul explosion.

To the wonderful Helen Littleton from ABC Books at HarperCollins who rang Skinnyfish at exactly the right time to ask if we were interested in a Gurrumul book, and to Julia Collingwood and Madeleine James who along with Helen has shown too much patience and understanding towards us. Thanks also to Matt Stanton's art direction to which the final package owes so much.

Thank you especially to Robert Hillman who has approached the task of writing a biography on someone who never speaks about himself, with great humour and a love of the task that is well beyond just doing a job. A big thank you to our partners Michelle Dowden and Kirrily Pfitzner — the journey of Skinnyfish Music and this project would never have realised its potential without their complete support and understanding.

Lastly Gurrumul's mum Daisy and dad Terry for the love and care that got their son to where he is. This book would not have been possible without their consent and the trust placed in Michael and I over these last few exciting years.

And thank you Gurrumul — our *Gathu* and *Wäwa*. We love you.

Mark Grose and Michael Hohnen

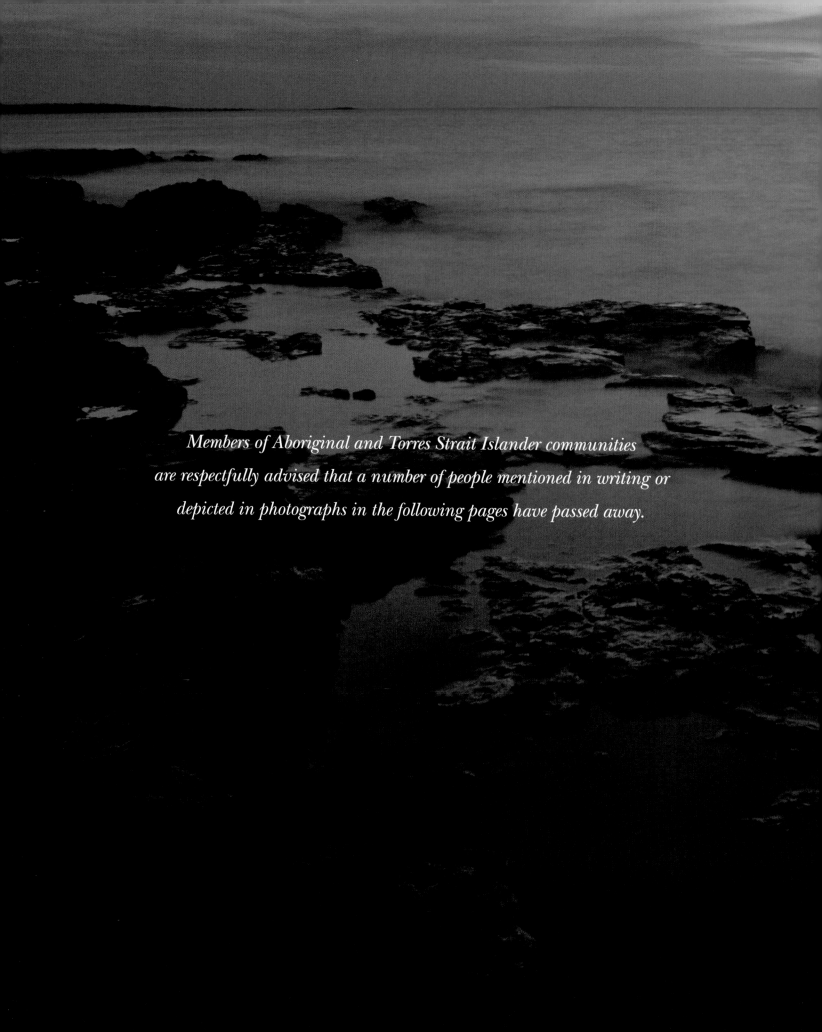

*Members of Aboriginal and Torres Strait Islander communities
are respectfully advised that a number of people mentioned in writing or
depicted in photographs in the following pages have passed away.*

GURRUMUL

HIS LIFE AND MUSIC

Listen

We come away from listening to Gurrumul with the word 'beautiful' on our lips. But where that beauty comes from, its richness and complexity — that's the wonder.

I've heard everything, but I haven't heard this before.

It's Geoffrey Gurrumul Yunupiŋu singing in Gälpu, Gumatj and Djambarrpuyŋu, Indigenous languages of north-east Arnhem Land and Elcho Island. A few thousand people in the world speak these languages but even those who don't know a word of them are drawn to listen. The song tells of Gurrumul's spirit ancestor Gopuru searching out the path of his kin, people he loves and honours. Gopuru takes for himself the freedom of the north-west wind skimming the sea; of the tall clouds that mass on the horizon. The wind has a name, Dirrmala, and the clouds have a name, Wanatjal. In the exuberance of his liberty and the joy of his quest, Gopuru soars and dives and becomes at once everything that shines, everything that moves with force and grace; waves, clouds, sea, wind.

The voice that has so captivated me, Gurrumul's voice, enjoys the same liberty as that of Gopuru, and undergoes the same transformations. It has a surface that shimmers like the skin of the ocean, a suggestion of powerful currents beneath. At times it fills out and floats like the clouds above the Arafura Sea. Whatever the song calls for — this song, the next and the next — the voice can accommodate: poignance, vigour, introspection, tenderness, soaring celebration, playfulness, wonder, and at times, a caressing sensuality.

And something else. Listeners come away from a Gurrumul performance eager to speak of beauty. But there are many beautiful voices, some at the top of the charts, some negotiating the nuances of a Schubert score. What Gurrumul's voice brings to his songs is a beauty wrought by a culture that has endured for millennia, holding fast to its integrity over two thousand generations.

Gurrumul's people have lived on the Australian continent through ages when the seas declined, and when the seas grew huge again and took back valleys and rivers and mountain ranges. They have experienced times of astonishment, dread, wonder and delight that lasted, not for moments or hours or days, but centuries; epochs of plenty that unfolded over a thousand years followed by a thousand years of struggle and hunger. The oldest narrative of the Australian continent in all its moods and secrets belongs to Indigenous people. It was the genius of Gurrumul's ancestors to uncover those secrets, so that they now inhabit Gurrumul and fashion the words of his songs. The beauty of those songs, the beauty of Gurrumul's singing is intimately related to the song-maps we know as 'songlines' that trace the path of travellers across the land, through the air, beneath the surface of the seas.

We come away from listening to Gurrumul with the word 'beautiful' on our lips. But where that beauty comes from, its richness and complexity — that's the wonder.

Gurrumul performs in English on occasion, but the full vigour of his voice is only revealed when he sings in his mother tongue. Maybe he feels a greater confidence in the meaning of words shaped in Gälpu, but I think it's also to do with the sheer love of the language he's used since infancy. He sings from the inside in Gälpu. These are the words that first drew him into the world, first fashioned the shapes and feelings that have been with him ever since. Without sight, the words would have come to him with a greater intimacy, perhaps a greater sensuality, than a sighted child would experience. It's there in Gurrumul's song of longing, 'Wiyathul', that feeling of the words being caressed as they emerge:

> *Märrma' djilawurr ŋäthinana, nambawu larruŋana Guwalilŋawu, rirrakayyunmina liyanydja milkarri, nambawu larruŋana Murrurrnawu …*

This is a song that tells of the cries of birds in the bush: scrub fowls, comrades of the Gumatj people, seeking the path back to places that may no longer exist. The cries of the scrub fowls echo the yearning of the singer for lost and longed-for places of his own, for sites of remembered delight, of comfort.

The Gälpu language in which Gurrumul sings has another vital role, perhaps the most important of all. Gälpu preserves the element of the sacred in Gurrumul's songs. This isn't to say that Gurrumul performs for the broad public the sacred songs of his people, songs that complement rituals — only that everything Gurrumul sings about is, in a sense, sacred.

The languages of Indigenous Australians, once numbering in the hundreds, have roots in even more ancient languages, in which the idea of the 'sacred' was first expressed. This is where the sacred begins, long before it's recorded on paper; in the heart and soul of people like Gurrumul. The spirit beings on the sandstone walls of caves in the Kimberley and at Anthwerrke not only depict the embodied forces of creation; they express some of the earliest attempts of humankind to bring the land and the stars, birth and death, rocks, rivers and the breadth of the oceans into a sacred alignment. What listeners to Gurrumul's voice and music hear is not simply 'beauty' but something that is the sound of life itself being honoured in its mysteries, its sorrows, its raptures.

You've heard everything, or you thought you had. But listen. This is Geoffrey Gurrumul Yunupiŋu of Elcho Island singing in the language of his people.

'One day that will be me' —
Gurrumul and the Saltwater
members are Elcho's local heroes.

1

UP CLOSE

CHAPTER 1

Botany

This is where it all begins, the stuff of his genius: from the rapture

of his engagement with the songs of his people.

The studio is a converted dwelling in a quiet backstreet of Botany; the airport ten minutes away to the north; Botany Bay, where the first white settlers caught their initial sight of the Australian continent, another ten minutes to the east. You enter through a room that was once the garage but which now functions as a sort of *salon fumeur*: a pair of armchairs against the wall, between them a small table stacked with magazines. The magazines are mostly *Rolling Stone* going back years and years, but deep in the stack is a well-thumbed copy of *New Idea* (yes, *New Idea*), old enough to feature Princess Mary of Tassie three months pregnant. An Elvis poster is displayed on one wall, the King circa 1966, just on the cusp of the coarsening that would eventually overtake him. He's a great favourite of Gurrumul's, Elvis.

The sun pours in through the aperture left by the raised roller door. It's a perfect Sydney summer's day, not hot enough to drive you mad but hot enough to get you down to the beach. The sky is an even, unbroken blue from horizon to horizon, as if it has been painted onto the ceiling of heaven with a tin of house paint and a giant roller. The warmth conjures that tang of liberty that you experience in Sydney on such a day as this, as if any crazy thing you might want to try is wide open to you.

The garage opens directly into the control room of the studio, fitted with a monster mix desk, multitrack recorders, an interface unit, computer monitors, a mix compressor, a hard disk recorder, computer processors and a keyboard. It looks like the cockpit of a spaceship, but more roomy. Electrical leads and computer cables run everywhere. A sofa sits against the back wall, away from the equipment. This is where you'd wait if your boyfriend's or girlfriend's band were recording, probably for hours — upright for the afternoon session, lengthways and semi-comatose as the evening wears on.

Beyond the glassed-in booth, another sofa rests against a wall with heavy vermillion drapes behind it falling from ceiling to floor in folds. A choir of mics are grouped on a dais,

The shoot for the cover of Rolling Stone *magazine in Australia. During the shoot Gurrumul asked: 'Did Dr Hook ever have to sit backwards for a photo?' He knew the song by Dr Hook, and saw the shoot as mainstream recognition of his contribution to the industry.*

DJILAWURR

Yä rirrakayyurruna Djilawurr manda, Goŋuŋa	Hear the crying of two Djilawurr, at Goŋuŋa
Roŋiyinana barrawalayu dharayarayu	Calling, thoughts going back to Barrawalayu, Dharayarayu
Yä bunbuŋa Djaŋadjaŋa, gulurrpuŋana	Building their nests
Yä ŋäthina, yä ŋäthina, Djilawurr manda gulurrpuŋana	Crying, crying, two Djilawurr calling
Gundawu wätthurruna dirrmalawu ŋurukuna	Calling out for that north-west wind, dirrmala
Rirrkay'yurruna wäyin Djaŋadjaŋa	That bird Djilawurr, calling out
Roŋiyinana Bekullili dhärriŋlili	Thoughts returning to Bekul, the old Makassan site
Yä ŋäthina, yä ŋäthina, Djilawurr manda gulurrpuŋana	Crying, crying, two Djilawurr calling
Djilawurr, wo..o gulurrpuma ŋunha marrtji wäyin	Djilawurr, that bird crying out
E..e rirrakay'yuna ŋunha marrtji Watjpalŋa	Crying out, that Djilawurr
Wo ŋurukuna wätthun ŋunha marrtji dirrmalawuna	Calling out for the north-west wind
E..e birrpuma ŋunha marrtji wäyin Rrumburaŋuru	Scratching the earth in the jungle at Rrumbura
Ŋuparana gurrwilŋayu dharayarayu	Following the bases of the jungle trees
Ya Gurrikurri Rrumburayu Galaniniyu	Oh, the jungles of Martjanba, Gurrikurri, Rrumbura,
Rirrakay'yurruna Djilawurr manda gombuŋa	Galanini
Roŋiyinana wäŋalili dhärriŋlili	Two Djilawurr calling out
Yä ŋäthina, yä ŋäthina djilawurr manda	Calling back to the Makassan sites
Gulurrpuŋana	Crying, crying, two Djilawurr crying
Djilawurr	Calling out
Djudukurrk giw giw	Djilawurr
	Djudukurrk giw giw

This austere version of the song that opened the robust second Saltwater album, *Djarridjarri*, defines what *Rrakala* hopes to accomplish by cleaving so close to the traditional. The Saltwater version creates a rich sense of worlds drawn together — the human and the non-human — while this version instead offers the skeleton of the poetry that supports the whole of Yolŋu culture. It's a choice between two types of beauty: one that asks you to look out into the world and one that turns your gaze inwards.

each mic costumed in a black cloth hoodie. It's a roomy space; the performance area hushed, welcoming, but empty at the moment. Gurrumul is expected to arrive any minute … or hour.

Gurrumul turns up in a taxi at three in the afternoon with his friend, mentor and collaborator Michael Hohnen. Michael takes Gurrumul's hand, tucks it under his arm and leads Gurrumul towards the studio. These two men — Michael, boyishly slim in his forties, and Gurrumul, shorter than Michael and broader — form a creative partnership unequalled in contemporary Australian music. And it's a genuine partnership. It's difficult to imagine that Gurrumul would have flourished over the past decade in the way he has without Michael's painstaking guidance. At the same time, Gurrumul's genius afforded Michael's particular gifts opportunities he might never have encountered elsewhere. It does no harm to think of it as destiny. Great talent rarely goes unrecognised, much less unexpressed. Thomas Gray spoke of the 'mute, inglorious Miltons', whose poetry, through circumstance, never found public acclaim, but there are probably far fewer unsung Miltons than Gray imagined. If there is a danger of a genius such as Gurrumul's becoming lost to the world, something happens; some shift in thinking that compels a Michael Hohnen to pack his bags and head north, searching out his own fulfilment and, in Michael's case, finding it in the company of a blind musician from Elcho Island.

Gurrumul, in faded jeans and an ancient brown T-shirt that's seen a thousand wash-and-rinse cycles, takes a seat near the stack of magazines while Michael organises the session with the sound engineer, Ted Howard. Gurrumul signals with a small gesture that the air-con has made the studio too chilly for a person who has spent his life in the wet tropics, and an adjustment is made. Now he moves his head in a slow arc, right to left, at the same time caressing with his fingertips the fabric of the armchair. Blind from birth, he has the habit of the unsighted of occupying a small space in which he feels secure, before fashioning a broader aural and tactile landscape; filling a canvas within his mind. His expression barely changes, and when it does it is to smile, sometimes secretively, as if wryly amused. He understands most of the English spoken within his hearing but is likely to respond, if he intends to respond at all, in one of Elcho's Indigenous languages. When he needs Michael's assistance, he gives a brief, two-note whistle, or if Michael is closer, calls for him peremptorily: 'Michael! Michael!' When he arrives, Michael speaks to him quietly in a mixture of Gumatj and English. One gets the sense of a profound rapport between the two of them, almost as if they are reading each other's thoughts and require only a type of shorthand to establish details. The rapport is evidently based on the respect felt by two artists of equal ability.

Michael leads Gurrumul into the studio and positions him beside an upholstered stool. A mic on an articulated arm is fixed just above the seat. Gurrumul's mobile phone rings and, as he responds, a shy delight spreads over his face. He holds the mobile pressed to his ear across the flat of his hand and talks to it in the way you would if you were speaking in a conspiratorial undertone to someone standing close. A song from yesterday's session is playing. Gurrumul holds the mobile up in order to capture the song for the person on the other end. Every so often he whispers into the phone. Then something in the voice — his own voice — seems suddenly to demand more concentration. He lifts his head higher and weaves it from side to side, intensely committed to what he's hearing. With his head raised, the whites of his sightless eyes show more distinctly. The face, on which so little expression appeared a few minutes earlier, is now all expression. He frowns, he smiles, he frowns again, maybe puzzled, maybe thinking of adjustments that need to be made to the song. He's hearing more than anyone else can hear, as if his ears distinguish not just the broad dozen points of an aural compass but a hundred. Still holding the mobile up to catch the song and still whispering, he shuffles within a small perimeter around the stool, lifts his free hand to stroke the back of his head, listening to what has been created with a force of concentration that seems to take him back to his origins on Elcho.

During the triumphant journey of recognition he has taken in the past decade, Gurrumul has, as the lyrics of his song 'Gurrumul History' tell it, 'been to New York, to LA, to London'; he's collaborated on stage with established stars such as Sarah Blasko, Missy Higgins, Sting; he's been lauded by critics; he's been introduced to world leaders and the celebrated. But this is where it all begins, the stuff of his genius: from the rapture of his engagement with the songs of his people.

Michael and Ted Howard are listening intently to yesterday's take, trading comments in the argot of the studio. The song concludes with a type of incantatory chant.

Gurrumul calls: 'Michael! Michael!'

Michael says: '*Wäwa, wäwa*!' ('Brother, brother!')

Gurrumul calls again: 'Michael! Michael!'

Gurrumul isn't wearing headphones and the lapse of communication with Michael makes him briefly anxious.

Michael calls, a little louder: '*Wäwa! Wäwa*!'

Ted says: 'A problem?'

'No, just the headphones.'

Michael leaves the booth and is quickly at Gurrumul's side. He picks up the headphones hanging from the back of the chair and places them in his friend's hand. All of Michael's movements are nimble; he's developed a deftness in assisting Gurrumul that he's ready to employ at a moment's notice.

Gurrumul puts his mobile aside and readies himself for the session. He speaks to Michael about the choice of song.

Michael says: 'Maybe those *bäru* songs.'

'The *bäru* songs?'

'Sure. What do you think?'

'Okay. *Bäru* songs. Good.'

Bäru is 'crocodile'. The crocodile is related to Gurrumul; at the foundation of his identity.

'You good?' says Gurrumul.

Michael says: 'We're good.'

Gurrumul lifts his head and from his throat comes a torrent of song as broad as a river. Michael, standing at the keyboard, marks the progress of this astonishing flow with the rich chords of melded strings and synthesiser. Gurrumul is singing into the mic but he could as well be filling a cathedral with his voice; or some vast space with a broad blue sky above it. Just at a glance, a crocodile mightn't seem the sort of creature to conjure such a volume of emotion, such poignant yearning, but for Gurrumul the crocodile is related to the world in a wholly different way than it would be for, say, a student of reptile genera. A crocodile has a spiritual home in creation and exerts its power through the flow of streams, through the currents in the air that surrounds it, through the mud of the riverbanks, and through the notes of the song that Gurrumul is now singing.

Gurrumul's song flows on, fulfilling every superlative ever applied to his voice. Listening spellbound, you might find yourself thinking: Does anyone see a poetry of completion in this? Or at least the irony? The studio in which Gurrumul has raised his voice to sing of the *bäru* stands in the centre of a suburb that reaches down to Botany Bay, where the First Fleet anchored over two hundred years earlier.

He needs a smoke. He takes off the headphones and calls for Michael to lead him to the garage where he can light up. He's left his mobile back in the studio. When it rings, Michael answers it, with Gurrumul's permission. Somebody or other is on a flight up in the far north and desperately needs a few quid, or more, or much more, to continue the flight.

Michael says: 'I'll get Gurrumul for you.'

He takes the mobile out to the *salon fumeur* and puts it into Gurrumul's hand. Back in the studio, Michael explains. 'It's one of his relatives. He's on a small plane. The pilot won't take him any further without payment.'

'So what happens now?'

'Who knows? They'll talk, maybe reach an agreement.'

'How long will it take?'

'How long? It'll take as long as it takes. And nothing will happen here until it's resolved. That's the way it is.'

Gurrumul's made himself supremely comfortable in an armchair, one leg raised so that the ankle rests just above the knee of the other. Holding his mobile in the odd way he has, he enters into a type of conference. His voice is barely audible. A smile plays across his lips. He laughs, and it's a laugh of genuine mirth, maybe a note of playful wickedness in it. The studio has to be hired by the day, and that wouldn't be cheap. Gurrumul seems unconcerned, and Michael, too, appears perfectly sanguine. Is there a term in Gumatj that corresponds to 'Time is money'?

Back in the studio, Michael tries out chords on the keyboard, preserved on the computer by Ted Howard.

Michael says: 'Family is crucial. He brings his family and others along on decisions, big and small. He's one of the few people on Elcho who is financially secure, but there are maybe twenty men between him and any leadership role. He shows respect.'

That respect that Michael speaks of is cultural. The very role of 'respect' amongst Indigenous Australians extends further than it does amongst most Australians, for whom 'respect' may go as far as esteem or mean no more than tolerance. Indigenous Australians embrace the whole of another's culture, and his or her past stretching back to the dawn of time, in showing respect. Listen to Margaret Kemarre Turner in her account of the meaning of being an Aboriginal person, *Iwenhe Tyerrtye*: 'We as Aboriginal people, we always relate to other people, connect with them, no matter who we are. If I see an Aboriginal person I wouldn't just say, "Oh, he's another language speaker, different from me." No, I'll always say, "That person is one of us, he's part of us." And no matter who that person is I still relate in whatever they are, no matter where you're from, you know? Like, whether you come from the southern area, or the north area, or the eastern side, or from the west, Aboriginal people always got the similar way of doing things, saying things, and the way they act, and the way they relate, and how they're part of Land, and how they're part of people.'

If you had to name the quality that stands out in Margaret Kemarre Turner's account of Indigenous 'respect', you'd say 'generosity of spirit'. And, as a matter of fact, that generosity can extend beyond people who are 'one of us'. Think of the plaque on a wall outside the Jewish Holocaust Centre in Melbourne that reads:

The Jewish Holocaust Museum and Research Centre honours the Aboriginal people for their actions protesting against the persecution of Jews by the Nazi Government of Germany in 1938.

This plaque refers to the protest led by William Cooper and Bill Onus of the Australian Aborigines' League (AAL) in 1938, who had read of the violence of Kristallnacht in the Melbourne *Age* newspaper and couldn't stomach it without saying something. They carried a resolution of the AAL to the German Consul protesting the 'cruel persecution of the Jewish people and asking that the persecution be brought to an end'.

He's chuckling now, Gurrumul. He's like a kid, just for a moment. Then a more serious expression comes over his face and all at once he's nothing like a kid. He's not saying a word. He looks like a prince on a throne, grave and silent. Then he's smiling again. The glass on the framed portrait of Elvis on the wall above him catches the sun and gleams. You might be waiting a long time for this family business to reach a conclusion. So relax. Do as Gurrumul is doing and light a smoke. Enjoy the Botany sunshine. He'll resume the session when he's ready. The songs will flow.

When Gurrumul's own community watches him perform, each member feels a validation of his or her own language and culture.

CHAPTER 2

Arrival

The thing that singles Gurrumul out is not his blindness but innate musical savvy, his hunger to make melodies to fill the air with what he can imagine.

Even when Yolŋu babies are still in the womb they have entered a cosmos of relationships with kin and country. The birth itself and the gender of the child will alter the child's place in that cosmos, yes, but the mind of a Yolŋu child is not a blank slate, a tabula rasa, on which anything at all may be written. The child is its soul, and the soul has an ancestry. It is this way for Gurrumul, the first of Ganyinurra (Daisy) and Nyambi's (Terry's) four sons, all born on Elcho Island. He is immediately an honoured figure in his culture, connected intimately with the existing narrative of the Gumatj clan and the Yolŋu people.

Gurrumul is four months old before it is realised that he is sightless. His aunts, both those on his mother's side from the Gumal clan, and those on his father's side from the Gumatj, all act in the role of mother, according to custom. It is Daisy's sister Dhäŋgal (Susan) who first notices Gurrumul's lack of response to visual stimulus — not easy to detect because his hearing is hyper-acute and he will look in the direction from which a very faint sound is coming as if he is turning his gaze towards it. But Susan thinks, as she cradles him: 'Something is wrong.' A local medical consultation followed by a trip to Melbourne in his mother's care for further tests confirms that Gurrumul is totally and permanently blind.

Even the fact that Gurrumul is blind is catered for in the narrative of his tribe and clan. It is not a calamity. What might be thought of as affliction in another culture finds a readier acceptance amongst the Yolŋu. It is more thought of as an unexpected feature of the child's story, now revealed. The Yolŋu, in their beliefs and structures, are not deterministic, and it wouldn't be right to say that Gurrumul's blindness was 'meant to be'. Only that 'it is'.

The diagnosis makes the child that much dearer to his family. Siblings are told: 'You look out for him.' Gurrumul is able to live a childhood just like any other — the same games, the same dicing with danger, the same sources of delight. The kids of Galiwin'ku ride a bicycle at full speed down a steep hill to see how closely they can court disaster, and so does

Low tide at Mission Beach,
Galiwin'ku, Elcho Island.

GALIKU

Buŋgul, buŋgul, buŋgul, buŋgul, buŋgul bunana, djaw'
dhiyakuŋuna watawuŋu dirrmalawuŋu, djaw'
waṉa ṉirrpuna banuydjina bili wuḻungupayina, djaw'
barrŋbarrŋ dhuwalinydja galiku watawuŋu, djaw'

Dance, dance, dance, dance, dance is here, take it
From this northerly wind, take it
On the mast the flags are playing, take it
The flags torn by the wind, take it

Giḻaŋ, giḻaŋ, giḻaŋ, giḻaŋ, giḻaŋ, giḻaŋ, giḻaŋ, giḻaŋ,
wuyupthurrunana djaw' r..r djaw'

Giḻaŋ, giḻaŋ, giḻaŋ, giḻaŋ, giḻaŋ, giḻaŋ, giḻaŋ, giḻaŋ,*
fraying to pieces, take it

Barrŋbarrŋ galiku, waṉa ṉirrpu,
giḻaŋ, giḻaŋ, giḻaŋ, baṉjarrŋulili, wuḻungupa banuydji
ganydjarrwuyaŋina wuḏuminyba, gaŋgayparrana

torn flags, mast arms,
giḻaŋ, giḻaŋ, giḻaŋ, on the masts, shredded flags
shredded by the power of wuḏuminy, gaŋgayparra winds

Nhenydja buŋgul waŋana, watawuŋu dirrmalawaŋu
rrondhu marrtji ŋunha Mindharrŋura, Wilirrŋura Muthamul
nhumanydja rrondhu märi walala, mala Mandjikay, m..m m..m

You (flags) asked to fly dancing, from the northern wind
flags dancing there at Mindharrŋura, Wilirrŋura, Muthamul
you grandmother-flag mob, you Mandjikay families, m..m. m..m

Lomuyinana lomu Mawuyul, wäŋaŋura Yanhdhaḻa
Yulpa? Bäpadjambaŋba, wäŋaŋura Djulkayaḻŋi

Soft sands of Mawuyul, at the place Yanhdhaḻa
For who? For Bäpadjambaŋ, at the place Djulkayaḻŋi

Wiripunydja burakina Birrinydjiwala, Djindjiray Baḻawuku
Mäwuḻmirri, Gandjamarr Birrapirra
nhenydja ŋäthili, wutthurra wurrminyba
wäŋaŋura Seki Gurrumuru, m..m, m..m

Also playing there for the Birrinydji Djindjiray Baḻawuku
Mäwuḻmirri, Gandjamarr Birrapirra nation
you first, clash the knives
at the place, Seki Gurrumuru, m..m, m..m

Dhuwalana dhärriŋdja, Gäḏinŋura Djaltjunbi
dhiyaŋi Dhuwa dhawal, Girriwaḻa Ṉambatjŋu
Djarpanbulu, Raŋimula Gaṉdjitji
ṉirrpunydja burakina, Gätjiŋba, m..m, m..m

Here is the trepang oven, at the Gäḏinŋura Djaltjunbi (Bawaka)
this Dhuwa country, Girriwaḻa Ṉämbatjŋu (Yäŋunbi)
Djarpanbulu, Raŋimula Gaṉdjitji (Barrkira)
the mast flags flew, for Gätjiŋ, m..m, m..m

Wanhaŋuru buwapuŋala Ḻuku-ḏumdhunawala
Melwula Barrthanagaŋuru, Dholtji Manunu
yä märiwala, Ḏilingarra Yawunbaŋuwala
Bungurrukurruwala, Walaywalayunawala, m..m, m..m

Where have the masts come from to be with Ḻuku-ḏumdhuna
(ancestor)
From Melwula Barrthanaga, to Dholtji Manunu
Oh my grandmother families, Ḏilingarra Yawunbaŋu
Bungurrukurru, Walaywalayuna m..m, m..m (Warramiri nation)

Giḻaŋ'thurrunana dhoṯthinana Djalinda yuṯa, djaw'
giḻaŋ'thurrunana ŋaraka dhuwalinydja Yamaliny Daṯarrwaŋa, djaw'
Djanŋala miyamara Gapala namba Barrumbarru, djaw'
bili nhanbalay dhuwali namba Gätjiŋba, djaw'
giḻaŋ, giḻaŋ, giḻaŋ, giḻaŋ, giḻaŋ, giḻaŋ, giḻaŋ, wuyupthurrunana
        djaw' r..r djaw'

Raising a new folded flag, take it
'giḻaŋ' as it is raised up the mast, take it
Singing the country Djanŋala, Gapala, Barrumbarru, take it
Because this is marked for Gätjiŋba, take it
giḻaŋ, giḻaŋ, giḻaŋ, giḻaŋ, giḻaŋ, giḻaŋ, giḻaŋ, disappears from sight

*'giḻaŋ' sound of mast rope against the mast and a flag flapping.

The distillation of the album's achievements. This song celebrates the dense congregation of the Yolŋu clans, represented here by their distinctive flags. The banners catch the north wind in from the sea and come alive, whipping against their masts. Gurrumul names clans and places in a tumble of melody, imitating the playful force of the wind.

Gurrumul. On the beach, where the greatest danger is not drowning but being devoured by a crocodile, Gurrumul embraces risk with the same reckless disregard as his brothers and sisters, and knows when to run and in which direction when someone calls out: '*Bäru!*' Despite Elcho being poor, childhood for Gurrumul and most of the Galiwin'ku kids is a barefoot paradise.

Gurrumul does not use a white cane, he has no guide dog and has never adopted Braille, although he is given the chance. In 1975, when he is four, his mother and aunts take him on the long journey by air and train to Geelong, south of Melbourne, where the Yunupiŋus board with a Methodist family while Gurrumul is introduced to Braille at a specialist school. The experiment doesn't pan out. The Braille alphabet employed is English; Gurrumul speaks Yolŋu Matha. But the other reason for the failure is that neither Gurrumul nor his family thinks of him as handicapped. That's not the way he's been raised.

The thing that singles Gurrumul out is not his blindness but his innate musical savvy. That and his hunger to make melodies; to fill the air with what he can imagine. His mother and his aunts sit empty cans on the sand of the island's shore and put sticks of approximately the right shape into his hands. He experiments. This tin gives off this sound; that tin another, just a little different. He puts the sounds together. In his mind's eye, he sees the position of each receptacle. He makes adjustments; rearranges the drums. More tins are found — bigger, broader, deeper, shallower. The ecstasy of rhythm and the sheer glee of composition widens his smile until it takes up half his face. The adults say: '*Walutju!*' ('Wonderful!') The kids looking on clap and laugh.

A little piano accordion comes into his life; a toy one, twelve notes, provided by his mother, Daisy, and his father, Terry. He finds the keys with his fingertips and plays, joyfully. Then a guitar from his uncle, a right-handed guitar that left-handed Gurrumul turns upside down and plays left-handed, as he will for the rest of his life, this guitar and many others. Instruments come his way, proper instruments, including a Casio keyboard, and his accomplishment grows.

Gurrumul will in time master the piano, the guitar, electronic keyboards and the drums, but even in adulthood when he commands the use of the best-equipped studios in the world, it will be the instrument of his voice that will most impress. In the choir of the Methodist Mission on the island, he learns to sing the hymns that he will enjoy for decades to come, 'The Old Rugged Cross', 'Amazing Grace' and gallery hymns such as 'Lo, He Comes with Clouds Descending' and 'To Be a Pilgrim' that call for choristers to raise their voices to the rafters. His first languages are all Yolŋu Matha, not the English of these hymns, but the words are not as important as the quality of emotion he can convey, partly technique, partly instinct. When the time comes for him to fashion his own compositions and record them, he will move listeners to tears, and this is where he learns how to sing in that way; how to freight his voice with feeling: from the Methodists. His own songs will be more subtle, more complex than the hymns, but this is where it starts; this is the template.

The inspiration goes further. He learns, partly through the hymns, the broad Christian distinctions between right and wrong, complementing the moral scheme of his Yolŋu culture, taught by his father, Nyambi. All but a few of Gurrumul's compositions in later life will focus on clan beliefs and obligations; on the consolations of being one with his people; of reverence for custom. Songs such as 'Wiyathul', 'Djärimirri', 'Galiku' and 'Wukun' are hymns of praise for the Yolŋu way of honouring life, and are thematically related to the hymns of the Methodist choir. The Rainbow Serpent (*Wititj*) in 'Djärimirri' ('I was carried by Mother

Wititj/ I am a Rainbow Child') takes on the same comforting role as Christ the Saviour in the great standard of the Methodist hymnal, 'Jesus Lover of my Soul' ('Jesus, lover of my soul/ Let me to thy bosom fly'). At six and seven and eight years old, Gurrumul is already absorbing the influences that will earn him praise not just for his singing, but for his songwriting. Many of Gurrumul's original compositions are spirituals, in the accepted sense, and we can think of him as one of the finest songwriters in this genre our country has ever known.

Hymns are not the only influence on Gurrumul's musical taste. The kids of Elcho pick up what they can from anything that comes their way. Someone returns from Darwin with Dire Straits' *Brothers in Arms* on tape and everyone from five to twenty on the island sings 'Walk of Life', 'Romeo and Juliet', 'Money For Nothing', and daydreams of handling a Fender Telecaster in Mark Knopfler's finger-picking style. The Elcho kids, and this is especially true of Gurrumul, are attracted to strong melodies, usually with a backbeat. It's all catch-as-catch-can, these musical influences. Nobody comes back from a mainland record store with Janis Ian or Lou Reed, but Stevie Wonder — yes. And so Stevie Wonder gets into Gurrumul's head and makes him more aware of the possibilities of pop.

Schooling on Elcho is a little less haphazard than in some remote Indigenous communities, where attendance fluctuates depending on the availability of more attractive alternatives, and sometimes the weather. Gurrumul's school is Shepherdson College, originally a Methodist institution. Lessons are about as difficult as they could be for a blind boy, and often pointless. Gurrumul is at school some days, at home on others. As he closes in on puberty and his clan initiation, the real learning that's going on is conveyed by his mother, his aunts, his uncles; by Elvis Presley (who's mourned on Elcho as much as anywhere in the world after his death in 1977), Cliff Richard, Stevie Wonder. 'I've got a little song here, a little song with a lot of meaning,' says Elvis, and launches into 'In the Ghetto'. That rich reek of gospel — that's a lesson. The twelve times table — not so much.

The Elcho bush is dotted, invisibly, with sites of ceremony. Walking the roads of the island, leaving the graded red surface for the tracks that meander amongst the woollybutts, spinifex, canavalia and acacia, a tourist will remain unaware of the stories that whisper and shout to the people of the island. Gurrumul's initiation into the adult life of his clan is not his first ceremony, but it is the most important. Many more will follow. Of the initiation ceremony itself, little can be said without disrespect. Gurrumul's identity has been revealing itself in stages ever since his conception, and his initiation completes one further cycle of his growth into the skin of 'Gurrumul'. Another cycle has commenced.

Rock and country, like the early blues of the American South, do not require any great level of accomplishment for a passing grade. An okay voice and ten guitar lessons and you're ready for 'Your Cheatin' Heart' and almost everything in the Chuck Berry songbook. But Gurrumul, even as he enters a new cycle in his traditional life, starts a fresh cycle in his musical life. He can handle the guitar with some of the casual mastery of Doc Watson and he's bringing a respectable portion of Stevie Wonder's style to the keyboards. It's a sign of something special when you don't mark time at the standard that wins you steady praise but instead push on.

Alan James, who manages Yothu Yindi, a band on the cusp of greatness in 1989, calls on Gurrumul in Galiwin'ku to ask if he'll take over the role of drummer, and Gurrumul agrees.

Up until his recruitment into Yothu Yindi, Gurrumul has lived entirely in the embrace of his family. He's a brilliant musician, yes, but even so, likely to remain on Elcho for years to come with few opportunities to express his talent. He can play the guitar and keyboards and drums twelve hours a day, but without direct exposure to influences other than albums, he'll remain essentially a hobbyist. Not that he's yearning to plunge into anything frenzied; there's none of that restlessness that draws young men and women to the bright lights and big audiences of cities. It wouldn't be at all that realistic, for one thing. On many occasions, Gurrumul is able to challenge the limitations imposed by blindness, but there are many more times when he is compelled to accept them. If he never leaves Elcho, never records a single song, he will probably find enough satisfaction at home to save him from boredom, but when that call comes to join Yothu Yindi, Gurrumul is avid to take up the offer. He can enjoy himself without leaving behind the familiar. The band, after all, is clan; the band is family.

Family, but louder. It's as if Gurrumul has gone off on holiday with the groovy uncle of the clan, the one who drives a V8, wears wrap-around sunglasses and goes to bed at three in the morning. The Indigenous members of Yothu Yindi are Yolŋu, certainly, but Yolŋu who've adopted with relish those bits and pieces of whitefella culture that attract them. In fact, Yothu Yindi's act owes more to the culture and conventions of rock'n'roll than to Indigenous culture. It isn't a hybrid sound; it's foundationally backbeat, occasionally rootsy, sometimes down-the-line country. The Indigenous complement is restricted to the language of the lyrics on some songs; the use of the *yidaki* (didgeridoo) and ironwood clapsticks, and the presence on stage of men painted for ceremony performing stylised versions of traditional dances. The Yothu Yindi mission is to show deep respect for Indigenous culture even in the process of merging it with rebellious whitefella youth culture. 'Indigenous people are survivors,' says Mark Grose, co-founder of Skinnyfish. 'They're not purists. If they see something in white culture they like, they'll try it out.' As soon as he joins Yothu Yindi, Gurrumul is at the heart of something fresh and vital in the evolution of black–white relations in Australia. Even more than that, he is immersed in one of the most thrilling experiences that life can offer a young man, wherever he is in the world: playing his heart out on stage in a big, loud, no-mercy rock'n'roll band.

Yothu Yindi takes Gurrumul north, south, east and west, both in Australia and overseas. Along the way, he moves from drums to his favoured guitar and keyboards. Yothu Yindi is equal parts politics and music, but for Gurrumul, more the music than the politics, and music is his big contribution to the band. Particularly in the recording studio, where his feeling for the nuances lifts a number of tracks above the ordinary and imparts a more complex texture. It's a three-year stint with Yothu Yindi, curtailed when his more senior family members come to feel that the risks of playing with a band that's living the legend to the full is doing Gurrumul no good. In 1992, not long after the release of the talismanic *Tribal Voice* album, Gurrumul is out of the band and back on Elcho. He makes no protest. It is impossible for Gurrumul to rebuff the wishes of his family. The Yothu Yindi experience plays a crucial part in Gurrumul's development as a performer. Yothu Yindi, when all is said and done, is a stage act; a rousing piece of theatre, in the way that any band's time on stage is theatre. Even Yothu Yindi's discourse, as sincere and important as it is, plaits itself into the drama. Gurrumul takes from the Yothu Yindi years the invaluable experience of creating drama in music. He's at the heart of this company of impassioned performers, toiling mightily to forge a cohesive sound out of polemic, electric guitars, drumbeat, the clack of ironwood sticks, the animal drone of the *yidaki*, thudding dance steps, keyboard and chorus. Yothu Yindi takes the talented hobbyist of Elcho Island and thrusts him into an apprenticeship in the hot gospel of rock'n'roll. Is there anything Gurrumul might have occupied himself with over those three years that would have benefited him more?

Top left and right: *Gurrumul's father Terry dances with his son.*
Bottom left: Bill Peaches' Australia, *a TV program of the 1970s, visited Galiwin'ku and captured a young Gurrumul playing a small piano accordion.*
Bottom right: *All Yolŋu kids learn to sing and dance as they learn to walk. Being blind was no hindrance to Gurrumul.*

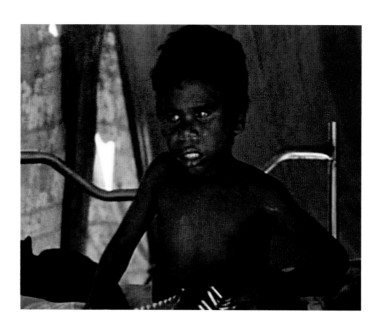

Roast wallaby for lunch.
Gurrumul is delighted.

Gurrumul is twenty-one when he leaves Yothu Yindi; he is twenty-five before another opportunity to shine comes his way. This hiatus in his career as a performer could easily have stretched for years longer, or might even have swallowed up the rest of his life — not an hiatus but a conclusion. Another man with Gurrumul's talents, compelled to while away the hours on a remote island, might have thought: 'I'm marooned, I'm rusting.' There's no evidence that Gurrumul gave any thought at all to the lapse of his career after Yothu Yindi, or that he even considered that he had a career. If he is home with his family, he's where he's happiest — bored at times, but it's where he wants to be.

The next knock on his door, in 1996, announces the resumption of Gurrumul's career as a performer. It's Gurrumul's friend and neighbour Manuel Dhurrkay. He tells Gurrumul that there's a *balanda* (white) guy from the TAFE in Darwin down the way ready to make a band; he's got the instruments, he's got recording gear, no time to waste.

And so Michael Hohnen enters Gurrumul's life. Michael is a TAFE music teacher with a brief to engage Indigenous kids, young men, young women in music making. He's temperamentally the right guy to send on a mission of this sort: ambitious for the kids rather than himself; happy with increments of reward, rather than an avalanche; an abiding respect for Indigenous cultures that never tips over into worship and, most importantly, an acute musical intelligence. He tells Manuel: 'Okay, you can't play any instruments, but you can sing. Find a drummer and a couple of guitarists to back you and we've got a band.' Manuel says: 'Ten minutes!' and away he runs. Desperate optimism of Manuel's sort is hardly ever rewarded, but it is on this day. Gurrumul with Yunupiŋu family members, Andrew, Nigel and Johnathon, are drafted into the band, as well as Joshua Dhurrkay. Lloyd Garawirrtja, Frank Wunuŋmurra and Adrian Garawirrtja make up the original company that will become Saltwater. Later, Kevin Djamina Gurruwiwi, Marcus Dhurrkay, Jason Dhamarrandji and Andrew Dhamarrandji joined.

It's not Gurrumul's intention to impress Michael with his craft and insight, but he can hardly help doing so. He's emerged from the Yothu Yindi years a seasoned performer. Michael places Gurrumul at the centre of the band that he's building. The mental note he underlines as he learns more about Gurrumul is that there's something fabulous to get out of him, when the time is right. It's more reggae than rock, the sound that Saltwater embraces; joyous and jaunty. Michael's mentoring makes all of the band members more alert to their potential. He points out pathways, develops their strengths, finds ways to enlarge the traditional complement of their songbook. Gurrumul, who might have had reservations about putting himself and all that he knew into the hands of a stranger from Darwin, learns to respect Michael's touch and tact and intelligence. Nothing is possible without an unspoken acknowledgment from Gurrumul and all of the band members that Michael knows what the hell he's doing and has some sense of destination.

The destination that Michael has in mind is an album. Saltwater is that good. Michael's initial hope is that the TAFE will finance the production and printing, but when that hope is dashed he and his friend Mark Grose, living on Elcho with his wife Michelle, set up Skinnyfish Music with Saltwater as its first client. The album, *Gapu Damurruŋ* (1999), is an enormously cheerful reggae and roots production recorded with Craig Pilkington down at Mount Bundy Station studios, south of Darwin. It attracts some attention over time, finds some airplay, wins friends amongst reviewers. But Gurrumul and his friends are not going to find it easy to commit to a program of touring in support of the album, not with all the obligations of ceremony back on Elcho. Without appearances to boost *Gapu Damurruŋ*, the album can only do so much. But that 'so much' is appreciable, 10,000 in sales, and Gurrumul and the band are encouraged.

At some point between *Gapu Damurruŋ* and *Djarridjarri*, Gurrumul becomes the father of a daughter, Jasmine, who has always lived with her mother, Rebecca, in Galiwin'ku, rather than her father. But Gurrumul sees her regularly. He only talks about Jasmine with his family members, although he once confided in Mark how proud he is that Jasmine has grown up so lovely, taking her schooling seriously. 'You know, Marky, she goes to school every day. What do you think, Marky? Every day.'

Two more Saltwater albums follow *Gapu Damurruŋ*. *Djarridjarri* in 2004 and *Malk* in 2009. Both albums reveal just how much talent was in the tap to begin with, and how beautifully judged Michael's suggestions and interventions have been. *Djarridjarri* wins the 2004 Deadly for Album Release of the Year, and Saltwater wins the Deadly for Band of the Year. *Djarridjarri* is also nominated at the 2004 ARIAs in the category of Best World Music Album. *Malk* (after Gurrumul's 2008 first solo album, but recorded in 2006) is a near-masterpiece, a concept album of inter-connected songs that still stands as one of the most sophisticated albums by an Indigenous band ever released. The Saltwater albums are the rewards of a carefully nurtured trust shared between the band members, Michael Hohnen and Mark Grose. It's no great strain for Gurrumul, Manuel and the other band members to share their culture with a mainstream audience; the more insight mainstream Australia enjoys into Yolŋu culture, the better. But that trust is on the line a hundred times in the course of a year. If an appearance has to be ruled out because of a clash with clan business, Gurrumul expects Michael and Mark to respect his priorities without argument. And they do. Such-and-such that was commited to months ago is now not going to happen, and the reason may be important or trivial, but it must be accepted. The more trust, the less there is to discuss.

In 2007, eleven years after Gurrumul and Michael formed their friendship, Michael returns to the mental note he made in 1996 — that there's something exceptional in Gurrumul that he might one day be encouraged to share. That mental note has been amended countless times since, and Gurrumul has revealed a great deal of what makes him unique on the three Saltwater albums. But he hasn't revealed everything. Not even Gurrumul knows how far he can go and what he can tap into. When Michael says: 'A solo album — good idea?' Gurrumul says: 'Okay, yeah,' not with the conviction of a man who has been waiting patiently to step into the spotlight and overwhelm an audience with his individual genius, but more as if he's saying: 'Do you think?' Michael talks of an album made up entirely, or almost entirely, of songs in language — songs like 'Djärimirri' and 'Galiku', already recorded on the Saltwater albums, but given a quieter, sparer setting. 'Just your voice, *wäwa*,' says Michael. 'Maybe some guitar, piano.' Gurrumul says, 'Guitar, piano, no worries,' but he's thinking, secretly: 'He's mad.' All the same, he's prepared to go along with what Michael has in mind. Eleven years of deepening trust — well, Michael could have proposed a medley of Gilbert and Sullivan patter songs in Gumatj and Gurrumul would have given him the benefit of the doubt.

The album *Gurrumul* is recorded in Craig Pilkington's studios, now located in Coburg. Whatever reservations Gurrumul has, he gives everything he's got to the project. And day by day, this extraordinary leap forward — Gurrumul and some thousands of years of his culture, in all of its power and mystery — develops such haunting beauty that Craig and Michael exchange glances almost of alarm. It was just an idea, Gurrumul solo, but for the idea to fulfil itself in this way is spellbinding. Michael calls Mark Grose and in his excitement, makes the astonishing prediction that this solo album will sell twenty thousand copies. Mark says: 'Twenty thousand?

This photograph and the one opposite were both taken in 1937 and show Michell Banburawuy (Malangatj) Garrawura, who was Gurrumul's great-grandfather and Terry's grandfather. Dutch settlers on Elcho Island referred to Michell as the chief of Garrawurra tribe, which was one of the two main tribes on Elcho. In the photograph opposite, Michell is with his wife Dhatu Garrawurra and their daughter (standing) Badayka Garrawurra, who is Terry's mother and Gurrumul's grandmother. The baby in the coolamon *is Terry's mother's sister, Baŋarra Garrawurra.*

Really?' And Michael says: 'I'm not kidding. Twenty thousand.' Try two hundred thousand. Try four hundred thousand. More. And this at a time when the sale of CDs over the counter at record shops is fast becoming a phenomenon of a past era.

The week of recording in Audrey Studios is the great landmark of Gurrumul's creative life; one of those arrivals that seems, in hindsight, to have been marked on a map years earlier. The delight in Gurrumul's face as he discovers, on the beach at Galiwin'ku, what happens when you whack a tin can with a stick — that moment is there in the studio, and it's there on the album. Every new landmark in the days and nights of Gurrumul's life to come is a point on a path leading from that moment of arrival. *Rrakala* will follow, a new album that evolves, thrillingly, from the first; and performances in concert halls all over the globe; accolades and awards and the praise of his peers; songs from the heart for the American president; for the Queen, for the Governor General; an outing in cap and gown to accept an honorary doctorate in music from Sydney University. That, 'Yeah, good' is almost all that Gurrumul is prepared to say about any moment of achievement. Nor does he ever attempt to explain his art, other than to make a technical suggestion here and there.

But there is an occasion in a studio in Byron Bay when Gurrumul goes further. These sessions in Byron have been running for a week. He's telling Michael about the new song he's written; a song that he'd tried out in Avatar Studios in Manhattan. It's a song he loves, and when he feels this way about a song he demands to hear the tape over and over. After each playback, he says, 'Play it again, yeah.' After he's listened with intense concentration three times, he leaves his stool and settles into a big, embracing leather armchair that he's made his own over the week. He says suddenly: 'Michael! Look!' This must be important, to bring that imperative note into his voice. He's cupped one hand, as you might when you intend to fill it with water. Then he brings his cupped hand to his head, tips it, and taps his forehead, or a little above. At the same time he's frowning in the rigour of concentration, and it's as if he's enacting what he requires of Michael. He bows his head, keeping up the gentle tapping.

He says: 'This is the deep part, the deep part of the mind. You know?'

Michael says: 'No.'

'Listen,' says Gurrumul. He taps that area just above his forehead again. 'See? The deep part. Okay?'

This is what Michael does know: he's being tutored. But it's not clear to him exactly what he's meant to understand.

Gurrumul says: 'In the song, at this part you should play the bass … you know …' He's struggling to think of the word.

'Bowing?' says Michael. 'I should use bowing?'

'Yo!' says Gurrumul, relieved of the burden to describe something he has never seen, only heard. 'Bowing! Yo!'

Michael asks his friend: 'What's the song called?'

'Ulminda,' he says, lifting his chin and grinning.

'Ulminda?' says Michael, and he's smiling, too.

'Yeah.'

'Really?'

'Yo. Ulminda.'

'Ulminda' is the name Gurrumul gave to Michael's wife Kirrilly a year or so earlier.

The age-old tradition for learning drums in the bush is to get as many tins as possible and practise, practise, practise. Gurrumul is a beautiful drummer and here he is honing his skills.

Julie Herd on Elcho

'This one,' says Daisy, showing the baby to Julie Herd, 'this one is Gurrumul.' She's cradling the infant in her arm, leaving one hand free. Julie knows that Daisy's baby is blind, but it's difficult to tell. The main indication is the alert movement of his head as he tracks the voice of his mother.

Julie, who is seventeen, not yet of the age when a woman employs all the sweet phrases that became familiar when she cradled a baby of her own, says: 'Gummumul?'

'No,' says Daisy. 'Gurrumul. Gurr-u-mul.'

'Gurrumul?'

'Yes. Good. Good. Like that. Gurrumul.'

Daisy is twenty-two, slim and lovely with a cheerful ease about her and a brilliant smile. She helps out in the household on Elcho Island in which Julie and two friends have been invited to spend a month's holiday in early 1972. Over the next few weeks, Julie will come to know Daisy and the baby well, and not only Daisy and Gurrumul but Daisy's daughters and her husband, Nyambi (Terry), her sisters, brothers, aunts and uncles, nephews and nieces and cousins galore. Julie writes two letters a week to her parents in distant Geelong, where she and her friends are training as primary school teachers. She writes:

> There have only been people on Elcho since World War II when Mr Sheppy (Shepherdson) began flying people here to protect them. Mr and Mrs Sheppy are still here. He's always flying around the place. The Yolŋu will charter a plane like we'd hire a taxi ...
>
> Last night Greg and I went to a play at the church — 'The Birth of Christ' — put on by the Yolŋu kids and choir ... The people here love to laugh at each other. Then we went with a couple of boys we know to a stage just down the road where they played guitars and sang. They have three electric guitars and an amp. It was great. The Yolŋu are very musical ...
>
> Right now Daisy (our house girl) is singing songs from the hymn book, while Greg accompanies her on guitar. She has a beautiful voice. We'll tape her next week ...
>
> Fifty per cent of the Elcho population is under sixteen. There are about 200 guys on the island who can play the didgeridoo. I'd always learned that only one man in a tribe was able to play it ...
>
> Last night Garr, a Yolŋu friend of Greg's came around and we sang and they played music

Julie Herd holds a very young Gurrumul.

for quite a while. Did I mention our house girl Ganyunurra (Daisy). Although only about the same age as Garr, she turned out to be his '2nd mummy'!

The Yolŋu still hunt and fish a lot. The Yolŋu kids often fish and hunt crabs and oysters down on the beach … Yesterday 4 of us and 7 Yolŋu boys went up to 'Bible Camp', a place about 15 miles up the island. They borrowed a small 4-wheel drive which did an excellent job, with 11 of us on board! The road up was quite rough in places as it had rained the night before … If a tree falls across the road here, rather than shift it, they will build a detour road around it … a practice I would say which was typical of the Yolŋu … Six of the guys took their rifles and headed off into the swamp to shoot wild geese … They came back with 6 wild geese which they plucked (a bit!) and roasted on an open fire …

Yesterday (after the outdoor movies, a western) the guys were running around with their guns pretending to be Indians. They call themselves 'Apaches' … In the western films, the Yolŋu always barrack for the Indians! Garr's other name is 'Ben Casey'. Lots of the Yolŋu tack names onto their own – e.g. Cliff Richard, Elvis, etc.

We slept in this morning and Greg came up and told us that Gannarrbul [Dorothy] (Daisy the housegirl's sister and Djingalu's wife) was waiting to see Roz and I. She'd been waiting an hour. She presented Roz and I with a string of beads each. They are really beautiful. She also gave Roz and I a tribe [tribal name]. Mine is 'Gometch' (Gumatj). Djingalu calls Roz and I his daughters and has promised Roz to Greg. Gannarrbul and Garninarul [Ganyunurra] (Daisy) stayed for lunch, which was quite a scream. Daisy has a great sense of humour and also very good English …

Last night was one of the highlights of the trip. Daisy and her family arrived around – sisters about 19, 16, 15 and 3, brothers about 15 and 20, Daisy's three little kids (including Gurrumul), and the 19 year old's husband and baby. Later in the evening, Daisy's parents, husband and young sister arrived too … We had a fantastic night. We sat outside on the grass and sang and laughed, the girls also danced … They've all got wonderful senses of humour — especially Daisy, who's an absolute nut. They're a gorgeous looking family …

Last night Djalangi and a friend came around and we went with them to a platform where the boys were playing guitars. There were about 200 of them there, from babies to 25. As soon as we walked in a bunch of girls jumped around me, stuck an hibiscus in my hair and asked me if I would twist. The girls here always play with my hair — they say it's 'so fine and soft and straight'. Daisy and her sisters were here too – as mad as ever. We went back to her place after and talked to her family — her father is a real old gentleman …

At the end of the holiday, Greg leaves his guitar with Daisy's family as a gift. This is the guitar that Daisy's brother-in-law, Djuŋa (David) will, a few years down the track, present to Gurrumul. And in a moving completion of this cycle of coincidence, Julie, decades later, will send her terminally ill niece in Queensland a copy of Gurrumul's first album, for solace.

Opposite Top: Gurrumul's Aunty Susan holding her son, Nigel. The smiling boy on the left is Kevin Djamina Gurruwiwi, who in later years made a reputation for himself in the Northern Territory tourist industry. All his life, Kevin remained as cheerful as he looks here. He guided and influenced Gurrumul throughout the Yothu Yindi and Saltwater years. On tour, his knack for comedy and satire delighted everyone. Opposite Bottom: A family photo the three Gurruwiwi sisters with their family. Anne is on the left with her favourite red dress bought in Perth by her sister Dorothy, Susan is in the middle and Daisy is on the right holding her son Gurrumul. Below: A gentle arm is all that was needed to reassure Gurrumul.

Gurrumul (centre sitting) enjoys a day at the beach with his family. He was never far from a watchful gaze when growing up.

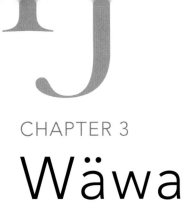

CHAPTER 3

Wäwa

This was the moment of confluence, when the flow of two distinct talents merged.

Great talent is not a solitary wayfarer, emerging one day, like a prophet from the wilderness, to harvest our acclaim. It is the friends it makes; the good fortune it encounters. What looks and sounds like no more than an above-average talent might reveal a phenomenal capacity for growth once exposed to the right influences. The release in 2008 of Gurrumul's first album of twelve songs marks the point at which the passion and mystery of the lives lived by Indigenous Australians reached into the culture of mainstream Australia and took hold. That album, *Gurrumul*, is the product of a powerful gift; good luck; an all-important capacity for growth; and the fresh influence of a white boy from the south with a double bass and a nagging sense of mission.

Michael, now in his mid-forties, spent his infancy and childhood in the Melbourne 'beach belt' suburb of Beaumaris, almost as far as you can get from Elcho Island and Galiwin'ku while still living on the Australian mainland. And as remote in manners and mores as is possible from the vernacular, clan-based life of the Gumatj. Beaumaris is comfy without being ritzy and, with the beach fifty metres from your front door, one of the daydream suburbs of white, middle-class Victoria. You can live on Elcho with the beach only fifty metres away, too, but you won't have a job, a house to call your own, or a Citroën parked in your garage.

He was the eldest of three kids in a happy, thriving family. Both parents — Geoff and Patsy — were ambitious for their kids, within reason, and nudged Michael and his brother, Ben, and sister, Lucy, into music lessons — but not with any great success. Patsy had to round up the kids from the outdoors and the beach whenever the music teacher visited. But at the age of thirteen, Michael was either encouraged or compelled to sit the entrance exam for Melbourne High — a government-funded secondary school with a select enrolment, not so far from Beaumaris. He passed the exam without difficulty and, only days after commencement, realised with a shock that worlds existed within worlds. At Melbourne High, he was not

When Gurrumul is asked a question in English, he rarely answers directly, but instead turns to Michael and says, 'You tell them.'

BANBIRRŊU (FUNERAL SONG)

Bon maḻikin Baṉbirrŋu
Djarrpirana Binininyala, Guyundu
Ya Buliyaŋu Dhaluwaṯpaṯtjin
Guṉdirrŋa Dhaluma guyuḻ ŋoyanhara
Dhaŋurr-wuykthunda
Ya djaḻaḻyunda, dhaŋurrma ŋaya ḏitjuwan guykkuykthuwan
djarwunuwan guykthuwan
Galmakḻi Ŋaypinyayu, gananan ŋaya
Galmak Dhupuḻa, Garrimaḻa, Ḏulunŋuru
Ya Waranyina
Na..a

Gathanan ŋaya, dhaŋu Gurruwurru Djarimi, Warradaymi
Bämbaṯ yirrwara guykthuwan ŋaya
yothuny nyäkuway ŋarru djarimiŋan Warraḏaymiŋan

Dhawuru bämbaṯŋuru, burralma ŋaya
Ya ḻupthuwan Wurrambayu, Milpuṉbuṉ

Ya Gaḻtjuwanŋu, ŋarrarra...
Ŋarrarra

Ancestor Baṉbirrŋu is tired, worn out
Ancestor Djarrpirana: Binininyala: Guyundu
Oh Ancestor Buliyaŋu: Dhaluwaṯpaṯtjin
Ancestor Dhaluma rests in the termite mound
Speaks, calling out
Oh the path, I return, speaking sacredly
of the fresh waters at Ŋaypinya
The sacred fresh waters of Dhupuḻa, Garrimala, Ḏulunŋuru,
I leave
Oh, the sacred waters of Waranyina
Na..a (tune of the sacred words spoken)

I hold this sacred shelter, the Ancestor Djarimi,
Warradaymi
I consecrate the shelter
My child becomes me, the Ancestor Djarimi, Warradaymi

From the sacred shelter, I join the sea
Oh, I am the Salt Water Ancestor Wurrambayu, Milpuṉbuṉ
Oh, I am the Salt Water ancestor Gaḻtjuwanŋu
(sound of the songs)

Although a funeral song, 'Banbirrŋu' is not a lamentation but a sacred song of solace for the departed, and for those in mourning. In some of Gurrumul's songs, the emphasis is on the agony of grief for one who has died. In this song, the Gumatj ancestor has entered a cycle of the Dreaming that takes in both the living and the dead. The solace for the departed is that he has embarked on a journey that never ends, and on the journey he partakes of the refreshment of his ever-present existence in the thoughts and dreams and memories of his kin.

simply prodded towards success with kind words and gentle endorsement, but driven towards achievement with exhortations. In this new culture of accomplishment, he was expected to establish a lofty standard and strive to reach it.

On your first day at school, you chose a sport and you chose a musical instrument. Michael chose rowing and the double bass. The school's string players were tutored by Imre Pallos, a Hungarian in his sixties who was passionate about the sounds that his pupils should get out of their cellos, violins and double basses. You got a rap on the head for slackness and a praising kiss for application. Michael earned more kisses than whacks.

If you're a kid of fifteen and you persevere with the awkward space between notes on the fingerboard of the double bass and the even more awkward 180-centimetre height of the instrument, maybe you've got the right stuff. Michael graduated from Melbourne High to the Victorian College of the Arts, mastered the unwieldy instrument and entered more completely into another world-within-a-world — that of the professional musician, with its insane working hours, second-hand cigarette smoke, bohemian camaraderie and steady diet of felafels purchased from street vendors at two in the morning. He hauled his instrument from venue to venue, playing in pit orchestras, chamber orchestras, jazz clubs, bars; he pitched in with pop bands, rock bands — bands of every complexion — along the way refining his craft and building up the musical savvy that would one day find its mature expression in his collaboration with a black kid on a distant island he didn't know existed.

Like music graduates everywhere, Michael was forced to think of teaching as maybe the only career path that would afford him any sort of secure living — the type of thing you do to please your oldies who insist you have 'something to fall back on'. He completed a Diploma of Education without developing any great passion for pedagogy, taking his casual approach as far as recording one of his practical exams on a cassette tape and leaving it on his lecturer's desk. In any case, he didn't go into teaching; he went into The Killjoys, a Melbourne indie outfit that emerged in the late eighties from the thriving Melbourne pub scene and prospered on the exceptional vocals of lead singer Anna Burley. He toured with The Killjoys for four years, playing with a dozen other bands over the same period, mixing and matching in whatever way was required of him.

What anyone who hired Michael in those troubadour years could rely on was terrific competence, but the insight and originality for which he would in time win such wide respect — that remained unexpressed. And yet, what he might do, what he could do, the potential within — it whispered to him. All the parties, all the launches, all the low-budget promo videos, all the towns, all the pubs, all the schemes, all the songs, even the applause — it can come to seem an endlessly revolving carousel of hype and self-indulgence.

He lived with a sense of lapse and drift. He was twenty-eight and for all he knew, the best of him might be a past-tense thing. Then at a party in London in 1991, he met Archie Roach. In Archie there was none of the toxic vanity and attention-seeking, none of the destructive hunger for flattery that had become the theme of Michael's disenchantment. Instead there was a stillness and privacy, a sense of a profound interior life. Archie's album *Charcoal Lane* had been released in Australia the year before to some acclaim. The standout track, 'Took the Children Away', told Archie's own story as a child of the stolen generation of Indigenous Australians but, in its sorrow and beauty, it had become the anthem of all those who'd suffered — the children, the parents, the families and the tribes. It was not simply meeting Archie that converted lapse and drift into conviction for Michael, but it made him curious about Indigenous Australia; made him embarrassed to know so little of the vital life of people who could call Australia home in a way that went far beyond the glib sentimentality of a pop song.

This curiosity had been aroused just as he was beginning to look at what lay in front of him in a more critical way than at any other time in his life. It was that existential moment when a revealing light fell on the choices open to him, and he knew in his heart that the choice he made would mean a world of difference, for better or worse. If Michael were to go on in the way he had, okay, he could make his living out of music more or less forever, and there were compensations to offset the repetition and superficiality of the gig-to-gig occupational cycle of a journeyman bassist: the bantering friendship, the breezy lifestyle, freedom from any real responsibility. But think of Archie Roach; think of the character in the man's face, the strength in his voice when he sang of the life he'd led. You can't get a face like that, a bearing like that by taking what comes along with a shrug of acceptance. So, if you want your own life to amount to more than the casual sum of your careless habits, do something. Do something.

He came back to Australia not knowing what the something was he had to do, only that it was crucial that he did it. And in the way that these things pan out, a friend suggested that he go north — just do it, pack up and go north, maybe to Darwin, or to Arnhem Land. He'd see something he hadn't seen before. For one thing, he'd see black Australians in the landscape they'd lived in for thousands of years; he'd see the Yolŋu. He'd see a culture that would astonish him. If he had something to offer, something to contribute, okay, do it. Go north.

He did; he went north. He drove a '69 Ford up one highway then another and another, all the way from Melbourne to Darwin, his double bass on the front passenger seat: the troubadour and his instrument.

In every life there's one legendary journey. It's the journey that makes you feel as if you're heading towards a beacon on a hill; a journey that has a true destination, not just the Point B you've reached after setting out from Point A. For Australians, the journey doesn't get more legendary than this journey of Michael's from the great southern city on the banks of the Yarra to the impossibly remote northern city facing the Arafura Sea. It's the journey of explorers Burke and Wills when they were chasing a dream of their own, and a journey that was negotiated in reverse, north to south, over thousands of years by migratory Indigenous peoples. It's also the journey that any number of Australians in the sprawling suburbs promise themselves they will make one day to fulfil a dream of discovering the 'real Australia'. For Michael in his '69 Ford with his double bass for company, it was both a journey and a leap of faith. If he broke an axle or destroyed the diff and it all became too much, that'd be defeat. Once you set out on this particular road, turning back would be a failure of the imagination. Burke and Wills expired in the mulga, of course, but that was poor planning, not lack of courage.

In 1995 Michael's DipEd landed him a job, at St John's Catholic College in the Darwin suburb of Stuart Park, teaching music to boisterous children, including a substantial number of Indigenous kids from all over the Northern Territory. It's a college with provision for boarders and most of the Indigenous kids are amongst the boarders. Teaching at a high school a million miles from anything mainstream may have looked like a comedown from touring with The Killjoys and taking the stage with chamber orchestras in the big, bright capitals of Europe, but

Michael loved it. He was struck by the exuberance of the Indigenous kids. Even away from their families, they were full of that glee you find in children who've made a playground of the world. The smiles and laughter were enough by themselves to endorse his decision to come north. And then there was Kirrilly, a fellow teacher at St John's; attraction, romance, and all at once the prospect of a much more settled life than any he'd known since Beaumaris.

He'd developed an appetite for change; he'd driven up the highway as far as he could go. Was he happy now? Yes, but more important than the happiness was the liberty of imagination he experienced; a type of quickening that left him free to think in a way he'd barely bothered with until a year or so ago. 'Identity' for instance — what was it? He'd seen how vital and vigorous a sense of identity was amongst Indigenous people. It meant to black Australians something that went far beyond the casual sum of the habits that define us in a consumer society. Indigenous people drew their strength from a belief in their spiritual connection to the natural world, and embraced their ancestors as if those who had died still walked the earth beside them. The Indigenous people of Arnhem Land and the whole broad region between the Gulf of Carpentaria and Joseph Bonaparte Gulf — Yolŋu, Gälpu, Dangbon, Woolna, Ngandi, Ngalakan, Gunwinggu, Rambarrnga, Wuningangk, Ngalkbun — inhabited two worlds, only one of which was visible to a white man like Michael, and the greater part of what they believed about life and who they were was rooted in that invisible world. That was the fascinating thing.

White people go north with intentions of every stripe, and it might be true to say that some of those intentions are naïve, some very worthy, some bloody awful. Best if you go with intentions like Michael's: to look around and learn. Just have an open mind and a receptive imagination. Darwin was a portal sketched in the air, no pillars and no lintel, but an opening to a very different part of the world. Having passed through that portal, Michael was content to wait for the path ahead to open for him. The sense of mission he'd brought with him remained intact.

Other doors opened. The Northern Territory University (now Charles Darwin University) had more supportive contact with Indigenous Australians than any other institution of higher learning in the land. Its commitment to Indigenous education included an arts faculty outreach program that aimed to develop industry skills amongst black Territorians in remote communities, like the one on Elcho. Three months into his St John's gig, Michael applied to the NTU TAFE faculty for a position on the program, and was accepted. With a van full of musical instruments he took the program as far south as Tennant Creek, and as far north as the Tiwi Islands.

You don't have to spruik all that hard to get black kids engaged with music. They're avid. Music and sport — Australian Rules especially — are the two destinations of ambition that black kids in any numbers really care about in the Territory, or even elsewhere. And no wonder. The only Indigenous heroes they have ever seen are Cathy Freeman, on the dais with a gold medal around her neck; or Lionel Rose, with both arms raised in a boxing ring in Tokyo; or Jimmy Little; Mändawuy Yunupiŋu; Michael Long; Cyril Rioli; Kev Carmody, standing up on stage as applause fills an auditorium. It's endorsement, spectacular endorsement that captivates them.

When Michael flew to Elcho with his cargo of instruments for a three-month stint of mentoring, he expected to find a thriving musical culture already in place, but maybe not quite as lively as it turned out to be. In Galiwin'ku, kids already had rock heroes like George Burarrwaŋa (known as George Rrurrambu) of the Warumpi Band to look up to, and Elcho

Michael listening to his adopted brother singing and playing, enjoying the moment and the music.

Gurrumul playing around after completing a great photo shoot for the magazine Dumbo Feather.

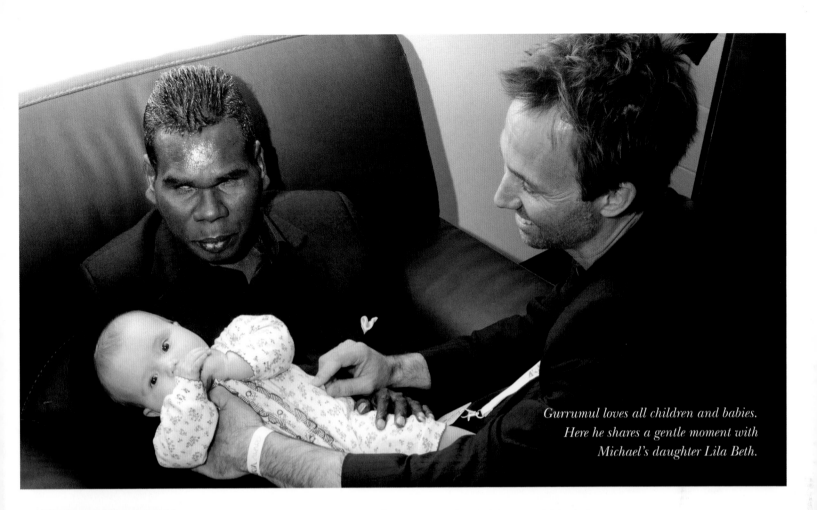

Gurrumul loves all children and babies.
Here he shares a gentle moment with
Michael's daughter Lila Beth.

'You speak, Michael.
You speak.'

was, after all, the very island that featured in the Warumpi and Christine Anu hit, 'My Island Home', written by Warumpi's Neil Murray. Another hero was Gurrumul, the blind black guy. The kids pointed him out to Michael: 'He been in Yothu Yindi, Gurrumul been every place.' Michael thought: 'Oh, really?' Michael had heard of Yothu Yindi, and he admired the band; he understood better than most the innovations of the Yothu Yindi sound.

The most importunate of the locals was a young bloke by the name of Manuel Dhurrkay, with an ego the size of Arnhem Land, but tremendously likeable at the same time. Manuel's ambition was to rock himself crazy, blaze a fiery path across Australian skies, win a million fans, settle into some Galiwin'ku Graceland. Manuel was the defining death-or-glory, music-mad young Indigenous guy, with just this one shortcoming: he couldn't play any instrument above a so-what level of competence. But he could sing. So when he turned up one day to be a part of what Michael was offering, Michael said: 'You need a band you can front.' Manuel sprinted off to recruit the people he'd need for a band, pleading, cajoling, knocking on every door he could find, and one of those doors was Gurrumul's.

Out of Manuel's charisma, Michael's patient mentoring and Gurrumul's rapid uptake, the Saltwater Band was born. On any given day all over the world, a million kids are struggling to build a band. It's a Bill & Ted, Wyld Stallyns, rite-of-passage thing. Nearly all of these bands fall apart before anyone hears of them, but not Saltwater, surely one of the best bands formed anywhere on earth on its particular day of foundation. Gurrumul played guitar, keyboards, sometimes drums, and this multi-instrumental mastery carried on through the rest of the members. Three Yunupiŋu family members, Andrew, Nigel and Johnathon; the Garawirrtja cousins Adrian and Lloyd; Manuel's brother Joshua, and Frank Wunuŋmurra changed instruments just for the novelty of it, without the sound suffering in the least. Manuel's vocals were full of muscle and sinew, perfectly judged for an outfit crazy for reggae and roots. Manuel sang in a Yolŋu language for the most part, and just as Gurrumul would later captivate us with the sound of Gumatj, so Saltwater showed what could be done with this language of East Arnhem Land and the Arafura coast.

Michael had savoured his good judgment in going north, but what Saltwater was achieving with his guidance added a rush of excitement. He began to see a way ahead for Saltwater, recognising that in Gurrumul, the *genius domus* of the band, something extraordinary had come the way of Indigenous music. He sat there, Gurrumul, his head weaving as if his blind eyes were searching out images he couldn't see, smiles coming and going, little whoops of pleasure and occasional cackles of laughter erupting from him, and Michael knew that he was experiencing a type of charisma he'd never before encountered. In Archie Roach, he'd seen the charisma of sorrow, a profound gravity. There was no great sorrow in Gurrumul, but there was that sense of a limitless life unfolding beneath the surface, as if his interior took in seas and storms and sunsets, towering clouds, the leap of dolphins catching the sun in a broad bay ringed by white sand, a crocodile lifting its head to roar. And he saw in Gurrumul, too, what he'd become aware of in other black Australians — that way in which they conveyed an identity not made up of individual components, but whole in itself, complete, reaching into the long ago, embracing all of time. But side-by-side with the confidence of identity lived a vulnerability, not to be entirely explained by Gurrumul's blindness. It was a vulnerability rooted in racial memory, as if Gurrumul and his brothers, like many other Indigenous Australians, knew of forces that could ride roughshod over their culture, and which had done just that in the past. Nobody who understood the life and experience of black Australians like Gurrumul would wish to violate their culture, but what of those who didn't understand, or even worse, those who misunderstood? Gurrumul, reaching for Michael's hand, was paying him the compliment of trust, something to be valued forever.

This was the moment of confluence, when the flow of two distinct talents merge. Michael would say: 'Let's try this,' and acted out the suggestion on this instrument or that. Or: 'Have you thought of this?' and demonstrated something the Saltwater boys hadn't yet imagined. Michael's credentials as an innovator impressed Gurrumul and all of the Saltwater boys, but what made him more welcome was his feel for the culture around him. This wasn't a white boy dispensing the largesse of his craft to a gang of benighted boys from the bush; this was intelligence, curiosity, a desire to learn, a foundational respect.

Saltwater was ripe for recording by 1998, but it would be murder trying to get anyone interested in a band from the Territory singing in a language nobody out there knew a thing about. You'd sell, what? — five hundred CDs, a thousand at best? Michael buttonholed people higher up the food chain at Northern Territory University, including his department head, attempting to drum up interest in a university-sponsored record label. It wasn't an outrageous idea; certainly not outside the theoretical scope of what the university had taken on with its musical outreach program. On the contrary, it fitted in beautifully. Imagine the rush those kids would experience if they could flaunt a CD with their own music on it. The department said: 'Maybe.' But at a staff meeting a little later, the suggestion of a record label was dismissed: 'Michael has been speaking of a record label that the university would sponsor. It's not going to happen.'

Michael by this time had met and developed a friendship with Mark Grose, the council clerk of the Galiwin'ku shire, who was as committed as Michael to making some sort of difference in the lives of black kids. Michael had spoken of the record label to Mark a number of times, and Mark thought: 'Pie in the sky.' In his role as council clerk, he'd listened to scheme after scheme proposed by visionaries up from the south, some of them plain nuts but a few fairly feasible. Each scheme was designed to transform the lives of black Australians, put some money in their pockets, empower them hugely. But it was talk, all talk, no sense of what would really be required to get a scheme up and running. Then one fine day Mark pointedly asked Michael if these Saltwaters actually had any talent.

'Yeah, they do.'

'You're sure of that?'

'I'm sure.'

'Because if you're sure, okay, we'll do it. We'll start a label. I'm serious.'

Despite everything we know of the way the world works; despite our loyalty to logic, to sturdy reason, it's difficult sometimes not to believe in destiny. The record label that Mark Grose and Michael Hohnen established in 1999 was Skinnyfish Music, which had no right to flourish, but did. Saltwater, a band fashioned out of a rapidly convened posse of Elcho

Islanders who had time on their hands, should have produced some sort of mongrel ska/reggae/roots/folk/rock/northern blues mish-mash, but instead it found the inspiration to fashion three albums that deserve to be part of the Australian music canon forever. Geoffrey Gurrumul Yunupiŋu, after a fruitful but rowdy few years with Yothu Yindi, emerging dazed and confused from the ordeal, should have faded into obscurity in Galiwin'ku, but instead realised his manifest destiny and changed the Australian cultural estate forever. Mark Grose, after years of wandering the continent, might well have spent more years doing just that. Instead, he discovered in his make-up a knack for marketing, sat with a telephone for twelve hours a day and made a hit out of Saltwater's first album. And Michael Hohnen, who, with less imagination, might have found himself in middle age playing gigs at hotel lounges on Mother's Day, pricked up his ears, headed north and discovered a genius.

Gurrumul performing as lead singer with his band, Saltwater. Stewart Dhawulu Wunuŋmurra is the dancer in the background. Saltwater's sound was big and sophisticated, almost from the beginning.

CHAPTER 4

Home

This is where he was named, where he became the crocodile,

where lore whispered in his ear and bound him to his ancestors.

This is where he became Gurrumul.

That's Howard Island with a fringe of fawn sands, just across from Elcho. Barely inhabited, just an outstation or 'homeland' down one end there, a few cattle, and perhaps ten people in all. But this is Elcho with its population of almost three thousand, including Gurrumul when he's home, and he's home today, Gurrumul and his entire family: mother, father, brothers, uncles, aunts, cousins galore. It might be possible later in the day to call in and shake hands, or it might not. The Elcho community has been celebrating the funeral rites of one of its members for a full week and may continue to honour him for another week. The schedule of observance takes precedence over all other business, and it may be — no one can be certain — that Gurrumul will be committed for the next few hours … or for the day … maybe even longer.

Mark Grose from Skinnyfish and Gurrumul's 'adopted' father says: 'It might sound strange, but funerals are the main industry on Elcho.' The entire community will commit itself to the rites, and even relatives no longer living on Elcho fly in from wherever on earth they find themselves when they learn of the passing. Funeral dishes to prepare, funeral feasting, funeral processions, singing, dancing, ritual tributes. People who are mourned on Elcho are mourned with vigour and feeling.

The funerals are usually held in turn. Those who died on a Monday will be honoured with rites before those who died on Friday of the same week. But it's not a strict rule. Some insuperable difficulty in getting those from afar to a funeral in time might mean that Friday is buried before Monday. And the backlog can see a funeral delayed for weeks after death; even longer. The ritual of farewell itself is so dense, so complex, so complete that it's impossible to predict when a break might occur in these serial obsequies.

Gurrumul's father Terry Nyambi
Yunupiŋu, a warm and generous carer,
who is immensely proud of his son.

BAKITJU

Ga nhinana ŋarra	I sat
bala ŋäthinana..a	And cried..d
roŋiyinana bala wäŋalilina..a	For my home
Nalilayu Gunyaŋara	Nalilayu, Gunyaŋara
Ga nhinana ŋarra	I sat
bala ŋäthinana..a	And cried
roŋiyinana Dhalpulmurruyu Ŋarrariyal	For my country Dhalpulmurru, Ŋarrariyal
Gawupuyu Bandirriya	Gawupu, Bandirriya,
U..u gunda Bakitju	Oh my Rock and strength, Bakitju
U..u gunda Rraywala	Oh my Rock and strength, Rraywala
U..u nhenydja ŋäthiya	Weep, weep for your home
Wo..o gunda nhäma Bakitju	Behold the Rock, Bakitju
E..e Rrakpala nhina ŋilimurru	We the Gumatj people live
Ŋurukuna gunda wo, Bakitju - Rirralinygu - Naŋuypurr	for that Rock, Bakitju, Rriraliny, Nhaŋuypuy
Wo..o nhina ŋilimurru Djurarr Rrakpala	We the Djurarr, Rrakpala, the Gumatj people
E..e ŋurukuna Gundawu	are of that Rock
Dharulŋura nhina yarrayarr'yun	We Gumatj sit contemplating under the shelter
Wo Rrakpala Djurarr	of our country
Mala waŋgany Djurarr Rräyuŋ	Oh we the Gumatj
	Together, one people, one spirit
U..u gunda Bakitju	Oh my Rock and strength, Bakitju
U..u gunda Rraywala	Oh my Rock and strength, Rraywala
U..u nhenydja ŋäthiya	Weep, weep for your home
Ga nhina ŋilimurru guluwunbuma, minygarrarrayun	We sit together, sharing under the shelter of our country
Mala waŋgany Rrakpala Rräyuŋ	Together one Gumatj people, Rrakpala, Rräyuŋ
Waŋganyŋura Dharulŋura	Under our shade Dharul
Dharriŋŋura Galupa	At Galupa where our Makassan relatives visited
Ga yäkthurra ŋanya latjukuŋa, ḻerrpuŋanydja	Take special care, look after
Bonalŋura dhuwalinydja Gapanyŋura Gopuluŋura	these mounded funeral sites Gapany, Gopulu
Bothaŋura ḻiyawayma	for our Gumatj knowledge and wisdom is here
Ga nhina Yolŋu märr-nininyŋu	Gumatj, people of the land
Makarr mulka Balalapu	Stay close and strong
Märrŋura nhina ḏitjpurrkŋura ḏuwarrmirriŋura	Keep (our) spirits strong in (our) Gumatj identity
Liyanydja nhina djirrmilyun	Keep our minds focussed
Ga dhuwalinydja wäŋa Mayaŋ-ŋaraka ŋilimurruŋu	Mayaŋ-ŋaraka is our place
Gu ŋilimurru nhina waŋganyŋura, Bonalŋura	Let's live together, on our ancestral lands
Liyanydja nhina ḏirrmalawu	Keep our thoughts fresh like the north-west wind
U..u gunda Bakitju	Oh my Rock and strength, Bakitju
U..u gunda Rraywala	Oh my Rock and strength, Rraywala
U..u nhenydja ŋäthiya	Weep, weep for your home
U..u gunda Bakitju	Oh my Rock and strength, Bakitju

'Faraway from home' is one of the foundational themes of Indigenous songwriting, in something of the way in which heartbreak has dominated Western poetry and songwriting since the time of the Provençal troubadours. It forms the subject of half of all Gurrumul's compositions. But not all of his songs of absence from country are loaded with grief. Indeed, in songs such as this, he is simply drinking from the great wellspring of Indigenous inspiration. Longing for country in this song (at the level of language) functions as a type of Top End blues: singing of heartache restores the heart.

All things considered, it might be better if I wander around the island making notes and attempting to look a little less foolish than I do, but really, what's the chance of that? Black slacks, shod feet, designer long-sleeved shirt, multiple layers of SPF 30+, and my notebook. I stop and write, 'Strange bird with silver feathers,' then march on until the next strange bird catches my attention.

This is Galiwin'ku, the main town on Elcho, with its three hundred steel-frame houses designed to withstand the full force of a cyclone when it comes. The houses are hemmed in on all sides by wet-season waist-high grasses and wild bamboo, and by the taller greenery of banana plants, palm trees, mango trees, frangipani trees and hibiscus plants. At the bottom of the town, the Arafura Sea, the cornucopia of coast-dwelling black communities, extends from East Arnhem Land to the Van Diemen Gulf beyond Darwin to the west.

Galiwin'ku is the name of the main settlement on Elcho, and although it is far and away the largest settlement on the island, a number of other tiny towns or camps are scattered through the forest and in the bush above the shoreline: Gäwa, Ban'thula, Djurrunalpi, Dhambala, Galawarra. The entire surface of the island in its every feature, reaching down to the lapping waves of the bays and inlets, bears Yolŋu names, and each name has its place in story and is connected to many others through ancestral activity that's made clear in the clansongs. The island is a dramatic web of narratives, more than a geographical entity. The air above it, the layered earth beneath its skin — all of it seethes with association. As I walk the island, I can't help but think of the science of its formation; of frigid epochs that lowered sea levels; of warmer periods that raised them; of vegetation bound to thrive in soils with certain mineral qualities. But this is not the island that Gurrumul knows.

It's a very beautiful place, this island at the top of the continent.

Elcho's fecundity also gives us some of the finest Indigenous art originating anywhere in Australia. Local artists Peter Datjiŋ Burarrwaŋa and Gäli Yalkarriwuy Gurruwiwi preserve all of the formal traditions of Elcho and Yolŋu art, while at the same time conveying something especially vivid. People from Elcho, raised in their clan culture, will know in an instant if a bark painting of fire tongues (the traditional diamond design in black and sepia) comes from Elcho, and from the hand of Peter Datjiŋ Burarrwaŋa, or if a feathered morning star pole is the work of Gali Yalkarriwuy Gurruwiwi. For someone like me, from outside the culture, looking at the work of these two Elcho artists it is very like looking at the forms and shapes and shadows of the island itself, as if Peter and Gäli had by some process transformed Elcho into a Cezanne-esque mosaic of intense colour and subtle design. But it's more than this, because the works also embody the narrative of the Yolŋu.

Not all the creativity of Elcho is channelled into painting and sculpting. Some creativity takes the form of satire, as in the case of Elcho's celebrated Chooky Dancers. But are the Chooky Dancers of Elcho showing us something uniquely Yolŋu? The Chooky Dancers who perform a part cabaret, part disco version of Zorba's dance, to Mikis Theodorakis' music? Well, no. But what the Chooky Dancers do superbly is to put on display something that we might lose sight of when we focus too intensely on the politics of north-east Arnhem Land — the Yolŋu sense of humour. Because the Yolŋu do enjoy a joke, and in the case of the Chookies, the joke is that we expect to witness the spectacle of Indigenous dance and instead see a satirical version of the well-known Zorba choreography, so beloved of tipsy guests at wedding receptions. These boys of fifteen and up who form the Chooky ensemble became overnight sensations when Big Frank — a Yolŋu elder and Yolŋu legend, and a man who likes a laugh — logged a clip of the dancers on YouTube in 2007. The boys were teasingly honouring a Greek friend on Elcho, who was leaving the island after a long sojourn, and all at once found themselves celebrated around the globe.

I enjoy an episode of Yolŋu satire myself when I stand on a roadside in Galiwin'ku with notebook and pen, recording everything I see. Kids are chasing each other through the tall, wet-season grass with spears made of green bamboo, laughing and shrieking. After a few minutes, I notice that the kids are now laughing at me. I glance around and see a skinny boy in baggy shorts and a loose I Heart Darwin T-shirt miming me with an imaginary notebook and imaginary pen. He has captured my earnest expression perfectly. 'We are slowly discovering,' writes W.E.H. Stanner in his 1956 essay on Aboriginal humour, 'that (the Aborigine) had a rich aesthetic capacity and an interesting metaphysical conception of life and the world; and I can testify from much acquaintance that he added to these a very marked sense of humour.' And how many times have I seen a wicked smile playing at the corners of Gurrumul's lips as he listens to the hustle and bustle of the people around him. Or this: 'Gurrumul, here's Robert again. He's just making some notes.' That's Michael talking. And Gurrumul smiles.

Now, this place I've arrived at, this open area near the church where boughs of brilliant foliage reach up from trees and form a line, Gurrumul was here a couple of years back at an extraordinary ceremony of mourning. The man being mourned was a member of the church community, but he was first and foremost an elder of the island's black community. It was thought only right that he be honoured according to the rites of each of his communities, and so here, beneath the trees, his kin, including Gurrumul's mother, Daisy, sang him into the embrace of his ancestors in Yolŋu language he had spoken all his life, then switched to English and sang the hymns of his second faith. At the change from Gumatj to English, the mourning party took advantage of the amplification on hand: a hand-held mic and speakers.

Gurrumul sat cross-legged in the dust, his head weaving as he followed the singing. Others sat close by, still and stern, but at the same time devoted to the passion of ceremony, since ceremony means the world to the Gumatj; ceremony, singing, the motion of spirits in the air all around. It was a dress-up occasion and the women amongst the chief mourners wore colourful skirts and loose, patterned tops, while the men wore smart, open-necked shirts and pleated trousers. At a certain point in the ceremony, the senior-most mourner — the eldest male relative of the man being honoured — dropped to his knees and bowed his head. The members of the mourning party shuffled to where he knelt and placed their hands on his head, on his shoulders, sometimes two mourners at once. Nothing in the expressions of those watching registered the change from Gumatj to Christian rites. It was an unbroken ceremony.

The wet season is coming to a close but the island still gets a drenching towards the end of each afternoon. The clouds thicken and darken above the Arafura Sea; the wind changes direction by fifteen degrees; a dozen fat drops of rain hit the red soil so lazily you can count them. A minute later, the clouds spill everything they've got, like warm water poured from a cauldron. Then it's over. The thudding of the downpour is succeeded by the more musical sound of trees shedding the storm drop by drop. The blooms of wildflowers become more vivid, as if varnished; the warm earth evaporates the moisture it has drawn into itself; wisps of vapour rise from the forest's understorey. Now the honeyeaters return from shelter and get back to work in their fanatical way, plunging their beaks into the miniature wells of small, blue, trumpet-shaped flowers.

Pools of red water form along the dirt roads wherever a small depression or slough has been fashioned by nature or by motor traffic. The vehicles of Elcho, all but a few of them four-wheel drives, wear an orange skirt halfway up the Duco of their bodies. On the road leading north from Galiwin'ku, I notice what I've been told to look out for — a tamarind tree, standing above a freshwater swamp. Every source of fresh water on Elcho is flagged by evergreen tamarinds (*djambaŋ*), planted by the Makassan traders, from south-west Sulawesi, who visited the island and a hundred other sites along the Arnhem coast from the mid-seventeenth century onwards. Hundreds of Makassan words have entered the vocabulary of the Arnhem tribes, Gumatj included, terms of designation largely, applied to objects or concepts that hadn't entered the scope of Indigenous languages before the arrival of the Makassans: *rrupiya* (money); Kayu Jawa (western coast); *lipa-lipa* (canoes); even *balanda* (white people), whom the Makassans had encountered long before the Yolŋu met them.

Gurrumul's name is itself Makassan, and that seems apt, because the Makassans brought something to East Arnhem Land that flourished here: new ideas, a creative quickening. Echoes of that quickening in the creative life of the Yolŋu can be detected in the scope of Gurrumul's vision as a songwriter. There's a broader liberty of reference in his songs than you find in some traditional narratives of the Yolŋu and, in places, a complexity of thought in the way images are juxtaposed, that might well go all the way back to that dimension of observation introduced from Sulawesi. The Makassan influence aside, East Arnhem Land has been a heartland of Indigenous ingenuity and creativity expressed in sculpture, painting and ceremony for a very long time. Gurrumul's individual genius can be seen as the most recent manifestation of a Yolŋu/Gumatj genius drawn up from the red earth over thousands of years. The Yunupiŋu sub-clan certainly think of its members as belonging to the aristocracy of Indigenous Australia; an aristocracy founded on imaginative brilliance and an Aboriginal version of old-fashioned chutzpah. Michael tells the story of a visit to Adelaide with Gurrumul in 2009 that illustrates the Yunupiŋu loftiness. In the lobby of the Hilton in Adelaide, there's Nigel Yunupiŋu making himself supremely comfortable on a plush sofa while waiting for check-in to be completed. Legs stretched out, his back supported by cushions, arms folded, gazing about over the petty comings and goings in the lobby like royalty enthroned. Michael's whispered pleas for him to take his feet off the sofa meet only with scoffs.

'Nigel, you must.'

'*Yaka!*' says Nigel — No!

'I'm not kidding, Nigel — put your feet down.'

'*Yaka!*' says Nigel, and again, '*Yaka!*'

Finally, Michael tells him that a security guard will surely come over and order him to put his feet down.

Nigel answers, with haughty disdain: 'He won't. I'm a Yunupiŋu.'

It's the fresh water that attracted people to Elcho in distant times. That fresh water complemented the bounty of the coastal waters, forests and swamps. If ever Elcho was an Eden, it was then,

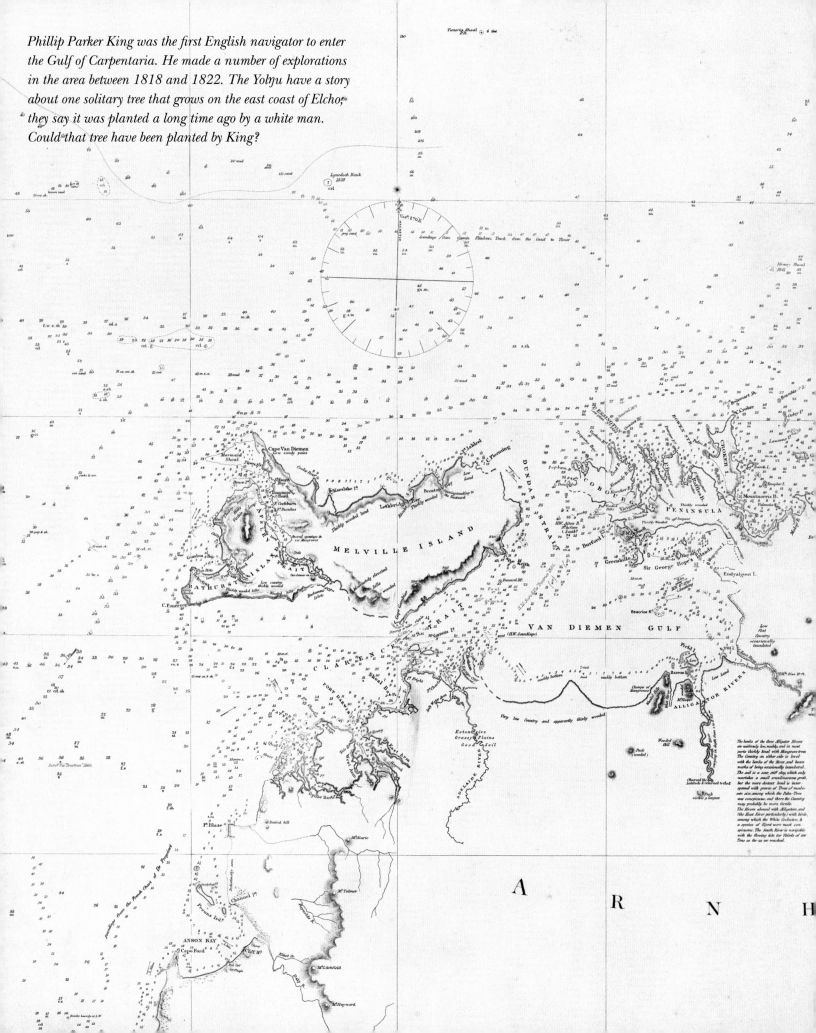

Phillip Parker King was the first English navigator to enter the Gulf of Carpentaria. He made a number of explorations in the area between 1818 and 1822. The Yolŋu have a story about one solitary tree that grows on the east coast of Elcho; they say it was planted a long time ago by a white man. Could that tree have been planted by King?

Chart
of
THE NORTH COAST OF
AUSTRALIA.
SHEET IV.
BY PHILLIP P. KING,
Commander. R.N.
1818-21.

WITH ADDITIONS BY COMMANDERS WICKHAM AND STOKES. 1839

Lieut. Chimmo 1856, Fred. Howard Master, & M.S. Guy, 2nd Master, R.N 1865.66.

Magnetic Variation in 1876; nearly stationary.

	HWF & C.	
Arnhem	VIIIh Sp. rise 6 to 8 ft.	
Goulburn	VI	5 to 6
Alligator (East River Bar) VIII½	13	
Shoal Bay	VI	18 to 25	Np. 14 to 20 feet
Port Kents	VI	22

Current: —— Flood —→ Ebb —→

Var.ⁿ 3° O.E.

Cape Wessel

WESSEL'S ISLANDS

Cumberland Strait

Truant Iᵈ

BROWN'S STRAIT

Point Dale

THE ENGLISH COMPANY'S ISLANDS

C. Wilberforce

ELCHO I.

Cadell Strait

BUCKINGHAM R.

INGLIS

MELVILLE BAY

Melville P.

CROCODILE ISLANDS

CASTLEREAGH BAY

ARNHEM BAY

VIII

Low woody country

C. Arnhem

N. Goulburn I.

S. Goulburn I.

VI

Braithwaite Pt.

Junction Bay

Liverpool R.

Table Hill

VII

Goyder R.

Pine Palm Forest

The Coast engraved in hair line is taken
from the Map of Captain Cadell's
exploration of northern territory. (1868)

Low woody country

CALEDON BAY

C. Grey

A R N H E M ' S   L A N D

BLUE MUD BAY

Bickerton I.

PART OF

Daisy Gurruwiwi, Gurrumul's mother, had to find the love and courage to raise a blind baby in a remote community. From his birth in 1971 up until the present day, Daisy has encouraged her son to embrace his musical gift and live life to the full.

Bäpa

The lyrics of Gurrumul's songs, reflecting his culture, rarely concentrate on individual experience, but instead reach out to encompass more general features of the Yolŋu story. Like a stone thrown into a waterhole, the initial splash is the impetus for widening wavelets, which eventually reach the shore, and subside. The verses of 'Bäpa', which is Yolŋu for 'father', can be listened to all the way through as a love song honouring Gurrumul's father Nyambi (Terry) but they actually commence with Nyambi, then reach across time and space to the ancestral past and to sites of spiritual significance. All the same, the tenderness with which Gurrumul renders the song these days (it was written fifteen years ago) is a tribute to his father, a generous and honoured man, employed for the whole of his occupational life as a master mechanic in Galiwin'ku, now suffering from an illness that restricts him cruelly. It was often Nyambi who took Gurrumul to ceremonies; who revealed to all of his four sons — Djanarri, Gurrumul, Bambung, Bawurramu — the lore of the clan, the wonders of the world, the difference between right and wrong. The role of 'father' in Yolŋu society is not the sole province of a child's biological male parent but extends to uncles, and further still. What Gurrumul manages to convey in 'Bäpa' is a love and esteem that places Nyambi amongst those men of his clan who have done the fullest justice to fatherhood in their attention and care. 'Bäpa' is the hand that rests on the child's shoulder, the voice that tells the child: 'Like this, do you see?'

In the early days of the Saltwater Band, Terry Yunupiŋu, Gurrumul's father, was an important inclusion in the touring party. He was there to make sure things were done right.

Gurrumul's sisters Valerina Birrarapi Yunupiŋu (left) and Jennifer Djapu Yunupiŋu.

the sea yielding dolphin, yellowfin, shark, skinnyfish, barramundi, turtles, lobsters, stingrays, mudfish, mussels, and the land, swamps, wallabies, lizards, magpie geese. Not that Elcho was ever the sole province of the Gumatj. To tell the truth, many of the Gumatj presently living on Elcho came here from elsewhere in East Arnhem Land, and different parts of Elcho are owned by different clan groups, so not everyone in today's Elcho community can count the island as his or her country. When the Japanese bombed the coastal towns of the Territory during the Second World War, the missions established further west (such as the Milingimbi mission, which started out on Elcho in 1921, then made a new home in Milingimbi, only to return to Elcho in 1942) moved their congregations to Elcho. Whatever the pedigree of Gurrumul in the annals of Indigenous habitation of Elcho, it is certainly one of the places on earth he calls home, together with Gumatj ancestral sites further east. And like all Indigenous Australians, Yunupiŋu or otherwise, 'home' means everything that has gone into the making of you; sea and sky, rusty red clay, the birds of the air whose cries reached your ears when you sat in the sand below Galiwin'ku with your mothers and your brothers.

That relaxed, open-air, sit-down format — mums, dads, kids galore, uncles, aunts, cousins, mates all enjoying each other's company — gets a thorough workout in Galiwin'ku; and for longer periods than people could afford in times past when the exigencies of hunting and gathering took up most of the daylight hours. If there's any shortage of aluminium-framed folding chairs, the more senior males have priority; the women will sit cross-legged on the ground, often at a short remove from the men. Sometimes there's a guitar on hand, maybe a ghetto blaster laying waste to local eardrums. The scene has its charms, until you realise it's underemployment that provides the leisure. People, wherever they live, can only stand so much leisure. In traditional Yolŋu society, what might be called leisure was integrated into the structure of a tribe's vital life; discussion, storytelling, negotiation. Killing time isn't the same thing.

The white man who had the greatest influence on Gurrumul before the arrival on the island of Michael and Mark was Harold Shepherdson, the Methodist minister who brought his mission from Milingimbi to the safety of Elcho in 1942, three months after the Japanese air force bombed Darwin and settlements along the coast. Shepherdson and his wife, Ella, established the mission close to the present site of Galiwin'ku, then a larger mission further north on Elcho. This was the second attempt of the Methodists to build a mission on Elcho; the first attempt, decades earlier, ended in failure, and when Bäpa Sheppy (as he was to become known) arrived, the island was without any settlement at all. Within a few years, vegetable gardens and a sawmill were able to employ a number of Sheppy's congregation; a clinic and a school served the entire black community of the island, and more people from the mainland. It wouldn't be going too far to say that the people of Elcho loved Shepherdson and Mrs Sheppy, and loved the mission. It was not only the energy and enterprise of Shepherdson that attracted people; the bible lessons, the hymns and songs (rousing tunes that had nothing to do with Christianity but were adored nonetheless), the school and the clinic made the congregation feel as if it were in the care of a man with a big heart. Sheppy and Mrs Sheppy knew the names of everyone on the island, and the state of health of all the children. If this was paternalism, it was nonetheless welcome.

The mission was a model of locally resourced development. Houses were built from local timber and carpentered by Indigenous tradesmen. From the house foundations to

Reverend Harold Shepherdson and his wife Ella, with several of the mission staff, on Elcho Island in 1952.

Brothers in Arms: Philip Yunupiŋu, Gurrumul and Andrew Yunupiŋu.

Lynette Baru Yunupiŋu, Gurrumul's niece; Valerina Birrarapi Yunupiŋu, Gurrumul's sister; and little 'Gamik' Sophia, also Gurrumul's niece.

Namul, Gurrumul's pooch, enjoying a photo opportunity after the return of his master from tour.

Small stage, small sound system, keen musicians, babies being held close to the stage, too many dogs on the basketball court, and hundreds of kids – it's concert night on Elcho.

Languages

The proliferation of Indigenous languages on the Australian continent during the long pre-settlement era reflects the stability of the tribal system. Wars, or at least conflict between tribes, weren't uncommon but annihilation of an enemy was. Languages that evolved attained maturity, and endured. The large number of Indigenous languages that have become extinct were lost entirely during the post-settlement era, when disease and displacement wiped out entire language communities.

Gurrumul speaks a number of Indigenous languages, in common with a dwindling number of Indigenous Australians who were raised in the culture of their clans. In Gurrumul's case, his range of languages all fall into the Yolŋu Matha (Yolŋu family) cluster. For Indigenous Australians, language is a highly fluid resource, but at the same time strictly delineated in its employment. The tongue spoken can vary according to circumstance and occasion. As a child, Gurrumul would have spoken his mother's Gälpu tongue, waiting until puberty to speak Gumatj in any consistent way. Language can vary according to dictates of courtesy — the mother's tongue used on some occasions, the father's on others. Indeed, the protocols of courtesy amongst Indigenous Australians are more complex than those of the Sun King's court. Language in all its subtleties is a great agency of order, honouring clan, hierarchy, kin, ancestors, neighbours and abiding spirits.

Gurrumul's languages facilitate the rhythms of singing so fluently that it could almost be imagined that they evolved that way. The relationship within sentences between vowels and the vowel completion of words provides an inbuilt, flowing cadence, as in, '… *ya ŋändi manda marrkapmirri manda, nhumanydja ŋäthinyanydja milŋurr Burarrapu …*' ('oh my mums, beloved mums, cry for the sacred spring Burarrapu …') A version of this singing cadence once existed in English, from the time of Chaucer to the Elizabethans, and its loss is apparent when Gurrumul sings in English, as on 'Gurrumul History'. The powerful, repeated stress on the first syllable found in Gumatj is not possible in English. Singing in his languages, with the first syllable stressed, he conveys an authority that remains even when he softens his voice. It is the flowing quality of Gurrumul's songs in language that exert such appeal to non-Indigenous ears. The songs never sound as if they had been 'written' but instead that they'd emerged spontaneously from Gurrumul's clan life.

Josephine Flood has written of Indigenous languages with painstaking care, informed by decades of close study. She says:

> All Aboriginal languages have a rich vocabulary and complex grammar … They have conjugation for verbs and declension for nouns, and many also have a gender system for nouns. The Dyirbal language of north Queensland has four genders — masculine, feminine, neuter and edible. The edible gender refers to food plants, a useful grammatical category in a rainforest environment with over 700 plant species, only a third of which are edible and many are poisonous. The edible gender was an ingenious way of teaching children the difference.

> Aboriginal languages each contain up to 10,000 words, a similar number to spoken English. Special features are pronouns that distinguish not 'you' singular and 'you' plural, but also 'you-two', 'you-many', 'we-two', 'we-many-of-us', 'they-two' and 'they many'.

The languages vary widely in vocabulary and grammatical structure but also generally resemble each other and usually employ a modest range of speech sounds of similar type. Words tend to be of two or more syllables and to end in a vowel. The main stress is usually on the first syllable.

Word meanings were extended to cover new items. Horses became known in the Sydney region as *yaraman*, meaning long-toothed one, and this name spread quickly with the colonists. Money was termed *gadna* signifying pebble by the Arabana of South Australia; telephone wires were known as *yooroo*, a spider's web, by the Gooniyandi of Western Australia. Aeroplanes were called *kantyal*, meaning eaglehawk, by the Wunambal in the Kimberley.

Gurrumul's daughter, Jasmine (Wangura).

the electrical wiring, everything was completed by locals. Apart from the benefit to the Elcho economy of hiring within the community, the finished houses stood as models of accomplishment. Out in Humpty Doo (it's a local gag, naming the 'suburbs' of Galiwin'ku after the suburbs of Darwin) the federal government has erected more than a hundred new houses to ease the accommodation crisis on Elcho. And they're fine, sturdy houses, but the steel-frame construction rules out the involvement of Elcho carpenters. Tradesmen from the mainland — whitefellas — have charge of the project. The sense of involvement of the local community is diminished, and when the houses are ready for occupancy, they will be accepted, gratefully, as a gift from Canberra, but they will never be thought of in the same way as the older, timber houses built by the community.

In the tall grass along the red roads of Galiwin'ku, shirtless and shoeless boys of the age of seven, eight and nine stalk each other with mock-spears of green bamboo. Their technique is fabulous — erect upper body at the moment of the spear's despatch, front leg planted well forward, balance enhanced by placing all the weight over the pivoting ball of the rear foot. These kids are fair dinkum. Mark Grose tells of a time when he was carting half a dozen Yolŋu kids around in his car and, from out of the mulga, a wallaby appeared. In an instant the vehicle was full of scrambling limbs with the kids breaking their necks to get out and give chase. 'Marky, Marky, stop here Marky!' Earlier in the day, these kids would have fed themselves on fried chicken from one of Galiwin'ku's takeaways, but the passion in their blood is still roused by the prospect of a slab of wallaby roasted on an open fire.

Gurrumul, in his childhood, Elcho all around him but invisible, drew into his being a way of understanding the world and himself that keeps him closer to those boys in Mark's car than to anyone outside his culture. He went to school here, attended church here, sang in the choir, nurtured his talent, grew to manhood, travelled from these shores to the other side of the earth and returned. This is where he was named, where he became the crocodile, where lore whispered in his ear and bound him to his ancestors. This is where he became Gurrumul.

The Yolŋu and their related clans believe that here the world began, in East Arnhem Land, with the sea before them and the land behind them. And 'believe' is too mild a term for their convictions: they have no doubt at all. This much can be said, at least: East Arnhem Land may well have been the first place on earth where humans succeeded in developing a sophisticated scheme of belief and regulation that left nothing in their experience unexplained; an integrated set of structures that provided a continuous narrative of a people from birth, through life and beyond.

Today after the rain, standing close to the dripping trees, I wait for the funeral to conclude; for the chance to say a few words to Gurrumul. But just for the moment, any questions I might ask, and any answers I might record, seem beside the point. Look at the mist rising from the bark of the tree trunks as the warmth within the wood evaporates the rain. The trees creak very faintly during this process. Best just listen. Be still and listen. This might be the sound from the beginning of the world.

Yolŋu

Gurrumul is both Gumatj and Yolŋu. 'Gumatj' is his clan, a sub-group of the much larger Yolŋu tribe, or language family. The name, 'Yolŋu', is translatable into English as 'person', but the meaning is denser than that, more like, 'us, the people'. The traditional estates of the Yolŋu take in a large section of East Arnhem Land reaching inland from the Gulf of Carpentaria and the Arafura Sea, including a number of islands, of which Elcho Island is the most populated. A number of languages flourish amongst the Yolŋu, all distinctly related. The tongues within the Yolŋu family of languages, or Yolŋu Matha, number forty or more, many of which are within the mastery of a Yolŋu adult. A few Yolŋu may also speak the languages of the neighbouring Ngandi, Ngalkbun, Rembarnga and Dangbon communities.

The Yolŋu clans embrace a highly complex system of laws, rituals and observances that cover the life experience of clan members from before conception to death and beyond. Cultural practices vary from clan to clan, but that which is shared between clan cultures is far more striking than the differences. Yet it must be said that the differences add to the vigour of Yolŋu culture.

The Yolŋu have enjoyed the bounty of their coastal domain for millennia, as well as that of the land. A rich strand of Yolŋu Matha is devoted to the Yolŋu experience of the sea in its rewards and moods and dangers. A number of Gurrumul's songs draw on his clan's close bond with the marine world, reaching back to a time (so the Gumatj believe) when the founding ancestors of the clan came from across the ocean and brought life to the land.

Before the arrival of white settlers in the late eighteenth century, most black Australians knew that the world extended beyond the lands they traditionally roamed, but only as far as the oceans. The experience of the Yolŋu was different. The coast of East Arnhem Land attracted visitors over the years from beyond the Yolŋu world. The tribal memory of the Yolŋu clans includes references to a people — the Bayini — who came to the Arnhem Land coast possibly as early as the fifteenth century. Various clues suggest that the Bayini were from South-East Asia, and may even have journeyed to the continent's northern coast from China. These mysterious people may have engaged in some rudimentary form of trade with the Yolŋu, but nothing on the scale of the trade the Yolŋu transacted with the Makassans of Sulawesi from the early eighteenth century to the early twentieth century. Exchange with the Makassans brought finely-woven cloth and metal implements (knives, in particular) into the Yolŋu world, as well as stimulants, such as tobacco. Of even greater benefit to the Yolŋu than the Makassan knives was instruction in the manufacture of sea-going craft, such as canoes.

The Yolŋu have a reputation for ingenuity and creative vigour, which may well have been enhanced by this contact with the Makassans. In the right circumstances (such as peaceful trade) exposure to technologies not yet imagined within your culture can have the reverberation of a thunderclap. One consequence of this exposure of the Yolŋu to the broader world was advance knowledge of the white men (*balanda*, a local rendering of the Makassan word, *hollander*) who would one day come to East Arnhem Land on a mission quite different to that of the visitors from Sulawesi. When the *balanda* did finally appear, the Yolŋu were not mystified. The Yolŋu evolved a sense of how extensively the world stretched beyond the sea's horizon.

'The Yolŋu,' says John Greatorex, 'look out at the world from a secure place. It's their culture that makes them feel secure. This feeling of security allows them to have reactions that a whitefella might think strange. Let's imagine that you say something a bit insulting to a Yolŋu man. He might make no response at all. It's not because he doesn't understand. He's thinking: "Oh, is that what you believe? Well, so be it." He doesn't feel under attack, as a whitefella would.'

John has lived with the Yolŋu for decades and, as much as any white man, he understands their subtlety.

'Somebody like Gurrumul,' I say to John, 'has to master two cultures, doesn't he? He might feel most secure with his own Gumatj culture, but if he has to, he can play a role and respond to the world like you and me. For whatever reason. Perhaps Michael has arranged an interview, something like that. He might find it tedious, but he'll go along with it. He knows how to do that.'

John sits back in his chair and gazes thoughtfully towards the ceiling of the room. 'Yes and no,' he says. 'I've seen Gurrumul being interviewed. After a time, he simply said, "Why are you asking me all these questions?" He said, "Why do you want to know?" It's a question of politeness. In Yolŋu culture you wouldn't ask questions in the way we do. You would assume that another person would tell you what he wanted to tell you and you'd be content to leave it at that. If you asked Gurrumul how long he was going to take to do something — some task — he'd think, "Why doesn't he just wait and see?"'

So it's to do with culture and manners. Perhaps there's a type of grace in Gurrumul's lack of interest in talking about himself. Listening to John — and there's something like grace in John's own manner — you do begin to see the intrusiveness in the interrogative format of the standard interview. Gurrumul seems to be saying: 'Stick around, look, listen,' as if anything of importance that we can learn about him will emerge through observation.

Keith Garadhawal Garrawurra, a highly respected member of Soft Sands Band, teaches a young boy a few tricks on a real drum kit. It is not unusual in remote communities to see young boys sitting under trees with upturned 20-litre flour tins, practising drumming for hours on end. Gurrumul learnt to play drums in exactly that manner, drumming on a collection of tins laid out by his family.

CHAPTER 5

Bapala

There was something waiting for him, and whatever it was,

it would have nothing to do with the expected.

There's a type of Australian male who requires a fair chunk of the continent and maybe half a lifetime to work out exactly what he's going to do with it. He's competent in a hundred ways: reliable, alert, intelligent and that's probably the problem. He's an amended version of a jack of all trades in that he's actually master of many, but amongst that many, he has not yet — in his thirties, then into his forties — matched his ambition to even one of them. Moving restlessly from job to job, his vision of satisfaction takes on complicated dimensions, and any prospect of fulfilment becomes more remote. He's left increasingly with a sense of some great work waiting to be done; some door not yet opened.

Mark Grose, who in the Yolŋu world is Gurrumul's adopted father, fits the profile of the exceptionally able Australian guy who spends half his life hoping that the second half yields more meaning than the first. But in his case, that portal to fulfilment opened for him on Geoffrey Gurrumul Yunupiŋu's Elcho Island, just when he'd run out of continent.

Mark commenced the journey that delivered him to the top of the continent from Victoria. He was a rural, working-class kid raised on a soldier settlement block in the far west of the state, at Casterton. It's one of those homely rural towns of the sort found all over Australia; shops and businesses lining the highway; two or three buildings of modest distinction; a couple of primary schools, a high school. Mark spent two years at Sacred Heart Primary, one of the two primary schools just off the Glenelg Highway.

Towns like Casterton flourish and flounder by turns according to rainfall and market prices for produce. Everyone can recall times of plenty, and everyone has known times of struggle. The block granted to Mark's dad on returning from the war, was neither large enough nor lush enough to survive the times of struggle.

Mark waiting for the tide to go out, Cahills Crossing, East Alligator River.

BÄPA

Warwuyu ŋarranha mulkana	Grief has taken hold of me
ŋarraku bäpawu	for my father
ŋuruŋuna guṉipunharayu	when the sun sets
ya..a, bäpa marrkapmirri	o..h, beloved father
Ŋäthina wilawilayurruna	Crying and crying
ŋuruŋuna djarrawalyurruna	when the sun goes down
ḻiya-wayma Bekuḻŋura	my mind there at Bekuḻŋura
yä..a, bäpa marrkapmirri	o..h, beloved father
m..m m..m m..m	m..m m..m m..m
Ŋäthina Djotarra maṉda	Two Gumatj ladies crying
garray Dhuwandjika Daylulu	ancestor boss ladies Dhuwandjika and Daylulu
ŋuruŋuna djarrapalwuyu	when the sun sets
ḻiya-wayma wäŋaŋura Gunyaŋarri	my mind there at the place Gunyaŋara (Bekuḻŋura)
M..m m..m m..m	m..m m..m m..m

Michael Hohnen: 'When Gurrumul first finished this song he was so eager for me to hear it that he turned up one day at the university and waited until all my classes were finished. He said, "Michael, this is about my father — Bäpa." Then he took me out into this back room, like a studio that I'd got going at the university, and played it to me with piano. He loves it. Just loves it.'

A song of tribute, along informal lines. The 'bäpawu' of the second line, 'my father' is, in fact, any father, and would serve any race.

He was seven years old in 1964 when the family was forced to give up on the farming life and move east to Geelong. Another primary school, then a tech, and the family was still struggling. It's the sort of utilitarian upbringing that prepares most kids for the expected, and leaves just a few with a hope that life will offer more.

Not that Mark knew it, but just as he was starting high school, a few kilometres down the road, an infant born blind on Elcho Island was settling in with a Methodist family. Gurrumul had been brought four thousand kilometres by his mother Daisy Gurruwiwi and his aunt Susan to have tests conducted in Geelong on his sightless eyes. Considering all that Gurrumul would come to mean to Mark some decades down the track, you'd have to agree with the writer who claimed that coincidences are small miracles preceding larger ones.

Mark had somehow retained from the Casterton years a feeling for life on the land, his vision embellished by the desire to make a better go of it than his father had. Or maybe this was the first manifestation of the romantic strain in his make-up, because Mark remains an example of what might be termed a 'sweat of your brow' romantic, placing as much emphasis on hard work as on inspiration.

He headed west from Geelong to enrol and board at Longerenong Agricultural College a few clicks down the highway from Horsham. The college took up more than a thousand hectares, a school of the outdoors where students learnt farming by doing it — raising merinos for their wool, prime lambs for slaughter, beef cattle and growing field crops.

Mark had enrolled at Longerenong in his mid-teens, but he'd be almost nineteen before he saw a certificate of any worth. After two years of college, he took time off to work at one thing and another, around the Wimmera and in Melbourne, always competent, never contented. He returned to school to complete Year 12, then accepted an invitation to fly around New Guinea with a couple of friends, not imagining where it would lead to.

But it did. It was in New Guinea that he began to comprehend all that lay behind the description of certain folk known as 'Indigenous'. In the hills and valleys of New Guinea, he saw people whose culture barely resembled anything in the culture in which he'd been raised. He learnt of rituals held dear, held sacred. What had happened was this: he had climbed a ladder and gazed beyond the walls of the life he knew. The colour and motion, the complexity and passion of that world both changed him and endorsed in certain ways the vague dissatisfaction he had lived with for years. There was something waiting for him, and whatever it was, it would have nothing to do with the expected.

One particular episode in New Guinea left a further legacy, one that would influence him in the years to come. He met a local kid, a boy of about fifteen, whom he liked a lot, even admired him in the way he went about his life. He spent half a day with him and managed to communicate without ever saying a word; just through a language of gestures. It was only when he was departing that he was told the boy was mute. 'I'd assumed that English was the issue — he couldn't speak it, I couldn't speak his language. But we'd been able to get on perfectly. His culture, my culture — it didn't matter. It was a revelation to me.'

Mark came home with an urge to make some sort of contribution to the cause of Indigenous Australians. All well and good, but what contribution? Teaching, maybe? He had no qualification. He was forced to concede that good intentions alone wouldn't put him in a position to offer black Australians anything of value, and so went to Perth with the idea of enrolling in a specialist course that would qualify him to teach Indigenous kids.

But not immediately. Instead, he found employment with a geologist — nothing fancy, factotum, junior grade. The job took him up into the Murchison, east of Shark Bay, and to the Hamersley Range of the Pilbara where he relished being a country boy back in the mulga once more — or the desert, at least.

It was in the midst of the sandstone, the salt pans and desert oak of the Murchison and the rich red palette of the Pilbara that he first came into contact with the black Australians he'd hoped to 'help'. He learnt something of their culture and, like anthropologist W.E.H. Stanner decades earlier, came to see that Aboriginal Australians looked at the world in a way that contradicted almost everything that a white man understood. He learnt the names of the tribes and clans of the region. In the caves of the desert, he became captivated by the raw power of the wall paintings, training his eye in a way that would eventually lead him to surround himself with museum-quality Indigenous art. He admired much of what he was able to grasp, of what he was permitted to see, but he saw the wounds, too: demoralised young men of his own age who fought a daily battle against despair and disaffection; no confidence at all in their future. Years and years down the track, Mark would make the sort of stand that Michael Hohnen made after meeting Archie Roach, committing himself to the rescue of young men just like those in the Murchison and the Pilbara, to work with might and main to get them up on a stage where they could experience equality outside of their own tribe for the first time in their lives. When Henry Reynolds writes of the history of black–white relations in *This Whispering in Our Hearts*, he's speaking of an engagement that began, for Mark, in distant New Guinea and took its first steps towards maturity in the Murchison.

Schlepping for the geologist offered Mark something, but not truly a way ahead. He packed his bags for Perth once more and enrolled at uni, chasing that teaching degree. It was a three-year course, and he gave it a year and a half, about as much as he could take of sit-down lessons at that time. Leaving uni, and Perth, he entered into a peripatetic period that took him north, south, east and west. He became a wool classer, a log snigger in the Grampians, a ticket clerk on the railways, a shearer in the Riverina. Earning a living at jobs of this sort nourished Mark's daydream of one day setting up as a farmer, but that daydream clashed with a more urgent need to be amongst black Australians. He took a deep sigh, returned to Perth and found the patience to finish his degree.

In 1984 Mark was put in charge of a classroom at last, but not in the location he'd first imagined. He was in Japan, parsing sentences and clarifying the subjunctive for the locals, a long, long way from black Australia, where thirteen-year-old Geoffrey Gurrumul Yunupiŋu was undergoing his rite-of-passage ceremony on Elcho. Mark was in the midst of a vocational muddle typical of this category of able men: very good at what they find themselves doing, but nagged by a sense of something more significant, more demanding up ahead.

Back to Australia again, and what was up ahead was the town of Derby on King Sound, east of the Beagle Bay Aboriginal Reserve. Mark accepted a job teaching black kids the skills of a station hand: riding, roping, branding and 'this is how you make your damper, right?' Also reading and writing and arithmetic. His convictions about what was needed in the lives of black kids evolved further, not to mention the level of his disgust with the institutionalised racism that Indigenous kids lived with every day.

Working with marginalised black kids is going to break your heart after a time, if you have a heart to break. What you want for them and what you can provide — there's a big gulf in between. Mark stuck with the program in Derby for almost three years but, with one thing and another, he wasn't quite in a job that attracted lifelong commitment. But exactly what would attract a commitment that lasted for years and years? God knows. Hire-and-salary doesn't do it for long, nor does anything that places you under the scrutiny of anyone you don't fully respect. A temperament of this sort is in its way a handicap. Unless you're in charge, that restlessness kicks in after a while and suddenly you're dragging your suitcase out from under the bed, a little bit sick of yourself, yes, but very sure you can't stay. And it's not quite true to call it 'restlessness'. What Mark was experiencing — and this had grown so familiar over the years — was a type of bad faith; a sense of being in a fraudulent position. He could teach the kids, but so could anyone. There was no feeling of contribution. One thing he noticed about his departure from Derby is that the kids he'd been teaching were not in the least surprised. A white bloke comes along, offers you a bit of this, a bit of that, then moves on. That's what some white blokes do — a bit of this, a bit of that, then move on.

By 1987, he was back in New Guinea with a couple of friends, leading adventure getaways for people with enough money to amuse themselves in this way. If he suffered from the sense of making so little difference in Derby, in New Guinea he wasn't even on the radar of black Australians. But in a short time he got himself back on the radar, this time involved with community education in remote regions of Western Australia. He trained black kids to do things that could make some sort of difference in their lives, gave them skills, like welding and carpentering. This time he had a long-term commitment, something that he hoped would stifle that feeling of being a fraud. Throughout the late eighties and early nineties, the TAFE that employed him moved him from one location to another, and eventually to Broome on Roebuck Bay.

A sense of mission is an uncomfortable thing to cart about, whether you're a priest or a prophet, or a farm boy grown to adulthood. It nags at you when you crave a bit of peace and, when it's not nagging, you wonder where the hell it's gone and wish it back. It's more awkward still when you have only a blurry idea of the mission itself.

Then one fine day he told an admired colleague, Mark Manado, that he made a terrific role model for the Indigenous kids he was instructing. Manado said: 'I'm not trying to be a role model. I'm just doing my job.' It was that Gordian knot moment that can occur when years of picking at a tangled mass is resolved with a single, clean stroke. Mark realised that Indigenous people were not some kind of sacred people or cultural icon that had to be tiptoed around. Manado showed him that Indigenous people want the same things that we all want and that Mark was simply a bloke doing a worthwhile job. That awkward sense of mission took on more manageable dimensions. The kids he was teaching gained something — just 'something', not 'everything' — out of his commitment, and that was it. This acceptance of the limited good he, or anyone, could do liberated him forever from the sense of being in a false position. How much benefit, after all, does wearing a hair shirt ever achieve?

Mark found another type of liberation around this time when he accepted once and for all that he would never become a farmer. Dreams are beacons or burdens, according to their

George Rrurrambu and good friend Tony Collins share a roadhouse coffee on the Saltwater tour. Tony Collins was the official tour documentary maker.

Flying to Elcho, one of the Crocodile Islands near Milingimbi.

His Island Home

Neil Murray's much-loved song, 'My Island Home', is a tale of longing based partly on the life of Murray's comrade in music, George Rrurrambu Burarrwaŋa, and partly on Murray's own experience. The lyrics of the song are fashioned in such a way that Neil Murray and George Rrurrambu (as he was always called, while alive) merge to form a single Murrambu figure, or persona, combining the two names. The 'island home' of the song is, of course, Elcho Island — George's home. Neil spent halcyon days visiting George (a member of Neil's Warumpi Band) and his family on Elcho, living on fish taken from the sea with line and spear. This merging of Neil and George dates from that visit.

A good song that dwells on a special time in a special place will often transcend the personal and take on a more universal quality. 'My Island Home' is one of those songs. It compels listeners who have never in their lives taken a fish from the sea to feel in their hands the weight of that long turtle spear, as if they were balanced in the prow of a boat scanning the blue water for turtles. The theme of the song is belonging; of recalling a place of heart's ease; a spiritual haven.

The haven of the individual listener may have nothing to do with the sea and its salt water. It is simply a place where you once belonged; a place of bounty. The song makes us believe that for each of us, there is 'an island home'.

George Rrurrambu died in 2007, at the age of fifty. He left behind memories of a cheerful, witty, and generous man, full of life, and ambitious for what his people might achieve with music. Gurrumul admired him greatly, and George foresaw the road that Gurrumul would take in the years ahead. At a time when Mark Grose and Michael Hohnen were facing criticism for having 'taken Indigenous culture to the marketplace', George encouraged Mark and Gurrumul to seize the opportunity of bringing Yolŋu culture to a wider audience. 'It's a good thing you're doing,' he said. 'A good thing for us Yolŋu, for sure.'

Christine Anu's version of 'My Island Home' came out in 1995, almost a decade after Warumpi's version on the album, *Go Bush*. The Anu version became a hit all over Australia, and partly through its success, has been accepted as one of the most important Australian songs of all time.

Clockwise from top left: Mark Grose, Managing Director, Skinnyfish Music with his great nephew Zane at Melbourne Zoo concert, February 2012; Michelle Dowden, Mark's partner, a strong supporter of Skinnyfish from the very beginning and of Gurrumul during his illness; Penny Arrow and Gurrumul's good friend and guitarist, Francis Diatschenko, enjoying the streets of New York; Penny Arrow, Andrew Bowles of Dramatico UK and Michael Hohnen outside Buckingham Palace during the Diamond Jubilee celebrations.

Top: Michael Hohnen, Shirley Dhamarrandji, Gurrumul, Charlie Yunupiŋu and Mark Grose after a successful concert. Bottom: Craig Pilkington has been Gurrumul's friend for many years, and it was at his Audrey Studios that Gurrumul's first solo album was recorded.

prospects of eventual realisation, and Mark's farmer dream had become a burden without his quite noticing. Sure, he carted his suitcase back to the southern states at regular intervals with the intention of settling on the land, but look what happened when he was up in the bush shearing woollies: unease at the absence of black faces. When Shakespeare wrote: 'There's a divinity that shapes our ends, rough-hew them how we will', he was summarising Mark's life. The divinity shaping Mark's end had in mind something along the lines of Skinnyfish Music, not a couple of thousand woollies bleating on paddocks up in the Riverina.

In 1993, when Gurrumul was emerging from his Yothu Yindi years, Mark came to Elcho with no other purpose than to catch up with Michelle Dowden, a woman he'd met on a trip back to Melbourne from the west. In Michelle, he'd happened on a kindred spirit; someone who shared his convictions about Indigenous Australians, and who had herself worked in Aboriginal communities in the Territory as a nurse and health services manager. A hundred things he'd be required to explain to any other person, didn't have to be explained to Michelle. It's a big thing when you meet someone who says, 'I know what you mean' and who actually does know what you mean. You can relax, and discard the roles you normally adopt; roles that have never pleased you in any case.

Michelle, with exceptional competence, was managing the clinic at Galiwin'ku; Mark, if he intended to remain gainfully employed, was due back in Broome. It happened that the Galiwin'ku Shire had just lost its town clerk, and no wonder; it was a demanding job, a budget of several million dollars to manage, a work force of two hundred to keep busy, and not much peace. Mark applied for the job, mostly because it kept him close to Michelle but another consideration was the chance to turn the whole operation of the shire around. He got the job.

He and Michelle became, in their commitment, a godsend to the shire community, including the folk of Elcho. Health professionals like Michelle can reveal an assortment of traits at managerial level. Some become tartars and establish a tyranny over their fiefdoms; some reveal a profound mediocrity once responsibilities multiply; some — and this is Michelle — bring to the job a calm competence and strength of character. As for Mark — well, the hazard for town clerks in remote communities is to become daunted by the thousand tasks that make up the job, so they buy a fleet of fancy four-wheel drives sporting the shire logo and leave it at that. It wasn't a hazard for Mark. He discovered in himself a knack for organisation and the candour to say no to nonsense and nepotism. Most importantly, though, were the lessons learnt from his twenty years (off and on) amongst black Australians. The big proportion of Indigenous Australians in the shire was, in fact, one of the attractions of the job. It would be difficult to imagine Mark wishing to run some metropolitan shire where a priority was the piquancy of the hors d'oeuvres served at official receptions.

Gurrumul was there on Elcho, but Mark was only aware of him as a figure in the background. He'd heard kids mention Gurrumul and Yothu Yindi in the same sentence, but it meant little since Mark had barely heard of Yothu Yindi. But he heard more about Yothu Yindi, more about Indigenous music, and much more about Gurrumul when Michael Hohnen came to Elcho in 1996 with his TAFE music program. Mark came to watch the black kids performing, and it meant something to his heart that music gave these kids what they'd gone most of their lives without once experiencing: the joy of an accomplishment and equality with white musicians.

Michael was a background figure in Mark's life for some time after their first meeting in 1996. Mark was impressed by Michael's professional expertise, yes, but his own experience of music barely equipped him to pick the difference between a reggae chorus and a Gregorian chant. It meant more to him that Michael wanted these Elcho musicians to succeed, at least on a local level. It was only when Michael helped with the formation of Saltwater that Mark began to take seriously what Michael had to say about the benefit a local record label had for the bands in the region. But where would a record label come from? Mark said: 'We'll do it.' What, build a record label without any capital, without a business plan, just based around the joyful antics of a mob of black kids from the bush? Yes, apparently.

Mark built Skinnyfish in the way that you might build a house by arriving on site with a hammer, a dozen nails, a length of two-by-four — and nothing more. He called everyone in Australia who'd listen to what he had to say about the Saltwater sound; he squeezed rotation out of radio station managers; he cajoled music shops into taking the album on board. He didn't think of blockbuster hits, only of fashioning a viable company that could offer artists such as Gurrumul ethical representation and reliable marketing. He went two years without a cent of income, supported financially and morally by Michelle. He made a brother of Michael, a son of Gurrumul, and bit by bit, a success of Skinnyfish.

Elements of everything he'd ever been went into Skinnyfish: the working-class kid from Casterton; the guy who'd become enthralled by the culture of black Australians and who'd poured his talents into providing something for the marginalised; the young man who'd discovered his own sense of beauty in the Murchison, gazing at the cave paintings of Aborigines; the sweat-of-your-brow romantic who'd been able to imagine something ahead, something that had meaning; and finally, the builder, the businessman.

A life that led to the embrace of friendship with some of the most worthwhile people on earth, after a journey that took in rural Victoria, Papua New Guinea, the Murchison, the Pilbara, Derby and Broome, would seem to many men a journey of enviable adventure and rich experience. And why not? Endless travel, liberty from many of the more tedious burdens of adulthood, girls galore. But the first freedom that Mark really enjoyed — the first relief from burdens of any sort — didn't come his way until he said to Michael Hohnen: 'We'll do it.' Commitment, the fullest possible employment of his skills and talents, the chance to give his sincere best to something worthwhile, the love of a good woman and of a blind black man who calls him 'Bäpa' — that was freedom. 'When I started to build Skinnyfish,' he says, 'I relaxed for the first time in my life. I calmed down. It wouldn't have happened without Michelle.'

It wouldn't have happened without Michael Hohnen, either. Think of Damon and Pythias, the great companions of Greek legend, who have come to exemplify honour and loyalty in friendship. The career of Gurrumul as a solo artist, and all that he has brought to Australian music, commences at this junction of the three individual journeys of three exceptional men: Gurrumul himself, out of Elcho; Michael Hohnen, out of bayside Beaumauris; and Mark Grose, out of Casterton, and about fifty other places.

A big tin shed, the back of a semi-trailer, a stage of bare earth – touring in the bush is all about making the most of what's on offer. The acoustics might be primitive, but when Gurrumul and the band come to town, the audience loves it.

Gurrumul performing live with a Martin guitar that Michael's Aunty, Margaret Keddie, gave him before she died. When Gurrumul performs live, no matter what the setting, he channels all his energy into every phrase as if everything is being recorded for life.

2
OF ELCHO

CHAPTER 6

Enmore

People want to leave the Enmore Theatre with everything they've heard from Gurrumul and everything they've read about him well and truly confirmed. And it is confirmed within the first spellbinding twenty seconds of the intro.

The Erkki String Quartet is on board for the Enmore Theatre performance. All of the guide string parts were written by Gurrumul just a couple of months ago, and then arranged by Erkki Veltheim, a friend of Michael Hohnen. Gurrumul loves strings. When he was a kid on Elcho he listened with his mum, his aunt Susan (Dhäŋgal) and his uncle Djuŋa (David) to the local Soft Sands String Band. Strings were to the soundscape of his world what a glittering stream would be in a visual landscape: a focus of enchantment. So on stage, Erkki, Veronique, Christopher and Patrick are at the back with their strings, Gurrumul at the front with Michael on the double bass and Francis Diatschenko on acoustic guitar. Other than a few boutique performances in small studio venues at the Opera House, this will be the first full concert in Sydney since the phenomenal success of the *Gurrumul* album, which has gone gangbusters all over Australia and is now triple platinum — more than two hundred thousand units sold.

And it's the Enmore, one of the three or four best venues in Australia for a concert of this sort. Snug in rowdy Newtown, just down from King Street, it bestows on anyone who performs here a certain cachet of acceptance within the milieu of the fully laid-back. Gurrumul appreciates what it means to be singing to a house like this, sold out for months. At the hotel before the 4 p.m. sound check, Gurrumul finishes dressing, then shuffles about with his head full of the occasion. 'Or'right!' he says — a little psyching to calm any jitters. Michael asks him if he's up for it. 'Yeah, I'm nervous,' he replies, and runs his hand over his head. 'How's the hair?'

With his reputation as a solo performer confirmed at Carnegie Hall, Gurrumul allows himself a moment of quiet pride. His expression says: That's the best I've played.

MARWURRUMBURR

Bili nhangu yalyuwan, ŋayim
munhaguyina nhangu ŋarruŋa nhäwu ..
yay yä, yay yä marwurrumburr

waripum nhan ŋarru m..m, ŋalthun bämbaṯli milkirilim gurruwurruḻi
ŋarru ŋarran butjikit, ŋarru ŋarran butjikit marwurrumburr
ŋarru ŋarran butjikit, ŋarru ŋarran butjikit marwurrumburr
m..m

ŋarru ŋarran butjikit, ŋarru ŋarran butjikit marwurrumburr
ŋarru ŋarran butjikit, ŋarru ŋarran butjikit marwurrumburr

ḏit ḏirri rriri, ḏit ḏirri rriri
ḏit ḏirri rriri, ḏit ḏirri rriri

Buŋanma nhan dhaŋu Maykuḻŋuwu, (wititj)
waripum nhan dhaŋu buŋan Djarrpiyanawu
Binininyala yay yä ya, yay yä yi marwurrumburr

ŋarru ŋarran butjikit, ŋarru ŋarran butjikit marwurrumburr
ŋarru ŋarran butjikit, ŋarru ŋarran butjikit marwurrumburr

Now it has cooled, the country
his night has come for ..
ya, ya ya, the cat

also he will, climb into the funeral shelter,
the cat will travel, the cat will travel
the cat will travel, the cat will travel

the cat will travel, the cat will travel
the cat will travel, the cat will travel

ḏit ḏirri rriri, ḏit ḏirri rriri, ḏit ḏirri rriri, ḏit ḏirri rriri

the scent of the smell by Wititj
the scent of the smell by Wititj
Bininyala ya, ya the cat

the cat will travel, the cat will travel
the cat will travel, the cat will travel

This song is known to Gurrumul and Michael as 'the pussycat song'. It celebrates the cat dance of the Gälpu — one of the clan's many ritual dances. (Others include the tobacco dance and the flag dance.) What a cat is doing in north-east Arnhem Land is a mystery, unless cats were brought by the Makassans. When Michael asks Gurrumul about the cat reference in the song, he gets three or four words. 'Oh, that's the cat dance,' and nothing more. In the last four years or so, Gurrumul has developed the comfort and security to do an encore, and he always chooses 'Marwurrumburr'.

The audience milling in the Enmore lobby has a different complexion from the audience that would gather here for, say, Nick Cave or Wil Anderson. We have a sprinkling of kids in their early teens accompanied by their parents and, at the other end of the spectrum, a complement of over-sixties. At a guess, the kids are here because their parents want them to witness what will likely be their first-ever experience of a headlining black Australian artist, while the older folk see in Gurrumul a vindication of their long-standing belief in the genius of the Indigenous people. Be that as it may, people want the music, above all. Gurrumul has been heard. Apart from the phenomenal sales of the album, various tracks have enjoyed terrific rotation not only on community radio, but also on the big-audience ABC stations in the capital cities and on the more culturally ambitious commercial stations. The prevalent view of Gurrumul's gift out in the community has been captured in rave reviews in the big dailies: 'he's a man with an angelic voice and to hear him is to weep'. This take on his voice can stand a little qualification, of course; Gurrumul's voice is angelic for moments on certain songs, but it is far too complex in what it can attain to leave it at that. And then the 'angelic' thing is liable to spill over and create a vision of Gurrumul as a semi-divine being who has emerged from the mulga of the Top End radiating golden light. He's not like that. In his make-up you find all the patterning of a gloriously intricate human being fully alive to the world.

Gurrumul has the sleeves of his suit jacket rolled up like a tradesman settling over his task; not a guy who's comfortably at home in anything with lapels. Michael and the Erkki players are sitting composed at their instruments. The first song will be 'Wiyathul'. In the audience there's anticipation. People want to leave the theatre with everything they've heard from Gurrumul and everything they've read about him well and truly confirmed. And it is confirmed within the first spellbinding twenty seconds of the intro. From this point on, it's all delight. This is the magic everyone craved. Even without any knowledge of the language, the audience knows that Gurrumul is singing of the beauty of his island; singing of sorrow, of longing and of the joy that comes his way; of peace and suffering; of love and loss.

The Enmore performance tonight marks the beginning of a new stage of Gurrumul's journey. The format of the concert will be played out over the years to come in capitals, regional cities and towns up and down the continent.

We can think of this journey as the celebration of Gurrumul and Michael's brilliant collaboration; of the arrival of a musical genius of the Gumatj people. At the same time, this journey maps the progress of reconciliation. When we lift our hands and applaud Gurrumul at the conclusion of a concert, we are also acknowledging what we did not always understand: that our land has a past of surpassing richness and variety, and it is this past that has given us Geoffrey Gurrumul Yunupiŋu's wealth of songs.

Redfern

About a spear's throw from the Enmore Theatre lies the suburb of Redfern, home to the most concentrated gathering of Indigenous Australians on earth. It was in Redfern Park, in December 1992, that Paul Keating delivered the speech that opened a long-postponed dialogue between black and white Australia; the speech that acknowledged the centuries of suffering of Indigenous Australians at the hands of settlers, colonial administrators, state and federal governments.

The audience of the sold-out show gathering in the Enmore at this minute came here by way of the portal that the Redfern Speech opened seventeen years earlier. Or if not the speech itself, the shift in national sentiment that the speech distilled. Paradoxically, or perhaps beautifully, that shift in sentiment gives Gurrumul the liberty to sing a dozen of his own songs that do not include a single phrase of complaint, a short distance from the radical heart of Indigenous politics in Australia. That's one of the joys of reconciliation: the right to escape stereotyping; the right to sing from your heart of your country, of your culture, without mentioning any of the familiar villains of the post-settlement era; the right, if you so choose, to step into the Dreamtime, seat yourself on a beach and gaze out to sea.

A media call for the Sydney Festival 2012. Manu Chao, the great Franco-Iberian singer and guitarist was also on the bill.

In 2008, Alan James and Michael Chugg introduced Gurrumul to Elton John in Darwin. Gurrumul played at Elton's TIO Stadium concert, following the support act. Gurrumul was barely known as a solo artist then, but after the concert, people who'd heard him came up to him in the street to say how much they'd loved his performance. Craig Pilkington accompanied on guitar.

CHAPTER 7

Nightcliff

'We'll find a table down near the pier and talk about Gurrumul.
The sea, the sunset, beautiful colours. And talk about Gurrumul.'

Yes, with pleasure, says Dorothy; she and her sister Anne will talk about their beloved nephew Geoffrey Gurrumul Yunupiŋu, a thousand stories, even more, but it will have to be after the tutorial they are giving at Charles Darwin University late in the afternoon. 'You come to my session at Charles Darwin,' says Dorothy, 'and then we'll speak about Gurrumul.' The subject of Dorothy's talk is the culture of her people, the Yolŋu. If it's right to speak of 'experts' in the culture of an Indigenous people, then Dorothy is an expert, but she's unlikely to refer to herself in that way. She was born into the Gälpu clan of the Yolŋu people and everything that a Gälpu girl or woman experiences is a part of her vital life. 'Expert' is a word from outside her culture, suggesting, as it does, objective study. Both Dorothy and Anne know from the inside something that cannot be taught, but can be explained, or illuminated, up to a point. She and her sister are prepared to shine a light on the culture of the Yolŋu to anyone prepared to listen, and that's what they'll be doing at the university this afternoon.

In a classroom at Charles Darwin University, with walls of a welcoming, buttery yellow, Dorothy and her sister Anne seat themselves in a relaxed manner and take questions from the audience.

'Yolŋu people,' says Dorothy, 'are in the world in a different way from white people — European people, *balanda*. A different way. A *balanda* thinks to himself, "The gold is in the ground, we better dig up the gold." But Yolŋu people don't want to disturb the ground. So we leave the gold there.'

Anne says: 'Different. We never think that we own the ground. We never think that we own the minerals.'

'I teach people at the Christian College,' says Dorothy. 'Twenty-one years of teaching. I show Yolŋu people things they don't know. We know some things, but not everything. I teach

DJÄRRIMIRRI

Ŋarranydja goḻanharawuy, ŋändiwuŋu Wititjkuŋu
ŋarranydja dhuwlala, yothu Djärimirri m..m

Ŋarranydja yothu Djärimirri, Djärimirri
Wititjkuŋu goḻanhara, Djärimirr..i m..m

Yurru beŋuru walmananydja, wakwakŋuru dhatam'ŋuru
Gudjuk walmana, raypinyŋura Garrimala m..m Dhupuḻaŋuru

Ŋarranydja yothu Djärimirri, Djärimirr..i
Wititjkuŋu goḻanhara, Djärimirr..i, m..m yothu Ḏimitjmi
yurru 1950s-dhunydja bäpa ŋarraku waṯthurruna
Muwalaŋgallili, Yanayanayu Wurrumbayu m..m Malpitjiŋuyu

Ŋarranydja yothu Djärimirri, Djärimirr..i
Wititjkuŋu goḻanhara, Djärimirr..i m..m
yurru ḻikannydja ŋarra dhuwala, Maralitja Dhar'yuna
Yothunydja ŋarra dhuwala barrmaḻawuy Wititjkuŋu m..m
Yothu Djärimirri m..m, Djärimirri m..m, m..m, Djärimirri

I was carried, by mother Wititj
I am, a Rainbow child m..m

I am, a Rainbow child, with a Rainbow
carried by Wititj, with a Rainbow

Emerged from there, from the waters lilies
Gudjuk emerged, from fresh water Garrimala m..m
Dhupuḻa

I am, a Rainbow child, with a Rainbo..w
carried by Wititj, with a Rainbow, m..m a child
of the Rainbow
in the 1950s my dad looked around
towards Muwalaŋgallili, Yanayanayu Wurrumbayu Malpitjiŋ
uyu (Point Bradshaw)

I am, a Rainbow child, with Rainbo..w
carried by Wititj, with Rainbow
I am Maralitja Dhar'yuna with my ancestors
I am a child conceived and carried by Wititj
a rainbow child m..m, with a rainbow m..m, m..m,
with a rainbow

*Wititj is the Ancestor Rainbow Python.

Michael recalls: 'I wanted "Djärimirri" for the first Saltwater album but there was some problem with it. Gurrumul said: "No, we're not doing it". He didn't say what was wrong, just, "No, we're not doing it". Then the second Saltwater album, and again Gurrumul said, "No, we're not doing it", the third album, "No, we're not doing it". But with the Gurrumul album, he didn't say, "No, we're not doing it," — he just started playing it. I said, "Brother, what're you doing?" He didn't say anything. So I turned to Craig and I said, "Right, we're doing 'Djärimirri'," and away we went, not an issue.'

'Djärimirri' is a song of unmixed pleasure, of affirmation — unusual in Gurrumul's repertoire, where sorrow and longing are often close by. The names of the Rainbow Serpent, Wititj, and of the 'Rainbow child', Djärimirri, are spoken with a reverential tenderness. 'Djärimirri' is sung with the voice softened, the tune itself savoured on the palette, the guitar accompaniment serving the song unobtrusively. This is the favourite song of Gurrumul's uncle, Djuŋa (David), and it's easy to see why, since it's what he most enjoys in his nephew — that gentleness.

them *balanda* things, good things. When I talk to you *balanda*, I teach you Yolŋu ways. Not everything. I can't teach you everything.'

Anne says: 'Some things. Not everything. Of course not everything.'

At the conclusion of the one-hour talk, the *balanda* who make up the entire audience thank Dorothy and Anne for their kindness and are thanked in turn for their attendance.

It's time now for Gurrumul. But why not eat as we talk? Dorothy suggests fish and chips down by the pier at Nightcliff. The Nightcliff fish and chips are much better than just very good, she says. Anne endorses her sister's plan. 'Nightcliff. They have a favourite restaurant. We'll find a table down near the pier and talk about Gurrumul. The sea, the sunset, beautiful colours. And talk about Gurrumul.'

The fish is barramundi, cooked in crisp batter. The taste is to die for, sincerely. The chips have the perfect crunch quality and the exquisite golden colour I hope for always but so rarely find. Out above the Arafura Sea, the sunset is more of a pastel composition than I expected in the tropics. The bleached skeleton of the pier reflects the last of the day's light.

My first question: explain *bäru* — the crocodile — as a totem creature. In all honesty, I don't understand *bäru*, I don't understand totems, I don't understand Gurrumul's relationship to the crocodile. Michael has explained it in this peremptory way: 'Gurrumul is the crocodile. He's not like a crocodile. He is the crocodile.'

Dorothy and Anne hear me out as they eat. In addition to the fish and chips, each of the sisters has ordered a complex salad made up of at least five vegetables with crab meat mixed in. Just for the moment, it's possible that Dorothy and Anne are more absorbed by the superb fare on the table in front of them than by my question. Nevertheless, Dorothy puts down her plastic fork and gives the matter thought.

'You say, "totem creature",' she says. 'That's wrong. Not "totem creature", just, "totem". You understand?'

'Just "totem"?'

'Yes. Now listen. Are you listening?'

'Sure.'

'In Arnhem Land, the crocodile goes way, way back to the creation story. Dhuwa, that is the mother; Yirritja, that is the father. Everyone in Arnhem Land is Dhuwa or Yirritja. One moiety is Dhuwa; one moiety is Yirritja. The crocodile is Yirritja. The crocodile is Gurrumul. So now you understand.'

Anne says: 'Dhuwa, Yirritja. One is the mother's side, one is the father's side. Dhuwa and Dhuwa, they don't marry each other. Yirritja and Yirritja, they don't marry each other. So now you understand in a proper way.'

Do I?

Anne, in the twilight, speaking in the gentle and deliberate way you might employ with a slow learner, explains that each moiety includes four groups, making eight groups within the two moieties. The four groups within each moiety are called skin groups. Your skin name comes from your mother, only your mother. Dorothy says: 'This is so we know where we come from. This is so Gurrumul knows where he comes from, and all his people. His mother gave Gurrumul his skin name, Gudjuk. But Gurrumul's skin name is not Daisy's. No. Only she gave

Gurrumul's aunt Dorothy Gurruwiwi and opposite as a child. She is known for her straight hair.

Gurrumul's aunt Anne Gurruwiwi.

Gurrumul his skin name. Now you know.'

I haven't come to court Dorothy and Anne's knowledge of their culture entirely unprepared. I've been reading, and what I've read suggests that Dorothy and Anne will eventually have to speak of the Dreamtime to explain the origin of skin names and totems, and what a task that will be! It's only over the past few decades that non-Indigenous Australians have begun to grasp the sophistication and profound involvement of what black Australians mean when they speak of the Dreamtime, of their Dreaming. To explain it to anyone born a long, long way from their culture, such as me — well, where do they start? To begin with, Indigenous Australians who speak to the uninitiated of the Dreamtime are compelled to treat the subject as if it were a subject, when plainly it isn't something that can be explained by adding fact to fact. Here is what the great essayist and anthropologist W.E.H. Stanner wrote in 1953 about his own struggle to fashion an understanding of the Dreaming and the Dreamtime:

> *The Australian Aborigines' outlook on the universe and man is shaped by a remarkable conception … immortalised as 'the dream time' … A central meaning of The Dreaming is that of a sacred, heroic time long ago, when man and nature came to be as they are; but neither 'time' nor 'history' as we understand them is involved in this meaning. I have never been able to discover any Aboriginal word for 'time' as an abstract concept. And the sense of 'history' is wholly alien here … A blackfellow may call his totem, or the space from where his spirit came, his Dreaming. He may also explain the existence of a custom, or law of life, as causally due to The Dreaming. A concept so impalpable and subtle naturally suffers badly by translation into our dry and abstract language. The blacks sense this difficulty. I can recall one intelligent old man who said to me, with a cadence almost as though he had been speaking verse:*

> *White man got no dreaming*
> *Him go 'nother way.*
> *White man, him go different.*
> *Him got road belong himself.*

Sitting here with this tasty food as Dorothy and Anne slowly disappear into the darkness of the night, I am really asking them to address themselves to a task for which there is no possible reward. I am the white man who goes down a road by himself. I am the white man who has no Dreaming. I read Sartre and Kierkegaard and Claude Levi-Strauss when I want to see further down that road and all I'm left with is a few interesting ideas, but no Dreamtime. Dorothy and Anne and Gurrumul know ways of telling stories and ways of hearing stories that I'll never master.

Dorothy says: 'You know "Djärimirri"? You know that Gurrumul song, "Djärimirri"? That one is an important song, "Djärimirri". If you understand that song, you understand Gurrumul and Dreaming.'

Anne says: 'Wititj, the Rainbow Snake. Gurrumul is a child of that Rainbow Snake. A child of Wititj. Now you understand. Good.'

Dorothy, relishing the crab salad, says: 'You have some, Robert. Have some.'

In fact, I don't eat crab. I'm not eating anything for the moment. The best fish and chips on earth, and I can't eat because I'm concentrating on skin names and moieties and crocodiles and the Rainbow Snake and asking myself: 'How does it all fit together? Can Gurrumul be both the crocodile and a child of Wititj?' I put the issue to Anne and Dorothy.

'Many, many people come here for fishing,' says Anne ignoring my question. 'So many! Those rocks down there, some days they're all covered with people fishing.'

Dorothy laughs, very lightly and with such mirth. 'All covered with people. They come down here to fish. They stand next to each other.'

Anne and Dorothy share a feminine East Arnhem beauty, soft and grave at the one time. Their generosity in talking about their culture is something you find again and again amongst Indigenous Australians, as if hope of saving white Australians from grievous unawareness springs eternal in their hearts. I once heard this from a woman who worked in an official way at Turkey Creek: 'They should be throwing hand grenades at us, instead they say, "Listen, I'll tell you something special."'

'So, you ask your questions about Gurrumul,' says Dorothy, and cleans her fingers with a paper towel. 'When he was a little baby, we held him like this.'

Both sisters, now silhouettes, mime holding baby Gurrumul and rocking him gently.

'And you sang to him? Your sister Susan on Elcho, she says she sang to Gurrumul when he was a baby.'

'Yes, we sang to him,' says Dorothy. 'All his mothers sang to him. Of course!'

'Many, many, many songs,' says Anne.

'We sang to him, "Wales, Wales, land of mists and wild".'

'We sang, "When the day is over".'

'"How great thou art" — we sang that many, many, many times.'

'"Kingston Town" — many, many times.'

Barely visible in the dusk, Anne and Dorothy sing a soft, yielding, soprano duet, swaying gently in unison:

Dear land of my fathers, whose glories were told
By bard and minstrel who loved thee of old
Dear country whose sires, that their sons might be free
Have suffered and perished for thee.
Wales! Wales! Land of mist and wild
Where'er I roam
Though far from my home
The mother is calling her child…
And:
Then sings my soul
My saviour God to Thee,
How great Thou art,
How great Thou art,
Then sings my soul
My saviour God to Thee,
How great Thou art,
How great Thou art!
And:
Far away where the nights are gay
And the sun shines daily on the mountain top …

This photograph taken in 1960 on Elcho Island shows a catch of stingray. Stingray when prepared Yolŋu style is a delicious seafood treat and one of Gurrumul's favourite foods.

Totems

The way in which many Indigenous Australians understand their existence has become more widely revealed to mainstream Australia over the past fifty years, but the role of totems in Aboriginal culture has remained a mystery. As it must, for there is nothing in Western culture that prepares the non-Indigenous for the profound identification of the human with the non-human. Some anthropological studies have sought to establish Aboriginal 'totemism' as a type of 'hunting magic' that allows the hunter to exercise power over the hunted creature by mimicking its characteristics. But more recent studies reveal that totems influence the lives of Indigenous people in more than one way. One of Gurrumul's many totems is the crocodile (*bäru*), as it was bound to be even before his birth. This is where one of the contradictions to the 'hunting magic' theory enters the picture, for those whom the crocodile inhabits do not hunt the beast, except in certain situations. Gurrumul reveres the crocodile, but the conditions of reverence are very complex. Although he might speak or sing of the crocodile in a way that celebrates its strength and cunning, if a big croc were to chase him on the beach at Galiwin'ku, he would do as any sane person would and run for his life. We might think of Indigenous totems — crocodile, cormorant, frill-necked lizard, taipan and many other creatures even extending to inanimate forms — as a type of sharing of the beginning. Gurrumul and the crocodile emerged from the same clay, as it were, with the same spiritual DNA. Totems honour that bond of shared origins.

The singing of these songs — an anthem, a hymn, a calypso ditty — appear to give Dorothy and Anne great pleasure. Their singing voices now and then give way to giggling. For a moment they seem as youthful as the girls of seven and eight I saw giggling in this same way on an Elcho Island beach. These are the songs of the Methodist Mission choir at Galiwin'ku. Like Djuŋa and Dhäŋhal — or David and Susan — on Elcho, Dorothy and Anne retain a great affection for the mission songs — many of which are not hymns at all — and for the mission experience altogether. Yet another mystery to puzzle over is the untroubled way in which Indigenous people who have come under the influence of missions such as the one on Elcho are able to accommodate the Christian narrative without surrendering their engagement to their far older cosmology. Gurrumul, who has gone as far into the passion of his people's beliefs as anyone, won't hear a word said against the famous rabbi of Nazareth. Michael Hohnen recalls occasions when he may have lapsed into satire when speaking of the reverence in a single Christian God, when the Yolŋu have their own system. 'It makes Gurrumul cranky. He says, "Michael, Michael!" He tells me to stop and goes off in a huff.'

In some ways, an Indigenous Australian raised in the deep culture of his tribe or clan will remain forever more rigid in what he or she is prepared to tolerate than a man or woman raised in the secular culture of white Australia. But in other ways, a man such as Gurrumul is infinitely more subtle and more supple in what he can grasp about the world and its ways than the average whitefella. Stanner says:

> … one has not succeeded in 'thinking black' until one's mind can, without intellectual struggle, enfold into some kind of oneness the notions of body, spirit, ghost, shadow, name, spirit-site, and totem … So long as the belief in The Dreaming lasts, there can be no 'momentary flash of Athenian questioning' to grow into a great movement of sceptical unbelief which destroys the given unities.

The 'given unities': that's what I'm trying to understand. I'll fail — of course I will. But in decades to come, Gurrumul's songs may have initiated a type of liberation, and people like me somewhere down the track will understand 'without intellectual struggle' what Dorothy and Anne are attempting to tell me.

And they are still attempting to tell me. The two sisters are now so filmy against the night that I can barely see them. But I can hear them.

'In everything, songs,' says Anne.

'In this tree is a song,' says Dorothy, and she must mean the she-oak beside us, whispering faintly in the breeze coming off the water of the bay.

Stanner writes:

> There are many such 'onenesses' … A blackfellow may 'see' as a 'unity' two persons, such as two siblings or a grandparent and a grandchild; or a living man and something inanimate, as when he tells you that, say, the woollybutt tree, a totem, is his wife's brother … There is also some kind of unity between waking-life and dream-life: the means by which, in Aboriginal understanding, a man fathers a child, is not by sexual intercourse, but by the act of dreaming about a spirit-child. His own spirit, during a dream, 'finds' a child and directs it to his wife, who then conceives.

In this way, then, Gurrumul was conceived.

Stanner writes: 'Through the medium of dream-contact with a spirit an artist is inspired to produce a new song.'

In this way, then, Gurrumul writes his songs.

But my understanding of totems and dreaming, of skin names and unities remains objective. I will have to accept that I cannot enter into the subjective embrace of Yolŋu culture through intellectual effort. That wonderful scholar of Indigenous culture, John Greatorex, who has lived amongst the people of Elcho Island for twenty years, suggests that there are now two Dreamtimes: one that the non-Indigenous have fashioned to suit their understanding, and one that is lived by black Australians. How could it be otherwise? Twenty, thirty, forty thousand years of living and dreaming in Arnhem Land; millennia after millennia of sunsets and summers and drenching rains; of listening to the sibilant roar of the crocodile, the chirrup of scrub fowls — that's what it takes.

'In this tree is a song,' Dorothy says. But what can I hear? A whispery sound in the she-oak's needles produced by the night breeze coming off the dark water of the bay.

I'm about to ask one more question, but Dorothy says: 'You can't see your notebook. Too dark. Best now we go.'

An intimate sunset concert at a National Art Awards show
in Darwin in August 2007.

CHAPTER 8

Zoo Diary

When Gurrumul sings his crocodile song I have to
wonder if the zoo's own crocs, fifty metres away,
are lifting their heads to listen.

As the beasts of the Melbourne Zoo begin to bed down (it's strictly a nine-to-six day for most of them), Gurrumul and the band make their way from a hire bus to the grassy area set aside for this evening's concert. Why a zoo should be sponsoring twilight concerts throughout the late summer and early autumn is a mystery, but the music lovers of Melbourne are attracted by the idea and stream in through the turnstiles just as the animal lovers are streaming out.

Gurrumul takes a chair in the greenroom where he'll remain until Michael leads him to the stage. Gurrumul's partner Bronwyn sits on the floor, a blanket beneath her for comfort. The supporting musicians hover over a laptop displaying the running order of songs for the evening. It's in the nature of musicians never to settle for doing one thing at a time when it's possible to do three or four; to tune and adjust their instruments as they listen to someone giving them vital information about an upcoming performance; or, if the instrument is out of reach, to find a way to start a second conversation in counterpoint to the first one, and then a third. This is what's happening around the laptop. Michael Hohnen makes alterations to the running sheet while at the same time settling something with Tony Floyd, the drummer, as Tony talks over the top of Michael's head to the guitarist Craig Pilkington, Gurrumul's friend and the man who has co-produced some of his albums.

Gurrumul, in his chair, turns his head to catch fragments of everything that's whirling around him, but he says nothing. He's the guy at the centre of everything, but at the same time he's not. What he'll be doing this evening is already settled; he's simply waiting to start. This sitting-back role is in part an enforced thing: a blind man can't wander about sticking his finger into various pies in the way sighted musicians around him can; the blind are compelled to master a type of patience and discipline that the sighted never need bother with. But it's also cultural, Gurrumul's stillness. Frenzied activity is not a feature of Gumatj life. In a number of his songs ('Galupa'; 'Mala Rrakala'; 'Bayini'; 'Warwu') Gurrumul celebrates sitting with his

*Southern summer. At this Melbourne Zoo concert in February 2012, Gurrumul performed
with a blanket wrapped around him and a bar heater within touching distance.*

MALA RRAKALA

Ga nhina ŋilimurru mala Rrakpala	We sit, we the Gumatj people
Ga nhina Yolŋu mala Ganyawu	We are the Ganyawu people
Wo mänha nhäma yarryarryunara	Sit together, look out beyond the seas, contemplate
Wo mänha nhäma mäwula-wuḻkthunara	Look out, tides change, contemplate
Wo..o mala Rrakpala, mala Rrakpala	Oh Gumatj nation, Rrakpala
Wo..o yi mala Ganyawu, mala Ganyawu	Oh we Gumatj, sharing our identity through Ganyawu
Ga nhina nhäma guṉda Gunyipi	Sit, look out, the Rock, Gunyipi
Ga nhina nhäma guṉda Rraywaḻa	Sit, look out, the Rock, Rraywaḻa
Wo..guṉda nhäma Bakitju	Sit, look out, the Rock, Bakitju
Wo..guṉda nhäma guṉda Rirraliny	Sit, look out, the Rock, Rirraliny
Wo..o mala Rrakpala, mala Rrakpala	Oh Gumatj nation, Rrakpala
Wo..o yi mala Ganyawu, mala Ganyawu	Oh we Gumatj, sharing our identity through Ganyawu
Yuw nhina ŋilimurru, mala Rrakpala	Yes, we sit together, the Gumatj people
Yarryarryun Rräyuŋ, Djurarr, Rrakpala	Sit together, the Gumatj people Rräyuŋ, Djurarr, Rrakpala
Mala waŋgany dharulŋura nhina	One people, we sit under our shade
Djurarr Rrakpala	Gumatj people, Djurarr rrakpala
Wo..o mala Rrakpala, mala Rrakpala	Oh Gumatj nation, Rrakpala
Wo..o yi mala Ganyawu, mala Ganyawu	Oh we Gumatj with our shared identity through Ganyawu
Wo ḻithara Watjapa, rerri Galaṉarri	Oh, the sunset, redness across the sky
Ga ḻithara Watjapa, nhäma Djekulu	The sunset, see the brilliant redness across the sky
Wo warwu gorruŋala, Rrepa Djäpana	Thoughts and reflections there as vivid colours
Wo warwu gorruŋala, miny'tji Garrumara	of the sunset, Djäpana
	Thoughts and feelings there as the colours
	of the sunset, Garrumarra
Wo..o mala Rrakpala, mala Rrakpala	Oh Gumatj nation, Rrakpala
Wo..o yi mala Ganyawu, mala Ganyawu	Oh we Gumatj with our shared identity through Ganyawu
Wo..o mala rrakpala, mala rrakpala	Oh Gumatj nation, Rrakpala
Wo..o mala Ganyawu, wo mala Ganyawu	Oh we Gumatj, sharing our identity through Ganyawu

A song from *Djarridjarri*, the second Saltwater album, and once again, altered in mood. The percussion is gone and the guitar intro is sombre rather than footloose. Sung solo at a lower tempo, 'Mala Rrakala' becomes a deeply felt hymn of praise for the enduring bond amongst the Gumatj.

Gumatj brethren; thinking, reflecting, remembering:

Ga nhina ŋilimurru mala Rrakpala	*We sit, we the Gumatj people …*
Ga nhina nhäma gunda Gunyipi …	*Sit, look out, the Rock, Gunyipi …*
Ga nhina nhäma gunda Rraywala …	*Sit, look out, the Rock, Rraywala …*

So he's thinking; remembering. Watching him, I don't get the slightest impression of vacancy; more of a mental journey that takes him close to the smell of the sea breeze.

Michael tells the tech guy: 'Okay, we'll start with a bass solo,' and the tech guy puts it on the laptop. 'You've got that? Bass solo?'

'Yep,' says the tech guy. 'And that's it?'

'Then the pussycat song.'

'Pussycat song?'

'The pussycat song. After "Galupa".'

Ego Lemos, the East Timorese folk singer who'll open for Gurrumul, is in a micro-rehearsal with Craig Pilkington, the guitarist. Ego says: 'Three times, okay?' Then he sings: '"It's my right, it's my right, it's my right to be free." Three times.'

Out on the grass people are scouting about for a place to spread a blanket. Close to the stage is good for atmosphere but not so good if you want to watch everything on the giant screen that rears up beside the prefabricated proscenium. Those who attempt to take advantage of a spot outside the roped-off area that's good for both atmosphere and screen viewing are hustled back inside the rope by security guards. One of the guards speaks into his crackly two-way in the time-honoured manner of security people everywhere: 'Guests in restricted area. Repeat, guests in restricted area.'

Up on stage, Michael tries out the amplification and signals to one of the stage crew. 'My vocal,' he says. 'I can't hear it if there's any feedback. Check one, check two …'

Gurrumul backstage tugs the zip of his leather jacket up as far as it will go then settles back into stillness.

Ego Lemos and his guitar take the audience on a sprint through the politics of East Timor with his songs of liberation. His first songs are in Tetum (one of the official languages of Timor). Such a cheerful guy as he is, with his huge smile and jaunty porkpie hat with a bird-of-paradise feather, it's difficult for Ego to convince the audience that he's serious when he speaks of things that imprison the human spirit. 'It's my right to be free,' he sings, and it sounds more like a celebration of his geniality than an anthem of the oppressed. The audience was not in favour of enslavement before Ego began to sing, so there are no conversions to liberation. But everyone is glad to have heard Ego's songs, everyone loves him except for the line of security guards standing solemnly just below the stage.

At the first hint of dusk, black clouds of starlings rise high into the air from the Canary Island palms and the lilly pillies that hem in the audience. A chorus of bellows and grunts and shrieks breaks out from here and there in the zoo's precinct — perhaps the creatures are protesting at the arrival of this second wave of visitors for the day.

The recorded voice of Gurrumul's uncle Djuŋa Yunupiŋu tells the audience of his pride

Occupational health and safety anyone? Note the open bottle of water. Gurrumul seems to always avoid such hazards on stage more adroitly than most people.

in his nephew, 'a hidden treasure that the world is experiencing today'. A storm of applause greets Gurrumul being led on stage by Michael who protectively holds Gurrumul's hand under his arm. One of the striking images from any Gurrumul concert is this moment of the impassive star being led by his friend. Michael has never attempted to coax a big, happy showbiz smile out of Gurrumul, who has a fabulously wicked sense of humour and smiles in his private life as much as anyone, but not so often on stage. In any case, Michael's and Mark's influence on Gurrumul is limited in certain situations; there are times when they struggle to get him to say 'hello', let alone grin. It's the members of his family and the elders of his clan who can reach Gurrumul when they wish to; before anything else, he's Gumatj.

Under Michael's other arm is a big, furry blanket, just to have on stand-by in case the two-bar electric radiator sitting beside Gurrumul's chair fails to keep his Territorian bones warm. And it is in fact getting a little chilly as the Melbourne dusk settles in. Michael takes his seat to the left of Gurrumul and cradles his double bass to his shoulder. He leans into the mic to welcome the audience, then introduces himself with word play: 'I'm Gurrumul's Muse … ician.' A few more words to explain what's happening in the first song, then Gurrumul's familiar, 'Mmm … mmm … mmm … mmm … mmm' opening to 'Wiyathul' as the sky darkens and the starlings settle.

That two-bar radiator is going to be crucial. An autumn night in Melbourne is not an autumn night in Arnhem Land.

A Gurrumul performance moves an audience in a way that goes beyond the pleasure of seeing a black Australian acknowledged for his gifts. The Skinnyfish mailbox brings testaments of joy and tears each week from people who've seen him live on stage, on television, on YouTube, or heard his albums. Here at the zoo, women and men listen with tears running down their cheeks. Only a few in the audience, if any, understand Gurrumul's Gumatj and Gälpu lyrics, so it must be the quality of tenderness in his voice that gets to them. Many of the mail correspondents mention the 'spiritual' quality of Gurrumul's singing and claim that his voice acts on them like the Sermon on the Mount set to strings. A woman in Perth listened to Gurrumul in hospital when she was seriously ill and found 'great solace'. A man wrote to say that his daughter put the first album on in the midst of a door-slamming domestic dispute and, within minutes, he and his wife (the door-slammers) were sitting on the sofa together, renewing their vows. Another fan writes: 'I am crying and do not have any reason for it except this wonderful voice with all this wonderful music … I have peace in my heart … thanx [*sic*] … I feel small and humble.' And: 'Geoffrey your voice brought tears to my eyes, my friend … Bless you, brother.' And: 'So proud, Gurrumul brings tears of love to my eyes.'

Almost any music in which you detect tenderness and beauty will provide relief of one sort or another, but maybe there is something especially comforting in Gurrumul's voice. His uncle Djuŋa (David) says that Gurrumul's singing comes from a place in his being where he dwells with his ancestors and the guiding spirits of his people. We're privileged to hear something that has its roots in his Dreaming, yes, but his musicianship takes him a long way beyond his heritage.

Look at him now up on the stage employing all his craft and musical savvy, a picture of concentration. He may well be singing from some core where his ancestors dwell, as Djuŋa says, but he's also a consummate musician who knows exactly what sort of spell he's weaving. His fans amongst his fellow performers — Missy Higgins, Sting, Elton John, to name a few —

know that the professional musician in him is just as important as the Gumatj in him. Without that savvy, he's not about to bring tears to anyone's eyes; not about to make anyone feel at peace. His great achievement has been to retain his spiritual integrity as a black Australian from Elcho while giving full expression to his musical brilliance. His own clan and the wider Indigenous community of Australia have embraced his music and his success in a way that wouldn't be possible if he'd compromised his Gumatj heritage. What we get from Gurrumul can't be faked.

A rapid light show of camera flashes issues from the darkness, shrouding the audience as one after another the songs spread their spell: 'Wiyathul', 'Djärimirri', 'Bäpa', 'Djilawurr' and then 'Wukun' at the grand piano. When Gurrumul sings his crocodile song I have to wonder if the zoo's own crocs, fifty metres away, are lifting their heads to listen.

At times, though, Gurrumul is labouring. The temperature is down to 17 degrees Celsius and if it falls one-tenth of a degree lower, that big woolly blanket is going to get a work-out. Meanwhile, the cohort of security guards — some very robust folk amongst them — are losing their patience with people who insist on walking along the path. The path that skirts the grassy area is a no-go zone, God knows why. 'Sir, I've asked you before, please keep the path clear, have I made myself understood?' And while this is being sorted, Gurrumul is well into his sublime 'Wukun' on the piano, glancing once or twice directly at the source of disruption in the crowd. Well, maybe not 'glancing', unless he has amongst his gifts a type of echolocation talent. But he doesn't miss a note.

On the fringe of the crowd sits a family of Somalis: mother and daughter (about twelve) kitted out in hijab, the father and son as jaunty as each other in embroidered skullcaps. By their expressions, they're well into the Gurrumul sound, but it is a strange thing to think of people from a distant culture responding in this way to the oldest culture at all; people who haven't witnessed all the stages of Indigenous triumph and sorrow over the decades; who have only at this late stage entered the narrative.

At the conclusion of 'Wukun', Gurrumul sits at the keyboard with his head raised taking in the applause. The stage lighting leaves his sightless eyes in deep shadow. Michael has left his perch to lead his friend to the front of the stage. Those in the audience who were seated climb to their feet, raising their hands above their heads to clap. The Somali family remains seated except for the daughter who is clapping rapidly with her hands just under her chin, glancing down at her mum and dad as if to say: 'Go for it! Come on!'

The applause dies down as Gurrumul, Michael and the supporting musicians leave the stage. In the greenroom, Gurrumul leans close to Michael and whispers something, very likely, 'How do people live in this cold?' Michael is already in the midst of multiple conversations with the stage crew, with Mark Grose, with Tony Floyd the drummer. For the space of a few seconds, Gurrumul is left standing alone; this small, sightless man from whom you would not expect very much if you hadn't heard him sing. He turns his head left and right, waiting for the hand that will lead him to his chair.

Hey — you in the fancy silk shirt!

We're in the guests-only lounge of the hotel in Melbourne, sipping Irish Breakfast tea; something to temper the gravel of Michael Chugg's voice. That voice is, of course, one of the most authoritative in the entire Australian music industry. Chugg's judgments as a promoter over the decades, often in defiance of convention, have been vindicated again and again. He's wearing a charcoal grey silk shirt with the sort of brief collar that fashion designers call 'the Karsai look' — a compliment to the well turned-out president of Afghanistan — and beautifully tailored black slacks. He has this to say about Gurrumul.

Gurrumul is a special person. A special person. I knew him first when he was with Yothu. Much later in 2008 up in Darwin — Elton's tour — Gurrumul was singing after the support act, at interval. I'm in Elton's caravan and there's a speaker in there so you can hear what's happening on stage. I'm talking to Elton, one thing and another, and this voice comes over the speaker. Elton looks up. 'Who's that?' This beautiful voice. I tell him 'That's Gurrumul'. Elton says, 'Has he got a CD?' Yeah, he's got a CD. Elton says, 'Can you get me forty of them?' What, forty? 'Forty. I want to give them to friends.' So I found Mark Grose, Gurrumul's manager, and I said, 'Mate, have you got any CDs with you?' Mark says he might be able to get his hands on two or three. 'No, no. I need forty for Elton.' Mark has to drive somewhere to get them, back to the office or somewhere, half an hour each way. He's back with the CDs and I give them to Elton. Elton's still a fan of Gurrumul's. He loves him. Gurrumul's a special person.

During the launch concert for Gurrumul's first album, held in a formal venue, Mark's wife Michelle had to ferry footwear out to a number of Gurrumul's family members waiting at the door. The dress code said: 'No shoes, no entry, no exceptions.'

CHAPTER 9

Dreaming

The Gurrumul who would one day thrill so many with the emotional intensity he can bring to a song is right here in the photographs of his childhood.

Music and Australian Rules are huge on Elcho. Footy is played with a fierce abandon; music of all sorts is embraced with something of the same instinctive urgency. Footy is played by both sexes; music is more likely to be taken up by boys than girls, but everyone is a fan. Gurrumul's house is situated at the back of the footy oval, almost in the shadow of a set of goalposts. The music capital and the sporting capital of the island, side by side. The houses in this off-oval area form a small suburb of Galiwin'ku. Beyond the dwellings extend the ironbarks, woollybutts and acacias of the island's forests, with their understorey of tussocks and hammock grass, east to the coast and northwards to the bulbous upper tip of Elcho. It's a country town, Galiwin'ku, and although employment plays next to no part in the daily life of the community, it's easy to imagine ten thousand other country towns in Australia in which footy (not always Australian Rules) and music are the essential sources of inspiration for kids and teens. The big difference between the recreations of the Elcho kids and those in white country towns is that footy and music form the outer limit of ambition; there is nothing beyond. No farm boys on Elcho working beside Dad to keep the place going; no kids taking up apprenticeships with the local plumber, carpenter, electrician; precious few getting ready to leave home and join their mates in a share house across the road from a city university. Those stepping stones of transition from school to life in the wider world — no, not so many stepping stones in Elcho, other than footy and music.

In Gurrumul's unfenced front yard, women sit chatting under the broadly spread boughs of a leafy tree. Four or five kids from two years old up to maybe eight, the youngest naked, loll about in the sun. Their interest in a visitor from the mainland, with a notebook and forty questions to ask Gurrumul, is exhausted in about one and a half seconds.

The questions in my notebook have been compiled more in hope than anticipation. Gurrumul, famously, does not give interviews. He has less than zero interest in talking about

Sunset at Mission Beach, Galiwin'ku, Elcho Island.

GURRUMUL HISTORY
(I WAS BORN BLIND)

I was born blind, and I don't know why
God knows why, because he love me so
as I grew up, my spirit knew
then I learnt to read the world of destruction
united we stand, divided we fall
together we'll stand, in solidarity

Ŋarranydja dhuwala Batumaŋ
ŋarranydja dhuwala Djarrami
ŋarranydja dhuwala Djeŋarra'
ŋarranydja dhuwala Gurrumulŋa
m..m

I heard my mama, and my papa
crying their hearts in confusion
how can I walk? Straight and tall
in society please hold my hand
trying to bridge and build Yolŋu culture
I've been to New York
I've been to LA
I've been to London
ŋarranydja Gurrumul

United we stand, divided we fall
Together we'll stand, in solidarity

Ŋarranydja dhuwala Barrupa
ŋarranydja dhuwala Dhukuḻuḻ
ŋarranydja dhuwala Maralitja
ŋarranydja dhuwala Ŋunbuŋunbu

Y..e, wo wäŋawu Garrapala
Dhamutjpirr, Dhamuŋura

I am Batumaŋ (ancestor)
I am Djarrami (ancestor)
I am Djeŋarra'
I am Gurrumulŋa (ancestor)
m..m

I am Gurrumul

I am Barrupa (my ḻikan)
I am Dhukuḻuḻ (my ḻikan)
I am Maralitja (my ḻikan)
I am Ŋunbuŋunbu (my ancestor)

Y..e wo of the country Garrapala
Dhamutjpirr, Dhamuŋura

What sounds like a steel guitar on 'Gurrumul History' is actually an electric guitar, a beautiful Fender Stratocaster. Michael's suggestion to Gurrumul was that the acoustic ambience should be varied a little on this track. It's one of only two songs on the album that employ lyrics in English — a deliberate tactic of its author, Gurrumul's uncle Djuŋa, designed to draw in a non-Indigenous audience. Gurrumul embraces this song like no other, but the sensibility of the lyrics is actually more his uncle's than his own. The 'God' who 'knows why' is the loving Christian God, who has made His way into the song directly from the Elcho Methodist Mission.

himself; it bores him. He's not without media savvy, but the entire price of fame argument (make yourself available to people with notebooks and tape recorders even if you're on a drip feed in intensive care) makes him yawn. Mark Grose says: 'He might answer a couple of questions. Or one.'

The first question in my notebook reads: Gurrumul, if you think back to your childhood, when did you first become conscious of music? And can you remember your response? Did it delight you? Did you have any inkling as a child of the role that music would come to play in your life? It might be necessary to settle for a quarter of an answer to that first of forty questions.

Mark Grose heads off to rouse Gurrumul while I make a self-conscious attempt at small talk, which is recognised for what it is and politely ignored.

Within two minutes, Mark returns not with Gurrumul but with a woven rug; a big one. He spreads it on the grass under the tree only to be told by the women that the rug cannot be placed where he's spread it. The women's instructions are specific: the rug has to be spread over there — there! — three metres away, but still in the shade of the tree. The reason for the veto of the original site goes unexplained, but it may have been that the rug was within the proscribed area surrounding a small cemetery of five graves on the south side of the front yard. Cemeteries of this sort are found all over town, in the care of a particular clan or sub-clan. But another twenty reasons could just as easily explain why the rug couldn't be left where it was. The skin of the earth to an Indigenous Australian is not what it is to the non-Indigenous. An interwoven narrative marries each feature of the landscape to each other part.

But Gurrumul. Where is Gurrumul? Those forty questions, where's the man who can answer them?

Mark says: 'He's asleep.'

'Asleep?'

'He's asleep. But David [Djuŋa] and Susan [Dhäŋgal] are happy to talk about Gurrumul. David is his uncle, Susan is his aunt.'

David seats himself on an aluminium-frame beach chair and leans forward with his forearms resting on his knees; Susan makes herself comfortable on the rug. David, in his fifties, with abundant grey hair, and a rather complex grey moustache, has the look of a man who has not left much of life's bounty unexplored. All the same, one of the great pleasures in his life these days is the recognition that has come his nephew's way. It is David's recorded voice that is played to the audience before the start of any Gurrumul performance, speaking of his nephew as 'a hidden treasure'. Not so hidden any longer, but David must remember times when Gurrumul was less appreciated.

Susan is a slim, graceful, soft-featured woman, also in her fifties. Her own pride in her nephew hasn't been broadcast in the way David's has, but she seems to welcome the opportunity to speak of Gurrumul now.

'Susan, when you think back to Gurrumul's childood, when did you notice him first becoming aware of music? Can you remember how he reacted? Did it please him as a little kid, hearing music?'

Susan nods and smiles. 'He always loved music. From the beginning. Right at the beginning. But before that you know, I held him when he was a little baby, not even three months, and I thought something wasn't right with his seeing. Something was wrong. We took him to Melbourne to see the doctor. I was so worried for him so we took him to Melbourne.'

'And the doctor diagnosed blindness?'

'The doctor said he was blind. Yes. It was what I thought in my heart, here, what I thought that he was blind.'

'And there was nothing that could be done?'

'There was nothing could be done. The doctor in Melbourne said, "He is blind from birth". But it made no difference to him. He was happy. Back here in Galiwin'ku he was happy like any child is happy. Everyone looked after him in the family. Daisy and Terry, his mum and dad. His sisters, his brothers, everyone looked after him. His aunties, everyone in his family looked after him.'

'And his uncles,' says David.

'His uncles, his aunties, everyone looked after him.'

David says: 'He had a gift,' and he touches his chest above his heart.

Susan says again: 'When we took him to Melbourne, I was worried for him. It was what I thought. He was blind from birth. But here, everyone looked after him. Everyone protected him and helped him. When the children played, he played too. Just like children always play, he played with them. On the bike — hoo! He rode his bike down the hill over there, down the hill, very fast. The other children, they stood here and here, in different places. They shouted out, "Go straight! Go straight!" And: "Don't hit the tree!" Like that. "Go straight!" He was laughing! Just like children.'

Susan lifts one hand to push back some stray wisps of hair.

'And he enjoyed music?'

'Of course! Always!'

David nods in agreement. He is prepared to defer to Susan, once his wife, now his ex-wife, biding his time to contribute. Courtesy, certainly, but also sensible discretion. Ex-wives on Elcho have memories as long as those of ex-wives anywhere else in the world.

Susan says: 'When he was three he made up his own music. Three! We taught him how to play drums. Not real drums, tins, all different tins. Flour tins, jam tins. All different ones. Flour tins, sugar tins, jam tins. Any tins.'

David says: 'I put them on the ground for him so he could play with a stick.'

Susan says, after a pause: 'We put them on the ground. All different tins.'

'And he enjoyed that?'

Susan says: 'Yes! Hoo! Enjoyed it very much, very much. He made his own music.'

Mark, listening in, says that he has some pictures in the car of Gurrumul as a kid pounding away on the improvised drums, and heads off to find them.

'Then Daisy gave him a piano accordion,' Susan continues, 'and he played that.'

David says again: 'He had a gift,' and once more he touches his heart.

'He listened,' says Susan, and taps her ear with a finger. 'His hearing is special. Special hearing.'

David leans further forward and clears his throat. 'To hear what Gurrumul hears, you must be blind,' he says. And then: 'When you listen to his songs, you must make yourself blind like him. You understand?'

'He listened to a band we had here one time in Galiwin'ku,' says Susan. 'Gospel band. Soft Sands. It was called Soft Sands. He listened to the band and you could see on his face, "Wonderful! Wonderful!" He loved Soft Sands.'

'It was a string band,' says David. 'Soft Sands String Band.'

Susan lifts her eyebrows. 'I said Soft Sands.'

David says: 'Soft Sands String Band.'

Susan makes a brief, dismissive motion with her hand. 'And to church. We took him to church, to chapel. He listened to the singing, gospel singing. He loved that. He was in the choir. First in the junior choir, then in the senior choir. He learnt how to sing.'

Mark has returned with the pictures — coloured snaps, eight by twelve centimetres. 'Here we go.' He lies them out on the rug and taps one that shows a small boy squatting over a half-dozen upturned tins. The boy is beating the tins with two sticks. The expression on his face is one of intense concentration mixed with glee.

'Gurrumul,' says Mark, with the affection that's always there whenever he speaks of Gurrumul. Mark is Gurrumul's adopted father, and Mark's wife Michelle is his adopted mother. It's not a legal adoption — of course not; Gurrumul is forty-one years old and was in his mid-twenties when Mark first met him. It's a title that recognises Mark's role in Gurrumul's life; a role that has developed over fifteen years. 'Adoption' confers a special status on a man or woman from outside the tribe or clan. It honours the dependability in the adopted parent, as if to say: 'In all ways, you show me the love and concern of a blood parent.' Its true importance is that it places a person from outside the clan within a spiritual context. Gumatj culture — and this appears to apply to Indigenous cultures generally — demands a foundational structure to accommodate any relationship: the structure of close kin — brother, cousin, mother, father, aunt, uncle; of friendship, and many others, reaching into the seethingly populated ancestral past. If the context of 'friend' becomes too limited to encompass your role in the life of someone like Gurrumul, the context is broadened and refined and you may, like Mark, become 'father'. This happens in other cultures too, but in Indigenous culture it isn't optional. If you can't be placed, you're more or less invisible, or at best, a blur, a smudge.

Susan, too, delights in the pictures; she laughs, she shakes her head fondly. 'Happy,' she says. 'Like all children. Happy.'

Mark climbs to his feet. 'I'll check on him,' he says. 'He might be awake.'

Susan and David's little picnic of conversation here under the tree attracts a regular trickle of visitors, some from Gurrumul's family. They sit and listen for a minute or two, establish that nothing's going on they haven't seen or heard before, then wander off, disappointed in what's on offer.

Here's another picture of Gurrumul, maybe five years old, holding an entire roasted wallaby, and looking enormously pleased with himself, like an apprentice warrior home from the hunt. The wallaby has been cooked, hide and all, its lips drawn back from its teeth into a grin that mirrors Gurrumul's. In another picture, Gurrumul, still five or six, stands smiling amongst a whole mob of little kids. Mark wanders back from his Gurrumul mission, lifts his baseball cap and runs his hand over his head. 'Nope. Still asleep.'

'They came here,' says Susan, 'what do you call them?'

'Who came here?'

'The big meeting. What was the name?'

David says: 'First Revival Church.'

'First Revival, yes,' says Susan.

'First Revival Church,' says David.

Mark says: 'It was an outreach thing. Across the Northern Territory and Western Australia. An outreach missionary.'

'We took him to that,' says Susan.

Mark has spoken on an earlier occasion of the type of appeal that the church — any church — has for Indigenous people: 'Their faith is spread pretty thin. The beliefs that come

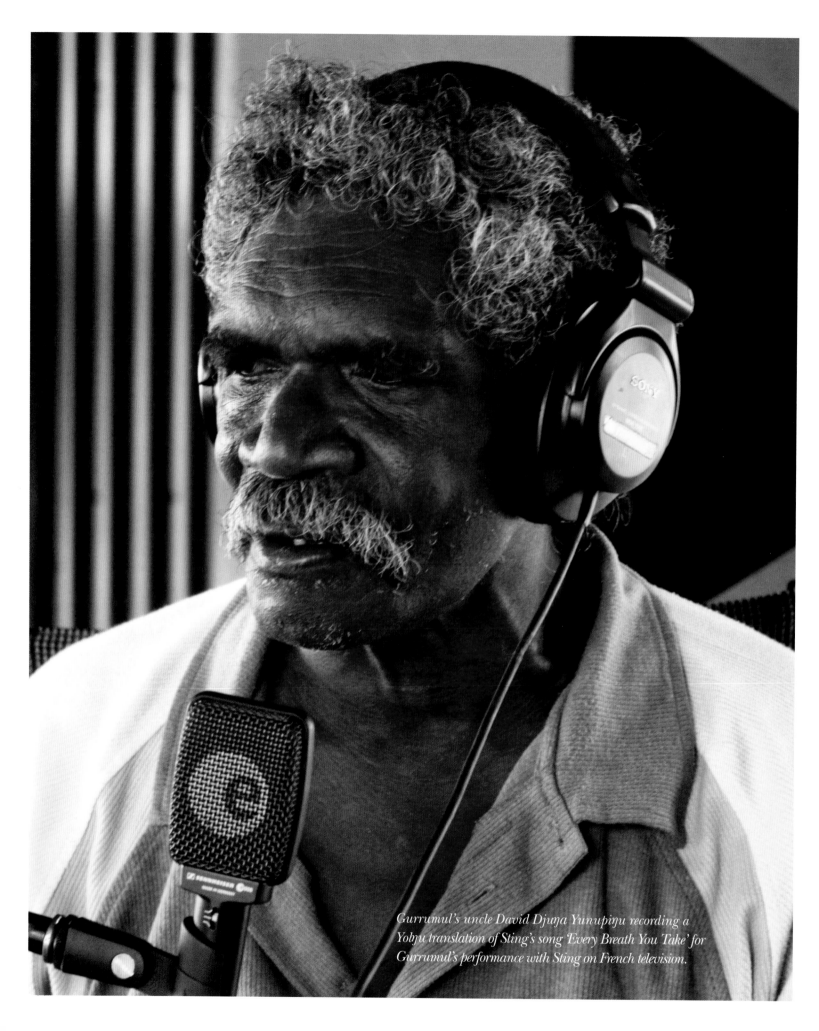

Gurrumul's uncle David Djuŋa Yunupiŋu recording a
Yolŋu translation of Sting's song 'Every Breath You Take' for
Gurrumul's performance with Sting on French television.

Susan (Dhäŋgal) Gurruwiwi, Gurrumul's aunty, when asked how does Gurrumul write his songs answered 'he writes them on his heart'.

from their culture — much, much deeper. People are attracted to the ceremony of the church, and the singing. But it's a surface thing.'

'And he enjoyed the music at the revival meeting?'

'Oh, yes. And at school. He learnt some more music at school,' says Susan.

'A bit of theory, maybe?'

'Some music. What do you call them? Scales. He liked it. Always happy. Like all children.'

David says: 'I gave him a guitar for his own, with fishing line strings. I taught him three chords for the guitar. And I took him to ceremonies. You know, ceremonies? I took him to ceremonies so that he knows his culture. He learnt all his culture, sat and listened to everything. He had a gift, here, in his heart.'

What does Susan make of this long contribution from her ex-husband? She picks at a grass burr in the rug, then takes up one of the pictures of Gurrumul and studies it with a smile.

'I saw that gift he had,' says David.

'And you encouraged him?'

'Oh yes. Very much. And to write songs himself. Very much.'

'David writes songs, too,' says Mark. 'He wrote most of that "Gurrumul History" song.'

David nods, and for the first time a smile appears within the thicket of his beard. The song is the only track on either of Gurrumul's albums with a political message, mild enough, a type of propaganda for humanity: united we stand, divided we fall, together we'll stand in solidarity.

'My favourite song,' says David, 'is not that one. It's another one.'

'What is it?'

'The rainbow song, "Djärimirri". That one is my favourite.'

The Gurrumul who would one day thrill so many with the emotional intensity he can bring to a song is right here in the photographs of his childhood and in the warmth of Susan and David's recollections. The nostalgia you hear in the lyrics, and that quality of yearning — its source is the love and embrace of his family. Perhaps that's what Gurrumul wants to convey, as much as anything: what came into his heart as a child.

'And when he was older, you continued to encourage him?'

Susan says: 'Yes, when he was older we encouraged him.'

David says: 'I said to him, "Do what is in your heart." When he was seventeen, he asked me if he should go to Hong Kong with Yothu Yindi. I said, "Go. See the world." It was in his heart, so I said, "See the world. Go." If something is true, you must do it. I told him, "Tell the truth." In the song, "Gurrumul History", the words say, "I was born blind". That's the truth. Everything in his songs is true.'

Two shrikes are squabbling in the foliage overhead. My awe at the pervasiveness of Indigenous culture is such that I can't help but wonder if the squabbling of birds somehow fits into it, has a suggestion to impart. But maybe not. Mark tells the story of a Gumatj friend in Arnhem Land telling him one day: 'See that tree, Mark? See that tree with the yellow flowers? When that tree gets his yellow flowers in July it has a special meaning to Indigenous people. A special meaning.'

And Mark: 'Really? What does it mean?'

'Mark, it means we have to do our tax. That's the meaning of the yellow flowers.'

A new question: 'So you made up for Gurrumul's blindness with your love and care?'

'I will tell you something,' says David, and he adjusts his weight on the aluminium-frame chair in preparation; readies himself. 'We went to India with the church. You know India?

That's where we went, to India. Madras. Lots of poverty in India, everywhere you look …'

Susan has realised that the story her ex-husband is about to tell would better be told by her — so it seems. She says: 'We saw blind children. Many, many blind children. And I thought of Gurrumul when I saw the blind children. In India the blind children — nobody cared for them. Nobody. And I cried to think of Gurrumul. I thought, you know, "We will make Gurrumul happy, even if he is blind." Not like the children in India. No. We will make him happy and give him everything so he can be whatever he wants to be. Happy. Like all children.'

'Susan, do you still count yourself as a Christian?'

Susan says that she remains a faithful member of the church community. The interface between the Christian commitment of Indigenous peoples and their far more long-standing tribal heritage must be either highly complex or very simple. Certain articles of Christian belief — Holy Communion, for example, and the resurrection — match up in an approximate way with certain Indigenous beliefs, but perhaps the greatest appeal of Christianity to believers like Susan is the New Testament emphasis on love and forgiveness. At various times in Indigenous history after white settlement, missionaries from various churches may have been the only white people who gave the impression of giving a damn about what became of native Australians.

The reason for the question is really to preface another question, one that isn't asked, all things considered: 'Is Gurrumul also a member of the church community?' It would be better to ask that question of Gurrumul himself on a day when he isn't kipping. In all of the lyrics of his songs, the only reference to a Christian God is found in 'Gurrumul History':

I was born blind, and I don't know why
God knows why, because he loves me so …

But those lyrics were written by David.

And this question: 'Gurrumul's songs don't touch on politics very much. Is that deliberate?'

Just at this moment, a shape appears in the doorway of the house. Is this Gurrumul? Awake at last? Well, no. It's Nigel, Gurrumul's cousin. Or if not Nigel, someone who looks like Nigel but who is also not Gurrumul. In any case, the shape has stepped back into the darkness of the house's interior.

David shakes his head, the hint of a smile on his lips. 'Asleep,' he says quietly.

The shrikes overhead have settled into a mumuring domesticity.

'Politics,' says David, and he makes a gesture with his hand, turning it loosely about; a gesture which has the same universal meaning as a shrug. 'I always said to him, "Catch the beauty of my clan and my mother's clan." You understand? His songs are about beauty.'

In this, Susan appears to concur. Politics are not for her, either.

'About beauty,' she says. 'Everything is part of one. Everything. About beauty.'

Most of the women who were seated under the tree earlier have departed. Perhaps the overheard question-and-response format of the interview, which is alien to the way in which Indigenous people develop knowledge of another, became tedious to them. Gurrumul has become a magnet attracting visitors with notebooks over the past few years but, for the community on Elcho, life has continued in the normal way. No doubt the Elcho folk are proud of Gurrumul and his accomplishments with Saltwater band, as a solo artist and as a

Coconuts

Greg Pilkington has been a friend of Gurrumul's for fifteen years or more. He was with Michael Hohnen in the Melbourne band The Killjoys long before Michael took his ramshackle Ford up the highway to Darwin in the middle of the 1990s. He now has his own recording studio in Coburg, Audrey Studios, where Gurrumul's first solo album was recorded. He's respected as one of the most astute and conscientious figures in the Australian recording industry. We're talking in Audrey Studios.

I've been in Darwin when a big 4-wheel drives goes by and one of those ballads from the first album is blaring out, and it's a moment, you know, so beautiful both musically and culturally, because so many Yolŋu people see that album as a flag of pride. I'm closer to the first album than the second, Rrakala, because I was so involved in the first album, but I feel very close to both albums. Robert, you asked me about Michael thinking of putting strings on that first album, and I said to him, 'You know, I don't think it needs strings.' The thing is, there's a lot going on sonically at the top end of Gurrumul's voice — a lot going on. The top end of his voice is very airy, and strings work in that area too, and I thought that strings might get in the way of the complex harmonies in Gurrumul's singing. People really respond to that voice. You know, I think out there in white culture — that's a fairly blunt way of putting it, but you know what I mean — it might be a time in Australia's history when people out there are yearning for a connection with Indigenous culture. But I also think that when you're trying to explain the success of something artistic, it's difficult trying to pin it down to one, two, three or four factors. Regardless of the socio-political situation in Australia, it's also to do with someone being exceptional. Every now and again comes along someone exceptional, a Gurrumul, and it doesn't happen all that often. That's a voice that really draws people, and it might have nothing to do with politics or what's happening in our society. People are just drawn to whatever he's singing about, but they don't know why. I'll tell you a story about recording that first Saltwater album, Gapu Damurruŋ, up at Adelaide River. I was trying to get an understanding of the songs, just so that I could grasp the structure, where we start, where we're going to, all of that. I asked Lloyd (Lloyd Garawirrtja, of the Saltwater Band) what one of the songs was about — because this song was seven minutes long, and I wanted to understand it. And Lloyd says, 'It's about a coconut.' I said, 'Hold on. How can you sing about a coconut for seven minutes? And how can you make it sound so reverential, so beautiful?' Lloyd says, 'No, not just about a coconut. Much more. When the coconut's in the water, in the sea, and it's floating along and it finds a rhythm, and then it's on the beach, all of that.' And I thought, we might have a song about boy meets girl, boy loses girl, boy gets girl, a love song sort of thing. But this is a really, really beautiful, reverential song about the life of a coconut — amazing. Because people up in Arnhem Land, people on Elcho, the coconut is one of their totems, they naturally sing about it in a reverential way. When people are drawn to Gurrumul's songs, they're responding to the beauty, and it could be about a coconut or a scrub fowl, but it's still the beauty in the singing that's drawing them in.

one-time member of Yothu Yindi, but they are not about to go crazy. People on Elcho have known him since he was a little kid whacking Golden Syrup tins with improvised drumsticks. A thousand stories have unfolded in the community between then and now, and Gurrumul's is only one of them. I sense a suspicion of visitors from the mainland seeking to slot Gurrumul into the national carnival of celebrity. Maybe people here think whatever is written about him will stand as a travesty of what it means to truly know him. As a matter of fact, I feel a certain amount of suspicion about my own motives.

Susan is gazing, smiling away into the distance. The dappled light filtering down through the foliage plays over her face like the patterns you see on the silky surface of a dark stream. She's a beautiful woman, assured in her convictions, at peace, if you set aside a certain impatience with her ex-husband's opinions. You don't see that peace in David's face; for him, life is still a quest. Susan is content to talk about her nephew out of courtesy and for the enjoyment of it, but David wants his nephew and the Indigenous soul intelligently understood in the broader community; he wants those bridges he speaks about.

I look down at all the Gurrumul questions in my notebook left unasked:

9. Are you consciously attempting to reveal more of Indigenous culture to your audience in your songs?

10. The interface of black and white culture in Australia is changing, or so it appears, and I wanted to ask if you detect that change during performance, in the feeling that comes back to you when you're on the stage, in your rapport with the audience, as it were?

And:

17. In your song 'Baywara', you sing of the 'Mother creator', i.e. the female principle, so often invoked in your lyrics. Would you agree that female figures of great power represent a creative force that exceeds that represented by the male figures in your songs?

And:

40. The future, Gurrumul? How do you see the future unfolding, artistically? Are there further innovations you'd like to introduce both at a technical level and in the variety of motifs you employ?

Reading through the questions, you begin to understand why Gurrumul has taken to his bed.

'Well, if that's it,' says Mark, 'we might make a tour of the island. It's going to rain soon.'

Hands are shaken; thanks conveyed. Susan accepts a cigarette, which she conceals from Nigel, who would disapprove. David checks the notebook to see if his Indigenous name, Djuŋa, is spelt correctly. Beneath the tree, a small child is crouched over a line of marching ants, studying them in fascination. He extends a stubby finger and squashes one ant, then another and another. The women who'd been chatting under the tree a couple of hours earlier begin to drift back.

Gurrumul is left in the house, sleeping undisturbed.

Dreaming.

It's the annual Galiwin'ku Healthy Lifestyle Festival, and the jumping castles are on site.
Opposite: No swimming pools on Elcho, but 'tip the bucket' is a hot day favourite. And the beach?
A few too many crocodiles down there for little kids to cope with.

Training for football is always interesting but when it is on
a crocodile infested beach it becomes really interesting.
Here the young women of Elcho train on Mission Beach.

CHAPTER 10

Manhattan

Even when he's playing with a song he's performed scores of times,
he's attracted to improvisation; to capturing something he's been
exploring with his guitar or with his voice.

'Djärimirri' rolls through the studio, supported by strings and the deep burr of an organ. It's the most poignant of all Gurrumul's songs, this tribute to origins and ancestors, the sound you'd expect to hear as you wander the halls of heaven. At a complicated mast of mics, Gurrumul begins to harmonise with his own recorded voice. The engineer, Anthony Ruotolo, in a duck-bill baseball cap, nods approval. Michael Hohnen, wearing a daggy T-shirt of the sort worn for studio sessions, says to Gurrumul: 'You know what I reckon? Gumatj voice.'

He's not asking Gurrumul to switch from English to his native tongue; he's suggesting more of the true Gumatj timbre and cadence, like a cataract running over stones worn smooth by a million years of flow. This is to be an album that takes in more of the mystery and enchantment of Yolŋu culture.

Gurrumul says: 'Gumatj voice?' and he raises his head to the mics and sings.

'That's perfect!' Michael calls to Gurrumul. 'Perfect! Like a church song. It's so … so big.'

I don't want the sound to stop, ever, and it doesn't stop, overwhelming in its grandeur. And I think: 'Dear God, people envy Australia for the truckloads of minerals we claw from the soil, but this is what they should envy, the language of a blind black man made into song, drawn up from the soil and stored in his heart.'

Michael calls: '*Latju! Latju!*' — the Gumatj word for 'beautiful'.

Gurrumul says laconically: 'Yeah?'

'So beautiful.'

We're in Manhattan, West 53rd Street. It's 2012, three in the afternoon and summer in New York. The trees of Central Park, just up Seventh Avenue past Carnegie Hall, are in glistening foliage. The studio is Avatar, one of the premier recording spaces in the world. Housed in what was once a Consolidated Edison power station, the studio was known for many

BAYINI

Nhinana ŋilimurru, yarrayarra'yun	We Gumatj sat together
Dhuwalana wäŋanydja Gämbuthuwa	Here at Gämbuthuwa
Gu ŋilimurru yarrayarra'yuna	Let's sit all together
Manha nhäma, yarrayarra'yunara	Sit together, watch the sea, contemplate
Mawula-wuḻkthunara	The changing tide
Guṉda dhärranana nininyŋu Bakitju	Standing, the land-ancestor Rock, Bakitju
Yä, ḻuku-nherranmirri, bäpa ŋilimurruŋgu	Oh, our father, steadfast, strong
Nininyŋu Daymbawi, Djiḻawurr	Of this country, Daymbawi, Djiḻawurr
Waŋana dhä-milmitjpa, ḻakaraŋala	Spoke in the afternoon, told
Wäŋa nininyŋunha, Bayini	Of our land-ancestor Bayini
Aa Bayini, Bayini, Djotarra	Ah, Bayini, Bayini, Gumatj woman
Barrkuna runu'runu Wuṉbirrwuy	The islands Wuṉbirrŋwuy far away
Guṉda djirripuŋala, Wurrwaḻa, raŋi ŋorranana	The Rock caressed, at Wurrwaḻa, the beach lies long
Nhanukala bunana Wäḻunbaŋu Gulunŋura	They met him, Wäḻunba, at the island Gulunŋura
djomula dhärrana, Miritjaŋay	The Djomula trees, in long thick stands at Miritjaŋgay
Yä, ḻuku-nherranmirri bäpa ŋilimurruŋgu	Oh, our father, steadfast, strong
Nininyŋu Daymbawi Djiḻawurr	Of this country, Daymbawi
Waŋana dhä-milmitjpa, ḻakaraŋala	Spoke in the afternoon, told
Wäŋa nininyŋunha, Bayini	Of our land-ancestor Bayini
Bayini, Bayini, Djotarra	Bayini, Bayini, Gumatj ancestor
Djotarra, ŋäthi nhina, Djotarra	Gumatj ancestor, sits crying, Gumatj ancestor

A song of communion, related to the rites of the Gumatj expressed in 'Mala Rrakala'. Gathered as if in a congregation, the Gumatj sit on the beach and lift their gaze to the horizon, honouring the Ancestral Women — the Bayini of the title — who came over the sea in the Dreamtime to enfold the land in their power. Gurrumul's voice climbs in this song, as if reaching towards the Bayini, while the harmonies he sings remain murmurously subdued, suggesting the tenderness of the welcome extended to the women.

years as The Power Station, the preferred recording venue of a whole host of pop music greats. Bruce Springsteen was here for *The River*; the Stones for *Tattoo You*; David Bowie for *Let's Dance*; Dire Straits for *Brothers in Arms*; Diana Krall for *The Look of Love*; Sheryl Crow for *C'mon C'mon*. Also John and Yoko. Also Bob Dylan. Six studios all up, the most capacious with a domed ceiling, each clad in pine for the sake of the acoustics.

This is to be a session that will get down a few more tracks on Gurrumul's in-progress third album. By the time the album is ready to print, three or four or even five studios will have worked it over. You can do that these digital days — pick up a studio wherever it's convenient, tack on a little more, carry away the hard-drive, and put it all together when you're good and ready. You can preserve every little nuance of production, spend a day on a couple of verses in Vienna, sit down in Paris, in Moscow, wherever your itinerary and your budget takes you, and work on another verse. Every well-equipped studio gives you the same opportunities, and even looks the same: the pine cladding, gleaming mics, *Star Trek* consoles, pictures of the greats who've used the space and, like icons in a cathedral, portraits of the legends — Jimi Hendrix, James Brown, Aretha Franklin, Lou Reed. Avatar, though, is more than just well-equipped; it's state-of-the-art. For Gurrumul and Michael, having the freedom of a studio like this is the equivalent of handing a couple of guys the resources of NASA to build a rocket.

Michael may not have had all the sleep he could use after the experience of the Jubilee Concert in London, but his eyes are bright. And why not? This album with its creative leaps and exploration of the Gumatj world could well become the *Rubber Soul* of Indigenous music, reaching for something more complex in its resonances than anything that came before.

And Gurrumul does seem to have hit his groove, maybe relishing the opportunity the session gives him. That slightly satirical smile that at times plays at the corners of his mouth is right there. Sameness bores him. Even when he's playing with a song he's performed scores of times, he's attracted to improvisation; to capturing something he's been exploring with his guitar or with his voice. He's by nature somewhat circumspect, especially away from his family and clan. On those occasions when he's come up with a new song, he isn't likely to simply shout 'Hurrah!' and let Michael in on it. Instead he'll doodle with it within Michael's hearing, hunched over his guitar, humming words of indistinct Gumatj. It's a gentle type of tease, but also owes something to his shyness. Michael's ears will prick up and he'll say: 'That's new isn't it, wäwa?' Gurrumul, not ready yet to concede anything, will work a few phrases before giving a shrug of agreement — or not. It might be days later or even weeks before he'll bring it out again, this new thing. And Michael knows not to push or insist. He might be curious, he might even be avid, but he observes a choreography of patience, he and Gurrumul dancing around the new sound. And that's what's happening at Avatar; that's what the secretive smile's about, possibly: improvisations he's keeping to himself, new approaches, some of which Michael has suggested, some of which will come as a surprise.

Gurrumul and Michael have now moved on to 'Galiku', known as the 'the flag song' because of its references to the clan flags of the Gumatj — identifying emblems that catch the wind and whip about, as if they had come to exuberant life. It's principally a song about tribal dance, but the dancing and the whipping of the flags merge in a joyous shout of praise for the spirits that inhabit the north wind. In 'Galiku', everything the Gumatj language can express is gathered up and released.

Michael says: 'I just want to check a word in that third line.'

'Third line?' says Gurrumul.

'Yeah.'

Gurrumul lifts his voice and provides the third line of the 'Galiku' verse.

'Yes, but just let me listen to this third line on the speakers.'

'Okay.'

Michael adopts an intensely focused expression as the song plays through his headphones. He says: 'It sounds like there's one word in that third line you're singing different.'

Gurrumul says: 'Yeah, yeah. The high one.'

'Just try that third line again where you're singing higher.'

'Okay.'

And Gurrumul sings the third line once more.

'That's good,' says Michael. 'And we've already got the fourth line. We're going to play the fifth line, all right my brother?'

'Yeah.'

Michael comments to Anthony on the fifth line: 'See how he blends it in? Amazing.' And to Gurrumul: 'That's perfect.'

'Yeah, good?'

'Beautiful. Perfect.'

So, no grand announcements from Gurrumul when a new song's on the way, and not much warning of any improvisations, either; he simply does it. He can't embrace too much liberty of departure from the familiar because his songs are always derived from ancestral precursors, but he gives himself as much of the compass as he can afford. The message is: 'Follow me.' There's never been between Michael and Gurrumul protracted discussion of a song's destination. Point-to-point planning is alien to the Gumatj way of going about things. John Greatorex, the scholar of Yolŋu culture from Charles Darwin University, and who would know, has pointed out that a whitefella must find his way into Indigenous cultures by exercising more subtlety than he employs in his own world. The whitefella will take the study of meaning down to the sub-atomic structure of a message, but in Gurrumul's culture, you must 'find direction by indirection'. Gurrumul pays Michael the supreme Gumatj compliment of expecting him to understand what the hell's going on without having it spelt out.

Michael: 'Okay, so from the "*gilaŋ, gilaŋ, gilaŋ…*"'

And Gurrumul: 'Nah, wanna hear it first.'

'Okay.'

The recorded sections of 'Galiku' come over the speakers, but something's not right.

Michael says: 'All the rest of the verse first?'

Gurrumul: 'Hoo! Another verse.'

'Do you mean from the start of the song?'

'Nah. 'Nother verse there.'

'I'll play it from the start — you know, the start that you've already recorded the harmonies to, then the second verse, that's the whole song.' And to Anthony: 'Okay, that first version.'

Gurrumul listens, shuffling about, raising his head, looking casual but in fact being highly exacting in what he wants to achieve here.

From the speakers: '*Wana nirrpuna banuydjina bili wulungupayina, djaw', djaw'*…'

The '*djaw', djaw'* at the end of the line is the song's imperative exclamation, repeated throughout: 'Take it! Take it!' It's an exhortation to dance, to take the clan flag, to fill yourself

His Martin guitar clutched in his gloved hand, Gurrumul braves the chill of a New York winter. It's his second visit to New York; the first was with Yothu Yindi, years earlier. On this visit, he stays at the Waldorf and plays Carnegie Hall with the Adelaide Symphony. Bliss.

with the spirit of the north wind, and finally, to be alive.

But the playback isn't giving Gurrumul what he's looking for.

Michael tells Anthony: 'Maybe just go from the start again and have the mic open so that he can call out.' And to Gurrumul: 'Okay, we're going to go from the start again. You listen and you call out when you mean.'

'Yeah?'

'Yeah.'

The song fills Studio G, three lines, four, then Gurrumul calls out: 'Hoo!'

'It's that one?' says Michael.

'Yeah.'

'Is that the one you overdubbed?'

'Yeah.'

'Okay, good.' And to Anthony: 'I think we'll get him to record a third harmony on this one, rather than doubling the second.'

There's English, there's Gumatj, and then there's a third language in the studio, formed of murmurs, half-voiced words of indistinct origin, little whispery ripples, onomatopoeic rumbling, monosyllabic exclamations ('Hoo!) and brief bursts of laughter spanning three notes. All of it comes from Gurrumul, but Michael appears to know exactly what it means. It was said of Miles Davis that you were often expected to know what he wanted from you just by studying his profile while he gazed straight ahead. Over years of friendship, of mentoring, of listening and learning, Michael has developed an acute sense of the direction Gurrumul's creativity is heading at any given time. It's not merely a matter of cataloguing Gurrumul's habits; just as important is Michael's sensitivity to Gumatj culture. All human beings are both individuals and products of the culture in which they were raised. The influence of Gurrumul's Gumatj heritage, if traced on an outline of his body, would reach into every corner and niche, every limb and organ, like an anatomical map of his veins and arteries. The eloquence of his singing and his sense of beauty itself are as much an expression of his culture as of his individuality. His songs are aural landscapes more than narratives; even the people mentioned, often ancestors, are embedded in nature, or are in fact what we would call 'nature'. For Gurrumul, for the Gumatj, what the eye sees as it takes in plains and hills, the shoreline, the scrubby desert oaks, ant hills, clouds, woollybutts, acacias, the she-oaks of the shoreline, rocks and red earth is the story of a people, extending from horizon to horizon. Everything seethes with the deeds of spirits. All of this is with Michael in the studio, and it provides the same clues as Miles Davis' profile.

The verses of 'Galiku' are played over the speakers to Gurrumul again and again. Michael stops the tape ten times, twenty times, more — as many times as it takes to tweak a phrase or a single word. Gurrumul and Michael are equally hard to please. The songs are edited as if everyone who will hear the album is a fluent speaker of Gumatj, capable of picking up tiny nuances in Gurrumul's delivery. Such an admirable way to go about the process of recording Gurrumul; a genuine example of art for art's sake, making songs that only one exceptionally discerning listener in a thousand will entirely appreciate.

Michael, by some means but God knows how, keeps up with the rapid, tumbling flow of the Gumatj words as if he were a native speaker of the language. Of all the skills he brings to the studio, this ability to remain oriented in the midst of the flow is the most startling. And that's not the only thing he's doing, of course; he's also making artistic judgments that preserve Gurrumul's culture while fashioning something saleable for the marketplace. He stands on the frontier between these two cultures, reaching deftly for what he needs from each. Unless he gets the cultural complements right — the vernacular blended with high art — he'll end up with something grotesque, comparable to the dire results of Pavarotti attempting 'A Hard Day's Night'. The emphasis in the judgments that Michael makes is always the preservation of Gumatj integrity; he says that he has to 'take care not to influence Gurrumul too much'. Convictions like this go all the way back to the thoughts that filled his head when he made his journey from south to north years and years ago, his double bass on the passenger seat of his dilapidated Ford. He wanted to amend his sketchy understanding of Indigenous Australia, provide something of value if possible. What he's doing right now in Avatar is honouring his commitment. That 'something of value' is this new album, and *Rrakala*, the second album, and *Gurrumul*, the first.

'Anthony says he's hearing one word in that line a little bit sharp,' says Michael.

'Yeah?'

Gurrumul sings the word.

'Yeah, that one.'

Michael says to Anthony: 'I think what we should do … is get another harmony.' And to Gurrumul: 'There's one bit missing, and that's the "*gilaŋ, gilaŋ, gilaŋ, gilaŋ …*" the first time.'

Michael plays the verse again, with Gurrumul's harmonies rising high behind the melody. He says: 'See, you were singing further away from the mic that time. Okay, let's try it now.'

Anthony says: 'Still a little high. It's low then high.'

Michael to Gurrumul: 'You've got a high voice, wäwa. Just in case you didn't know.'

With persistence, the verse emerges with Gurrumul's harmonies tweaked. But Michael wants to try a new harmony.

'Okay, that's great, from the start to the end. Now can you just play around with another harmony? For this song. I want you to try, you know, another harmony.'

'Mmm,' says Gurrumul.

'You know, like when you and Johnno and Nigel sing together? You always do different harmonies.'

'Mmm. Yeah.'

'Okay?'

Gurrumul produces the sound of a trumpet, as if he were playing reveille. For the fun of it. He's enjoying Avatar. Now he adds the third harmony to the 'Galiku' verse, higher still, and the sort of thing he gets into with his cousins Nigel and Johnno. His voice has a fine range, not all that unusual amongst great singers, but he is able to employ that range without any diminishment of character, which is much more unusual. When Gurrumul is spoken of as 'a genius', what's being lauded is the character of a voice that can reach your ears coated in the red soil of Arnhem Land or as polished as a shell on the beach at Galiwin'ku.

Something else: the vigour in his voice, and what it owes to good health. Because this is a man who was so ill a year before today's Avatar stint that his family and his dearest friends —

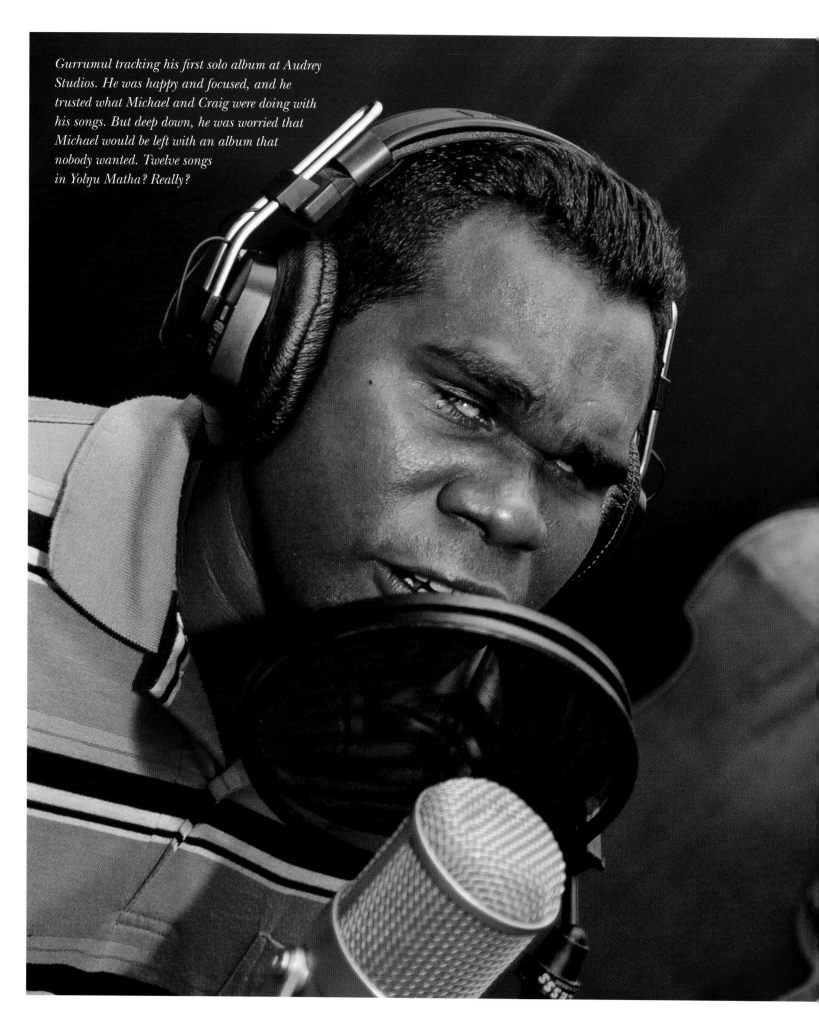

Gurrumul tracking his first solo album at Audrey Studios. He was happy and focused, and he trusted what Michael and Craig were doing with his songs. But deep down, he was worried that Michael would be left with an album that nobody wanted. Twelve songs in Yolŋu Matha? Really?

Michael Hohnen and Mark Grose, to name two — were themselves ill with worry, and preparing for heartbreak. 'He's a different man now,' Michael says. 'The change is unbelievable.' So that is there in his voice, too: a new lease on life.

The painstaking completion of the 'Galiku' harmonies goes on until finally Michael is satisfied. He says: 'Okay, that's it. I'll bring you in now,' and fetches Gurrumul from the performance area. He looks pleased, as if the session, rather than sapping his strength, has restored it.

Michael plays back the whole of the 'Galiku' version for Gurrumul, at the same time peeling himself a banana. 'Jimmy the mon-key!' Gurrumul sings, since no opportunity to recall Elcho's celebrity chimp is permitted to pass unobserved. Michael has in mind a *yidaki* (didgeridoo) accompaniment under the 'Galiku' verses and he plays a little recorded *yidaki* for Anthony, explaining its function, then imitating the *yidaki* sound to show how it fits. Gurrumul himself is a master *yidaki* player, scornful of what passes for accomplishment on the instrument elsewhere in Australia. And he's scornful now of Michael's imitation.

Michael says: 'Are you laughing at me?'

Gurrumul indicates that his friend has sinned against music, and art, and everything that a true didge player holds sacred.

'Maybe I'll lock you in that room,' says Michael, 'and come back tomorrow.'

Gurrumul needs a smoke, and is led by Michael to the highly circumscribed smoke-if-you-must area on an upper floor. Anthony and his tech guy have business elsewhere in Avatar, and Studio G is all at once empty and silent.

Outside, Manhattan is enjoying a summer evening. Still plenty of light in this city of architectural monuments dwelling dreamily in the clouds. And below the spires, the whole seething world hurries, but our guy (presently puffing away on a smoke) and the beauty of his singing — nobody passing him on a New York street would have guessed what he can do with a song.

It's a remarkable achievement from a toy keyboard in the dust of a remote community to a grand piano in a concert hall especially when you are self taught.

CHAPTER 11

Adelaide

Can you say that Gurrumul, Michael and Mark
have fashioned something at the top of the continent and
carried it all over the compass, and that its vigour will enrich
black–white relations in Australia?

It's Adelaide in the early autumn. I'm at the WOMAD (World of Music, Arts and Dance) festival in the Botanic Gardens, on a balmy Sunday afternoon, sunshine glittering on the leaves of the London planes and apple gums. People from every corner of the round earth have been singing their souls out all day. At the moment a band in the background from Jamaica (maybe) is rounding off its gig with a giddy version of 'My Boy Lollipop', Millie Small's jaunty ska hit of the sixties.

There's a 'One Perfect Day' thing going on here: the climate, the cheerful breeze in the tree canopies, the comfort of sitting on the grass, the kids behaving themselves in the outdoors (more or less), a holiday to follow on Monday and now, at this perfect time on this perfect day, the guy I especially came to hear, Gurrumul, is up on the stage with that voice coiled inside him ready to be released.

It takes in everyone, the WOMAD gathering, including a number of Indigenous folk close to the stage, making up about the same proportion of the crowd as they do the Australian population. The audience are all ages, including two beautiful girls of about eight and nine in the uniform of a swanky private school just down the road from the festival site. They've come to see the most famous black Australian on the island continent singing in his own tongue.

The stage is fabulously kitted out with speakers the size of wardrobes and maybe ten mics serving what will be a maximum of six musicians. A huge Kevlar canopy like a shade-sail rises high above the stage. Over to one side, a Yamaha grand stands waiting with the mic adjusted at exactly chin height for Gurrumul. The opener will feature just Gurrumul and his guitar, Michael on double bass, and one more acoustic guitarist. The musicians who'll take the stage

APRA Song Summit Sydney. This was the first industry showcase of Gurrumul's solo career.

GATHU MAWULA

M..m nhän ŋalma yarrarrayun, mala Dhurrkay
garmak nhäŋal balaṉḏi yarryarryunda mäwula-guḻkthunda
y..ä gäthu Mäwula, yothu ŋalinyuŋgu wäwawu Yotjiŋu
y..ä gäthu Mäwula, ḏirryuwan nhäŋa ŋirrimaḻin Burrayawaṯḻi
w..a m..m

Warwu guyuwan goluṉdjinan, ŋarru miny'tji-maypami
dhuwanma Galathi djäpanayina
y..ä gäthu Mäwula, yothu ŋalinyuŋgu wäwawu Yotjiŋu
y..ä gäthu Mäwula, ḏirryuwan nhäŋa ŋirrimaḻin Burrayawaṯḻi
m..m wäwa m..m

Watayu nhunany gaḏamanguwan, gaḏamanguwan
ŋarru dhambal ŋirrimaḻi miny'tji-maypamiḻi Burrayawaṯḻi
y..ä gäthu Mäwula, yothu ŋalinyuŋgu wäwawu Yotjiŋu
y..ä gäthu Mäwula, ḏirryuwan nhäŋa ŋirrimaḻin
Burrayawaṯḻim
y..ä gäthu Mäwula, yothu ŋalinyuŋgu wäwawu Yotjiŋu
y..ä gäthu Mäwula, ḏirryuwan nhäŋa ŋirrimaḻin
Burrayawaṯḻim m..m wäwa
yothu ŋalinyuŋgu wäwawu Yotjiŋu m..m

M..m what will we settle, we Dhurrkay nation
Saw the water like the arms of an octopus,
while the tide changes to go out
o..h daughter Mäwula, ours, bother Yotjiŋ's and my child
o..h daughter Mäwula, look back to the country Burrayawat
m..a m..m

Grief in my head, changed to Goluŋ, Galathi,
the colours of the sunset
o..h daughter Mäwula, ours, bother Yotjiŋ's and my child
o..h daughter Mäwula, look back to the country Burrayawat
older brother m..m

The breeze will make you clever, make you clever
to this place, colourful place Burrayawat
o..h daughter Mäwula, ours, bother Yotjiŋ's and my child
o..h daughter Mäwula, look back to the country Burrayawat
o..h daughter Mäwula, ours, bother Yotjiŋ's and my child
o..h daughter Mäwula, look back to the country Burrayawat
m..m older brother
ours child, bother Yotjiŋ's and mine

Gäthu Mawula means 'my son' or 'my daughter'. Gurrumul wrote this song to honour a female relative who looked after him when he and his then partner Shirley were living in Darwin. The song is not sung in Gumatj but in Dhuwal; nevertheless it conveys the traditional beliefs of north-east Arnhem Land. Shirley urged Gurrumul to write the song as a thank you for all the love and care. It is one of Gurrumul's troubadour songs, composed on demand, although with sincere feeling.

a little later wait with Mark Grose at the back. Bronwyn, tall, slim and beautiful, red hoodie tied around her waist, stands close to Mark, a shyness evident in her manner as she grasps a handful of his jacket sleeve for security.

The audience grows and grows until almost everyone at the festival site has settled onto the green grassy area in front of the stage. The 'Welcome to Country' address, which acknowledges the Kaurna people as the traditional owners of the land on which the festival site stands, has concluded.

Gurrumul on his chair at stage centre raises his head as if looking out over the audience, perhaps sensing in some way the number of people who've come along. His hair is as neatly barbered as ever but today it's slicked back with some sort of product, like Elvis in his early days. He lets his hand pick out the opening chords of 'Wiyathul', his song of place, of yearning. I've heard this song a number of times before today; I know its cadence perfectly, but still the opening notes — a type of keening, as if Gurrumul is preparing his heart for the words to follow — remind me all over again of what a voice like this can do. This is poetry, even before a single word is spoken.

Gurrumul raises his head a little higher as he moves into the lyrics: those two scrub fowls lamenting, their cries like those of women sorrowing in the same way. The lamentation recalls to the singer his own yearning for 'the jungles at Mutjwutŋa …'

rongiyirri rirrakayyu, y..ä barrawalayu y..ä Mutjwutŋa galaniniyu …

Barely one verse into the first song and you can see on every upturned face in the audience — the adults at least — the thought: 'Thank God I came …'

An Indigenous girl crouching on her knees at the front of the seated audience, tilts her head to one side, an expression on her face very difficult to interpret — is she puzzled? She's maybe six, maybe seven. If she is puzzled, it must be in a very compelling way because she's also listening with all the will and force of her small being. Her lips are moving, just barely. It's impossible to tell if she's shaping the words being sung by Gurrumul or whispering something altogether different to herself. Beside her, a woman who seems a little too old to be her mother but not old enough to be grandmother has let her chin rest on her chest. A boy of three or so who could be related to the little girl is standing with his bright red T-shirt pulled up, drumming away on the taut skin of his tummy. It's a happy, personal tattoo, nothing to do with what's happening on stage.

Michael, on his adjustable seat, is raised higher than Gurrumul to accommodate the double bass. The deep notes roll beneath the surface of the singing, supporting it in the way that a craft is supported by the current of a river: not just creating buoyancy but imparting a forward motion. The fingers of Gurrumul's left hand pick at the strings of his guitar in what you'd consider an upside-down way of going about it. The story that almost everyone has heard says that the right-handed Gurrumul as a boy was given a left-handed guitar by his uncle, Djuŋa Yunupiŋu (David) and the upside-down playing is the strategy that was forced on him. It works. And have you looked at his hands closely? — worn and seamed with an extraordinary cross-hatching of fine lines; the nails untrimmed, extending way beyond the flesh of each fingertip, like those of a Gypsy fortune-teller.

As in the gospel-inspired early blues of the American south, sorrow becomes solace in Gurrumul's song of loss and longing. But here's a strange thing. Although Gurrumul's voice can carry the freight of heartache with complete conviction, in many of his songs, including 'Wiyathul', the timbre reveals nuances that could accommodate everything from old-fashioned crooning to solid rock. In the DNA of his voice, a whole human genome of song is filed away. You can almost imagine — but don't, please! — that if the lapidaries of art music had found him before Michael Hohnen, he might now be singing blind duets with Andrea Bocelli.

The second song is 'Djärimirri' ('Rainbow') or 'Djärimirri Yothu' ('Rainbow Child'). The tune tells you something about the appeal of Gurrumul's songs to an audience unlikely to understand a single word of the lyrics. For the tune of 'Djärimirri' could almost have come from the English folk tradition, if you wanted to play it on a recorder with a squeezebox and fiddle for accompaniment. In Gurrumul's songs, melody is important; even when listeners can't follow the narrative in the lyrics, they feel engaged by the tune. Just as important is Michael Hohnen's formal training; the arrangement of a song such as 'Djärimirri' depends on the breadth of influence that comes with a thorough musical education.

'Djärimirri' is a song of blissful affirmation. The singer lingers on his origins in the totemic embrace of the Rainbow Serpent, the potent ancestral reptile of the Indigenous Dreamtime:

Ŋarranydja golanharawuy, ŋändiwuŋu Wititjkuŋu,   *I was carried, by my mother Wititjkuŋu,*
Ŋarranydja dhuwala, yothu Djärimirri …   *I am a Rainbow child Djärimirri …*

Gumatj could be a language created in song, so completely does it lend itself to music. The tenderness of the lyrics makes me glance down from the visitor box at the left of the stage to the girl who seemed so taken with the first song. The puzzled look is gone; she's leaning back with her hands braced behind her, legs stretched straight out, gazing at her bare toes. She may or may not be listening. But what I was hoping to see — the tenderness of her six or seven years floating on her face as if she herself might know what it is to be gathered into the embrace of Wititj — yes, that's there.

Gurrumul accepts the applause quietly. He turns his head to the left where Michael is sitting and Michael nods, just once. Hard to see how a nod to a sightless man can convey anything, but Gurrumul seems to sense it. He waits patiently for the applause to die down. His charisma is generated by the stillness of body and mind that, without warning, yields up the colour of his rich, textured delivery. It is a stillness like an eclipse, when the moon moves in front of the sun and in the darkness nothing stirs. Watching him closely, you become aware that the drama he generates has nothing at all to do with stagecraft. With each song, he relies on locating within himself the poise to commence, and finding that poise doesn't appear to be a matter of willpower; it's either there or it's not. And the poise can be influenced by something as seemingly trivial as the silver strand of mercury in a thermometer descending to an inconveniently low number. Like most Territorians, Gurrumul thinks that the only temperature range in which humans can sensibly exist is between 26 and 35 degrees Celsius.

Barbaric atmospheric conditions are one thing; at other times, Gurrumul is simply content to please his own sweet self. It's not petulance but stubbornness. Both Mark Grose and Michael Hohnen can recall without any great effort times when Gurrumul's obstinacy threatened to delay a performance. On one occasion, helping Gurrumul dress before a concert in Perth, Mark offered him a pair of socks — the one clean pair on hand — only to have Gurrumul reject them.

'What colour, Marky?'

'White.'

'Not white socks, Marky.'

'What's the matter with white?'

'Not white socks, Marky. Another colour.'

'What the hell does it matter?'

'Not white socks.'

'You realise I'll have to go out and buy them? You want me to do that? Go out and buy a new pair of socks?'

'Not white socks, Marky.'

If it's not the colour of his socks or the cut of his jacket or the state of his hair (Gurrumul is as vain as a peacock about his hair), his mood and demeanour can be affected by some disturbance in the cosmos of his spiritual life. Michael has known occasions when Gurrumul has fallen silent in a way that suggests something invisible to even the most culturally aware white man is working itself out. Michael says: 'It might be the anniversary of a death, it might be some clan observance. He doesn't tell me.' The spiritual life of many Indigenous Australians is the bonding agent of their being, never held distinct from other aspects of existence. When Gurrumul is 'performing', the stage all around him is inhabited by the phantoms of his heritage. And when he is not on stage, unwilling to respond to some question of Michael's about something or other — the order of songs for an upcoming concert, say — it might be that he's listening just at that moment to a question or message of far more importance; something of which Michael is unaware. When this happens, Michael and Mark don't pry, don't insist.

But not everything that happens on the stage comes down to Gurrumul's cultural heritage. Some of it — a crucial portion — is about good old-fashioned entertainment. Gurrumul loves to entertain. The relish he experiences when he hears the rising clatter of applause is purely to do with the thrill he's sent through the crowd. His uncle, Djuŋa, speaks with great pride of the bridges between cultures that his nephew has built. Bridge-building is a wonderful thing, but if a Gurrumul performance were only about construction, the audience would be left with the sound of planks being hammered to spars and little else.

Yes, Gurrumul loves to entertain, and loves to be entertained. Eighties disco — bring it on. Elvis, of course, with that rich reek of gospel that's in everything Presley from 'In the Ghetto' back to 'Love Me Tender'. Dire Straits; Iron Maiden. And yes, Sir Cliff.

The stage is filling up: two more guitars, and a very serious device that looks like a hurdy-gurdy crossed with a paper-shredder but it is in fact a very up-to-date pedal steel guitar. The masterful Tony Floyd is on drums; Lucky Oceans from Radio National is hunched above the pedal steel guitar; Ben Edgar and Francis Diatschenko handle another two guitars.

And there's comedian Stephen Teakle with his Barry Morgan shtick, just to lighten the mood for a few minutes. Barry Morgan and his World of Organs is a consummate funny-man turn; Barry in his beige safari suit exhibiting a mouthful of gleaming enamel and sporting the most pampered locks since the heyday of Farah Fawcett. The act satirises the radiantly smiling Wurlitzer guy from cinema matinees of yesteryear, but instead of 'The Indian Love Call', we're treated to Barry's organ and the full complement of drums, guitars and double bass blasting

Gurrumul has a habit of abbreviating people's first name using 'y' or 'ie' so his band members for this Womad gig are from left to right Frankie, Lucky, Mikey and on drums Tony or as Gurrumul prefers to call him Jimmy. Hidden behind Michael is Ben Edgar (Bennie).

Man at work, microphone positioned just right, guitar upside down, an armless chair, sleeves rolled up, we're ready to go.

out a country–rock fandango.

Gurrumul's enjoying the whole thing enormously. 'Take it away, boys!' he whoops, and the band jumps into the handover with relish.

It's maybe a good thing to lighten things up a little at the midway point of the concert; to remind the predominantly well-heeled, middle-class white folk out there that Gurrumul thinks of himself as no more than a troubadour from Elcho, a dab hand at the guitar with a pocketful of songs to sing. Also a man full of humour, eager to be amused, like so many Indigenous people.

At the same time, we should acknowledge what Gurrumul means to the people sitting in the sunshine. Black Australians such as Lionel Rose, Michael Long, Evonne Goolagong, Cathy Freeman, along with a number of other sportsmen and sportswomen — over the years they've been adored, applauded, lauded. But for many Gurrumul is the first black Australian in whom mainstream Australians have been able to rejoice. There's a distinction we can make between being exhilarated by Cathy in her aerodynamic hoodie powering to the finishing line of the 400 metres, and being moved to tears by a man whose poetry throws open the doors to a pavilion of emotion spanning grief, wonder and the sheer joy of being alive at the fringe of the sea. Gurrumul's art enlarges the world we carry within and adds an enriching complexity to our sense of identity as a people. The rejoicing is our gratitude.

I'm more aware than ever of what a hard day's night Michael Hohnen puts in at a Gurrumul performance. He leads the musicians on the double bass, sure, but at the same time he's making a whole series of judgments about how the concert is unfolding, filing away notes, making rapid appraisals of the audience response, keeping close track of the contribution of each instrument to the whole, measuring the complete body of sound against his concept of what he was hoping to achieve. He's producing even as he's playing, like an actor–manager of bygone days, bearing the burden of staging a demanding drama even as he pours his energies into one of the leading roles. Look at the strain of concentration on his face, and how he has to remind himself to give the audience the impression of relaxation — when relaxation is the last thing he can afford. It's a demanding thing for Gurrumul too — of course it is — but he can restrict his focus to performance. Mark Grose runs the crucial business and logistics side of things at Skinnyfish Music and relieves Michael of any fret in that way, but Michael remains the only person on earth with a steady vision of where this whole thing is heading creatively — Gurrumul's career, and that of another half-dozen names in the Skinnyfish stable.

Gurrumul moves into 'Bayini', his hymn-like tribute to the ancestral women (the Bayini of the title). The lyrics speak of the Gumatj gathered together at Gämbuthuwa above the ocean in rapt contemplation of the tide's ebb and flow, of the changing skin of the sea itself. Behind the Gumatj stands the ancestor rock, Bakitju, alive with masculine potency and endurance. Between the female and male sources of generation, the sea and the rock, the Gumatj honour the fertile mating of land and water and their own birth. There's a tender thoughtfulness in Gurrumul's introduction of the song. He calmly picks out the chords on his guitar, establishes the slow tempo, then settles into the murmured, '… Mmm … mmm …' as if he were invoking ancestral muses. As the words flow he lifts his tenor up to a higher register so that his voice takes on a soft, piping quality.

Nhinana ŋilimurru, yarrayarra'yun	*We Gumatj sit together*
Dhuwalana wäŋanydja Gämbuthuwa	*Here at Gämbuthuwa*
Gu ŋilimurru yarrayarra'yuna	*Let's sit all together*
Manha nhäma yarrayarra'yunara	*Sit together, watch the sea,*
Mawala-wulkthunara	*Think of the changing tide,*
Gunda dhärranana nininyŋu Bakitju	*Standing there, the land-ancestor Rock, Bakitju*

How far this extends into Yolŋu culture would be difficult to say, but in Gurrumul's songs the female influence is more pronounced than the male. This influence is there in 'Bayini', and it shows up in all of Gurrumul's lyrics, from 'Wiyathul' on the first album of songs, *Gurrumul*, to 'Djomula' on the second album, *Rrakala*. The feminine force is invariably the more active, the more creative. In 'Bayini' it is the fertile women ancestors who come across the seas, while the male principle is expressed as immovable stone. There are contradictions but, overwhelmingly, life unfolds at the bidding of women, or through the agency of feminine spirits.

We can say this, too: Gurrumul's own sensibility is informed by his experience of the maternal. It comes out as tenderness. The most influential people in his upbringing were his mother and his maternal aunts. Whenever you hear that throb of yearning in his voice, search the lyrics and you'll find he's appealing for maternal consolation.

Michael, in his role as MC, welcomes two guests to the stage: Natalie Pa'apa'a, a fine-featured Islander beauty, and Carlo Santone of the Melbourne roots band, Blue King Brown. Carlo on bass guitar finds some space near Michael; Natalie stands front and centre of the stage to share vocals with Gurrumul. You can see that Gurrumul takes a special pleasure in attracting guests to the stage, that camaraderie of musicians. The smile on his face and the way he lifts his head to 'glance' left and right suggests that he has some sort of vision in his head of this stage full of musicians.

He certainly has senses that take him a long way beyond what the rest of us can rely on. One of his former managers from the Yothu Yindi days witnessed so many examples of Gurrumul's uncanny knack of guessing what was going on around him in the visual world that he swore the man actually had the sight of a hawk. And Mark Grose says that Gurrumul can anticipate unscheduled phone calls from his nearest and dearest, as if he's homing in on intention from a thousand kilometres away. 'I'll say, "Better ring Michael", and he'll say, "No, Marky, Michael is ringing you now." Thirty seconds later the mobile rings and it's Michael.'

As Gurrumul throws to Natalie, he calls out: 'Go Natalie!' and Natalie goes, Carlo behind her on bass. This format that places Gurrumul amongst half a dozen or even a dozen musicians is much more what he's been used to over his performing life, rather than sitting at the front of the stage as the featured singer. Even in Saltwater, the fabulously energised band that he helped form after the Yothu Yindi days, it was usually his friend Manuel fronting. He is said to have next to no ego; no urge to draw the spotlight to himself and glory in the adulation of the crowd. The pleasure he gets out of a killer performance remains private.

'Bäru' is next, not the version from the studio session. It's a song that invokes the crocodile, a dominating creature in Gumatj culture as you might expect; the coast of Elcho Island is Crocodile Paradise. The classic recent headline of the *NT News* — a headline that could be printed a dozen times a year with no change but for the gender and age status of the person being pursued — reads: 'CROC CHASES SCHOOLGIRL'. It is said that Elcho folk have developed a nimble zigzag sprint to avoid becoming crocodile fodder but, every so often, the crododile wins the race. Marauding creature it may be, but the crocodile remains sacred. It's Gurrumul's totem, the crocodile. As Michael explains it: 'It wouldn't be right to say that Gurrumul identifies with the crocodile. He is the crocodile, and it's him.' The crocodile was Gurrumul's totem creature at birth and to remain so forever. What the crocodile means to him comes through in the exultant vigour of his singing. He's not a big man, Gurrumul, but he seems to expand and dominate the stage in this song, as if human and animal sources of strength in him had combined.

Michael has invited the audience to get up and dance, or at least take up the hissing roar of the crocodile at various points in the song's rendition. Amongst the audience of four thousand, a dozen or so feel inspired to take up Michael's invitation. A greater number shyly attempt to master the crocodile's roar. Most remain seated in the sunshine, feeling a little self-conscious. But the two Indigenous kids at the front, the boy and the girl, they're up to the challenge, and put down some moves that owe as much to disco as to their heritage.

A light breeze is swaying the tops of the tree canopies. We've reached that point in a performance at which an audience surrenders any prospect of disappointment, and is mentally fashioning the sentences that will convey the experience to friends not here today: 'Just astonishing, astonishing'; 'You missed the best thing, oh God you should've been there.'

Mark Grose, up at the back of the stage in his baseball cap, is sporting a smile as broad as the entrance to Luna Park. He's responding to the joy of seeing a vision realised. To Mark, Gurrumul and all of the Indigenous artists in his care embody change. From the beginning, he saw Skinnyfish as the means to an end, providing an arena in which Indigenous musicians could show their accomplishment, their originality. If Gurrumul's genius had been for stand-up comedy, or anything at all that wins applause and smiles, he would have been just as satisfied. He's seen young men, young women gazing demoralised at the horizon beyond, a wasteland stretching forever; seen enough of that to leave him heartsick. 'Up on stage, that's a black Australian in a situation an Indigenous person hardly ever experiences. That's equality.'

'Gurrumul History', the following song, largely in English, is as close as Gurrumul ever comes to anything confiding or to anything related to anthems. He gets into the song through a long entry of what might be termed meditative humming, familiar to our ears from other songs, and slow enough to suggest a ballad. His guitar gives out the perfect complement of contemplative chords, sitting just above the deep thrum of Michael's strings. He leans further forward than usual, more hunched, his head weaving a little:

> I was born blind, and I don't know why
> God knows why, because he love me so
> as I grew up, my spirit knew
> then I learnt to read the world of destruction
> united we stand, divided we fall
> together we'll stand, in solidarity

One of our finest drummers and Gurrumul's friend, Tony 'Jimmy the Monkey' Floyd.

The song to this point is a lament, its plangency seeking out a dramatic path close to sorrow. Narrative coherence, as distinct from musical coherence, is given no priority at all in Gurrumul's songs, without any cost to their impact. In the first six lines of 'Gurrumul History', the argument switches three times, without warning. But there is an overarching coherence that emerges as you study the narrative.

The opening two lines are a surrender, or submission to fate:

I was born blind, and I don't know why
God knows why, because he love me so …

The second line comes straight from the mission influence in Gurrumul's upbringing, but it might also reflect the familial lovingness in which Gurrumul was raised, as if the blessing of a divine love was channelled to him through those who had him in their care (his aunts, in particular). The 'world of destruction' in the fourth line again harks back, on the one hand, to mission teachings, to sin, to the Fall, but also takes in the more general tragedy of our humanity's hatreds and enmities. Locally, the suggestion extends to the calamity of violation, of all that is encompassed in such songs of the stolen generations as Leah Purcell's 'Run, Daisy, Run' and Archie Roach's 'Took the Children Away'. Gurrumul is never likely to write as pointedly of Indigenous politics as Roach or Purcell; no matter how grievous the wrong. Politics is not beyond the scope of his talent or his interest, but it is beyond the reach of his sensibility. There are no 'issues' in Gurrumul's songs; no calls to arms; no unfurling of flags. When he sings,

United we stand, divided we fall
together we'll stand, in solidarity

that is as far as sincerity can take him, and it is sincere; anything more trenchant would be forced and false.

When the song switches back to Gumatj, the pride in his voice is unmistakable, and not just the pride but also the authority:

Ŋarranydja dhuwala Batumaŋ	*I am Batumaŋ*
Ŋarranydja dhuwala Djarrami	*I am Djarrami*
Ŋarranydja dhuwala Djeŋarra	*I am Djeŋarra*
Ŋarranydja dhuwala Gurrumulŋa …	*I am Gurrumulŋa …*

That authority is not simply the relief of a man returning to his native tongue, in the way that a native speaker of English or Dutch might enjoy a break from struggling with a second or third language that doesn't come easily. Gurrumul's language is the living home of a culture, of beliefs, of pockets and niches of intimacy that can't be expressed in English. His English phrases will get him by, but in his own language a panorama of sunsets and thunderstorms bursts into life. The wind howls, a crocodile raises its head and roars, and he is home.

He's at the Yamaha for 'Wukun', a full-voiced song honouring the thunder clouds as they move across the sky connecting people and places. He's at ease on the piano, at least within the range of keys that sightlessness can accommodate, unless you're Stevie Wonder or Ray Charles. His entry to the song is gradual, but when he hunches closer to the mic and unleashes those rapid Gälpu vowels you're in a new place within seconds; somewhere that Gurrumul's extraordinary versatility hasn't quite taken you yet. Almost everyone who has written about Gurrumul in performance feels attracted to speak of his singing as 'angelic', but you have to go a hell of a lot further than 'angelic' to convey the ardour in his voice in 'Wukun'.

And listen to the pleasure he takes in naming places — Djarraraŋ, Milbunbun, Yarawarrtji, Yarrawaŋu, Galtjurrwaŋu, Wurrumba, Nukunuku, Maminŋu, as if raising his voice to sing of these sites refreshes and invigorates him.

The expression on Michael's face after the last song is one of welcome relief. Or more than relief: the performance was superb and the hundred or more artistic judgments he's put into getting the show up to that level have been vindicated. As the rapturous applause of the audience rises to a crescendo, Gurrumul at the front of the stage nods an acknowledgment, nothing extravagant. The supporting musicians — Lucky, Ben, Francis and Tony — know exactly where the spotlight is aimed and sit back waiting, professionally patient, for the cheering to die away. Out in the crowd, one of Gurrumul's most enthusiastic fans, a young woman who may have something a fair bit more potent than water in her Pump bottle, is singing out: 'I love you Gurrumul! Yoo hoo, Gurrumul! I love you!'

The audience begins to depart. Mums pack up their toddler kits — the colouring books, the pencils and felt-markers, the insect repellent, sunscreen, sugar-free chewy sweets, spare disposable nappies, sippy cups — and shove them into the pockets of the strollers. Everywhere, folk are reaching behind themselves to brush bits of grass off their shorts, their skirts and jeans. A mother close by calls to her husband or partner: 'Gordie went all that time without a wee!' The Indigenous lady with charge of the two little kids gets to her feet and, since I'm gazing at her, looks squarely back at me. Her cheeks are wet. What did this past hour mean to her? Would it be acceptable to ask? Maybe not. A small frown appears as she sees me lift my notebook to record her expression, her tears.

Can you say this, watching the dispersal of the audience, can you say that many of those who saw Gurrumul and Michael and the band today will take away something that goes beyond an episode of early autumn outdoor gladness? Can you say that the audience has added further impetus to something that was already well underway in the extended Australian community, something that will take years to develop its full force — a reappraisal of Indigenous cultures and of the ordeal of Indigenous Australians reaching back two hundred years? Can you say that Gurrumul and Michael and Mark have fashioned something at the top of the continent and carried it all over the compass, and that its vigour will enrich black–white relations in Australia? This blind genius from Elcho, this kid who was lucky he didn't break his neck tearing downhill on his bicycle at Galiwin'ku. Can you say what you want to say about him, that something has happened, something important has happened, and that Gurrumul is at its heart?

Backstage, Gurrumul sits as grave as a judge, hands on his lap, fingers extended along his thighs. Michael and Mark issue directions, answer questions, ask questions, study the screen of a laptop, call across the room (if a tent has rooms) to Tony, to Lucky, to some guy in a rasta snood who may or may not have any business being where he is. The whole show is off to the Shakey Isles for another WOMAD gig; much to do, too much to do, a thousand details to address. Tony Floyd the drummer says: 'Floyd. F — L — O — Y — D. Floyd,' and I take it down (accurately, this time) in my notebook. Gurrumul lets it all breeze by. He's in his Gurrumul zone, like, 'Let me know if anything that matters comes to the surface. Or not.' But maybe there is something there, just a hint of satisfaction that could have deep roots.

A long starlight session will follow the long sunlight session. The mums and dads and grans and grandpas will head on home, leaving the night's revels to the young and the beautiful. An announcement over the PA system reminds all of those who need reminding that UV rays remain 'an issue' until nightfall.

Gurrumul and Bronwyn are making their way through the crowd, Gurrumul's hand tucked under her arm. This is a shopping expedition, maybe; Bronwyn is said to love shopping. Nobody recognises Gurrumul, this small figure with slicked-back hair. The power that he controls on stage — it's not there at ground level. Bronwyn is whispering something into his ear, holding his hand now in both of hers. He moves his head left and right, picking up a panorama of sound. Suddenly he stops, and Bronwyn halts at the same instant. A band has started up at one of the performance sites. Gurrumul listens, head raised. Festival-goers pass on either side. As he stands still and alert in this way, the stage charisma returns. I can't take my eyes off this small figure drawing in the sound of the band. Then he allows Bronwyn to lead him on, and he's gone.

Francis Diatschenko, Gurrumul's guitarist, playing a Lebanese version of a Yolŋu song called 'Bäru'.

Backstage and onstage behind the scenes. Jamming with Francis and Michael, enjoying the rapport. Below: Michael checking Gurrumul's phone credit during a soundcheck.

Rock 'n' roll photography has a certain look and Tony Mott has captured it perfectly. Gurrumul has been told not to smile, but can barely restrain himself.

CHAPTER 12

The Poetry of Identity

Our taxonomies that fashion partitions in the natural world
have no equivalent in Indigenous cultures, where the human and
the non-human can merge and correspond, and where spirits
lie coiled in rocks and streams and clouds.

I was carried by my mother Wititj
I am a Rainbow child …
I am a Rainbow child, with a Rainbow
Carried by Wititj, with a Rainbow …
I am Maralitja Dhar'yuna with my ancestors
I am a child conceived and carried by Wititj …
Djärimirri, Geoffrey Gurrumul Yunupiŋu

A sense of identity starts with a story. The story gives us a role to play, and the role sustains us throughout life. Gurrumul's story of identity begins in the Dreaming, or Dreamtime, terms which the non-Indigenous find difficult to comprehend. John Greatorex, the scholar of Yolŋu culture, thinks it's futile for the non-Indigenous to grapple with definitions of Dreaming and the Dreamtime, so it might be better to simply say that Gurrumul could not have any identity at all if we were to insist that his life began on such-and-such a date and that before that date, he did not exist.

Gurrumul's identity was waiting for him — that belief forms the context of his learning; he had to be taught how to accept it. His culture provides a narrative for his very conception, and a further narrative for his blindness, each a tributary of the broad river of his individual story. Josephine Flood writes: 'A spirit child must enter the mother to give a baby life. Spirit babies lived on the branches of certain trees so that women who walked

WIYATHUL

M..m
Märrma djiḻawurr ŋäthinana, nambawu ḻarruŋana
Guwaliḻŋawu
rirrakayunmina ḻiyanydja milkarri, nambawu ḻarruŋana
Murrurrŋawu
roŋiyirri rirrakayyu, y..a barrawaḻayu y..a Mutjwutjŋa
galaṉiṉiyu

Ga namba Guwaliḻŋa, ga namba Warraḏika, ga namba
Yumayŋu, m..m

Yä wulman ŋäthinana, yä dhiyaŋuna ḻanyiŋdhu dhungunayu
yä bäpa Kamba-Djuŋadjuŋa, miḻn'thurruna bayma
Mayaŋ-ŋaraka
yä ŋäṉḏi maṉḏa, marrkapmirri maṉḏa, nhumanydja
ŋayathaŋana Ruypu Milinditj
yä ŋäṉḏi maṉḏa marrkapmirri maṉḏa, nhumanydja
ŋäthiyaŋa milŋurr Burarrapu
yä namba guwaliḻŋa, yä gunambal warraḏika, yä namba
Yumayŋa
m..m

M..m
Two scrub fowl crying out, looking for Guwaliḻŋa
the calls like women crying, looking for Murrurrŋawu
the cries returning his mind to the jungles at Mutjmutjŋa

oh place Guwaliḻŋa, Warraḏika, Yumayŋu, m..m

Oh the old man cries, from this drink
oh dad Kampa-Djuŋadjuŋa, home Mayan-ŋaraka
bright in his mind
oh my two mums, beloved mums, hold Ruypu Milinditj

oh my two mums, beloved mums, cry for
the sacred spring Burarrapu
oh the place Guwaliḻŋa, Warraḏika, Yumayŋa,

m..m

Gurrumul doesn't compose lyrics on the page. They are fashioned in his head and
remain there, unless transcribed. In the process of composing, he sits with his guitar and
develops the chords that will carry the lines. Many of the language phrases he employs
are drawn from a vast pool of idioms that have no author other than the clan. This song,
'Wiyathul', was not 'written' by Gurrumul at all, but by his cousin, Johnathon. But if
Gurrumul had written it, it's likely that he would have chosen the same idioms.
　　'Wiyathul' is one of the album's songs of memory, and some of the memories are
sorrowful. The repeated, 'mm … mm …' at the start of the song enacts either a sigh or
the ritual keening of Gumatj women in times of grief, which invokes healing.

underneath became mothers … a woman who wanted a child would go to a spirit centre, such as a waterhole, and wait with legs apart, or hope that a spirit child would follow her back to camp.' In Gurrumul's case, the spirit child who inhabited the womb of his mother was blind, and the child born of this conception is more precious for that reason. To the precious child, the lore and customs of the Gumatj had to be revealed. Words were whispered into his ear; his hand was guided to discover the shapes of things; that which his mother and father knew became part of him. Education amongst the Gumatj is a top-down process. Knowledge is richest in an elder, and it is the duty of the elder to ensure that his knowledge benefits the tribe. In Gurrumul's song, 'Wulminda', he honours the elder ancestor to whom he owes, in part, his own existence, since without the lore and wisdom of the elders, he cannot be the man he is:

Yakurr-wätjuwan, Yolŋuwa Dhawalmiŋuwa	*Sleep descends upon the elder-ancestor*
Muluymuluyyin ya Dhorupurra …	*Lying, resting, elder ancestor Dhorupurra …*

What is revealed occurs in regulated stages; Gurrumul was expected to understand certain important features of his culture at age four, age seven, age ten, and not before. The stages of learning continue well into middle age and even beyond. In Western culture, a precocious child might be permitted to acquire knowledge according to his grasp and appetite but, in Indigenous cultures, it would be thought immoral for a child of five to leapfrog into the domain of a ten year old. Precocity interferes with order and usually isn't welcome.

He is taught, in stages, the laws of relation, his obligations as the kin of a great many people. Margaret Kemarre Turner writes: 'Kinship holds Aboriginal people really close and strong, it holds everyone tightly together … [The principle of kinship] guides and cares for all the generations of people that have lived within the cradle of their Land. It's been like that always, stretching from the Creation, and it endures forever … If you don't relate to each other like this, nobody can know who you are.' He is taught the shapes and forms of his country; its pulse, the manner of its breathing, its moods, rewards, dangers, and such secrets as it is thought right for him to know, as a male.

Many of the lessons of country are purely practical — setting aside his blindness, there will never be any danger of him expiring in the midst of plenty in the manner of Robert Burke. At a deeper level, what he learns of his country becomes a structure of support, like a trellis that holds the woven tendrils of a flourishing vine up to the sun. His country and his family are not merely sources of consolation to him, in the way that the love of one's parents and being back in one's home town might be to a white Australian; Gurrumul is his country, is his family. One reason that the funeral rites of the Gumatj are so lengthy is that the death of kin is felt as keenly as if it were one's own spirit being mourned, one's own spirit being comforted, sung to rest.

He has been given his 'walking name', bestowed on him at the time he took his first steps. Later, he'll be given another name, more sacred, and told that it honours not only the life he will live but the life of his ancestors. His totem has been revealed to him; his spirit-being. It is the crocodile, *bäru*. Gurrumul honours *bäru* (also called *djambuyma*) in a song that he always renders with great feeling, no matter how often it is performed:

Gaŋgathina ŋolurrŋura, wäyindja Djambuyma	*Eager to leave the nest, ancestor Djambuyma*
Mari marrtjina wäyingu, dhärranhana	*Off hunting with unwavering determination,*
barraka'yu	*ready and poised*
Wäyin dhuwalinydja Gadumitjpal	*That ancestor Djambuyma, Gadumitjpal,*
Gurnyinmurru	*Gurnyinmuru*
Yä dhupundji mariwarra, ya dhupundji	*Ah, ancestor Djambuyma, ancestor*
warrarrinya …	*Djambuyma …*

Our taxonomies that fashion partitions in the natural world have no equivalent in Indigenous cultures, where the human and the non-human can merge and correspond, and where spirits lie coiled in rocks and streams and clouds.

Gurrumul's culture gives him a voice in which he can call out to a tree on the summit of a hill; a tree which has a name no less intimate to him than that with which he might address a friend, such as Michael Hohnen or Mark Grose, or his own mother.

His rite of passage into manhood is an ordeal. He shows that he can endure pain, that he can face dread. Knowledge kept from him in childhood is now revealed. This initiation enacts a death and a rebirth. His new name is that of a new being. In the time when the rites of passage were formalised, survival itself depended on a stoic readiness to face the ordeal of day-to-day nomadic life. It was important to draw a line in the sand, making the initiate understand that on this side of the line, duty, responsibility and knowing what is right and what is wrong can never again be set aside. Crossing that line is an acceptance of the seriousness of life.

Gurrumul has crossed that line. Everything he has been taught finds a deeper dwelling place within him than before. With the passing of each year, the culture of the Gumatj matures until well beyond the point at which any other culture can replace it. He knows of other cultures; he knows how extensive is the reach of the whitefella way. Like many other Indigenous Australians, he accepts that up to a point and, in certain circumstances, he has to walk the walk of the white man, but talk his own talk. The crucial thing is to accommodate the whitefella if that is necessary, but never to forget that line in the sand he stepped across at initiation. Michael might say to Gurrumul: 'Next week we sing in Sydney.' The elders of the clan might say: 'Ceremony is coming.' Ceremonies can vary in their importance, but if the one that is coming requires his participation, then Sydney has to wait. Living in two cultures is extraordinarily difficult for many black Australians, Gurrumul included, and one of the trials is knowing at what moment you say: 'Ceremony is coming. Sydney has to wait.'

The dances, the chants, the songs, the emblematic body painting; everything that goes with ceremony is now an integral part of his identity. He has danced on the beach with a fire casting a glow over the lapping waves; he has danced at hidden places amongst the trees, far from Galiwin'ku. The expression on his face when he returns might be exultant, or something else — remote, silent, secluded. Michael and Mark have enjoyed years of friendship with Gurrumul; have shared everything with him, not least their love. But there are times when neither knows what Gurrumul is thinking, where he is, with which world he is in contact.

The Gumatj have a history but it isn't a matter of dates and dynasties but rather of patterns and their disruptions; of stingrays that disappeared from the bays and inlets of the Arnhem Land coast during a time past, and of the strange cause of their disappearance, and of how they came back, and why. Any event that overthrows the time-honoured and expected can become history. Usually such events are related in narratives that might go on for days, and there's always a moral, since anything important enough to talk about should be more broadly illustrative. The great moral scheme of Yolŋu culture reaches into everything. Things happen for a reason. Events above a certain scale are patterned to comply with the scheme. Sometimes magic, or sorcery, is invoked as an explanation.

By the time he is a young man, Gurrumul is the living embodiment of his people's culture, an expression of that culture. But not entirely. Nature can never be content with clones. Individuality persists, and is accommodated by Yolŋu culture — or more than that, it is welcomed. This man is the clown of his clan; another is the philosopher; another is a notorious ladies' man. Individuality is easily accepted, but its approval is not quite what it has become in Western culture since the Romantic Revolution of the late eighteenth century; it is not enshrined. Western culture might honour the man or woman whose individual inspiration takes the form of a visionary program to smash the old and make everything anew, but there is nothing we know of that suggests upheaval of that sort in Indigenous cultures in the millennia leading up to white settlement.

Gurrumul, in adulthood, is both everything that is expected of him in his own culture, and everything expected of him in whitefella culture. If we wish to think of him as a genius, we can, but such a distinction means next to nothing to him, and his people would rather speak of him simply as a man who honours his clan and the entire Indigenous nation with his music.

Who is Gurrumul, then? He is Geoffrey Gurrumul Yunupiŋu, a troubadour, hailing from the sunshine and shoreline of the island of Galiwin'ku in the Arafura Sea. He is Gudjuk, another of his names. He is the beloved child of his clan, the father, the son, the brother, the uncle, the nephew. At a deeper level, he is a figure who emerged from the dreaming of his clan; and he has been here as long as the dreaming, in one form or another. He became Gurrumul and the only person he could ever have become was Gurrumul. He has sung of his identity in 'Gurrumul History', in these words:

I am Batumaŋ

I am Djarrami

I am Djeŋarra

I am Gurrumulŋa

I am Barrupa

I am Dhukulul

I am Maralitja

I am Ŋunbuŋunbu …

He is his ancestors, his totem, his country, his people. And he is the songs he sings.

The Dreaming

The terms the Dreamtime and the Dreaming are English language approximations of a range of words in Indigenous languages that refer to tribal and individual origins and to the foundation of spiritual engagement with the world. Nothing could better convey the extraordinary effort that many Indigenous Australians are required to make in negotiating Western culture than the difficulty they face in explaining Dreaming. It does not include an eschatology; there is no emphasis on judgment, no detailed account of beginnings, and is free of the stress on purpose that is entailed in the program of the Judeo-Christian god's creation. We might think of the Dreamtime as the period of the soul's creation, and Dreaming as the vital influence of the soul in our lives. Indigenous Australians express reasonable satisfaction with the use of Dreaming and the Dreamtime as workable headings for what can't be fully translated into English, but why this should be is a mystery. Perhaps it has something to do with the transporting quality of a dream experience, or in other words, 'something like dreaming'. What we can say is that the Dreamtime seethes with narrative drama; it is the elemental poetry of Indigenous Australians, and a great deal more, but complete understanding would require a thousand generations of living on the Australian continent. W.E.H. Stanner devoted years of patient thought to the Dreaming and reached this conclusion:

> *Clearly the Dreaming is many things in one.*
> *Amongst them, a kind of narrative of things that*
> *once happened; a kind of charter of things that still*
> *happen; and a kind of logos or principle of order*
> *transcending everything significant for Aboriginal man*
> *... it is much more complex philosophically than we*
> *have so far realised.*

Gurrumul's mother, Daisy Ganyunurra, in ceremony.
'I had white ochre all over me for a funeral and a Dhapi
(initiation ceremony). He said, "Mum, why have you got
ochre on you? What's going on, are we at a funeral?" And
I said, "Yes." He asked, "Can I paint myself?" "Yes." He
started to dance around in ceremonies, that's how he learnt
without seeing because he is blind by listening for the clap
sticks for the songs.'

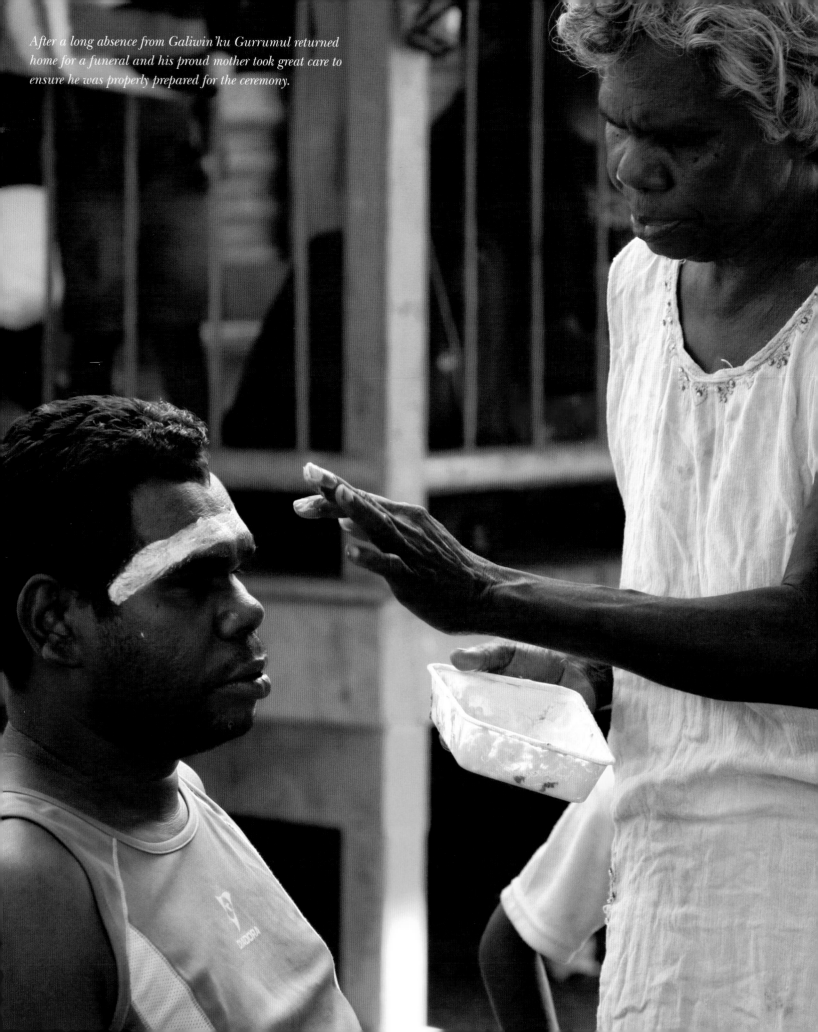

After a long absence from Galiwin'ku Gurrumul returned home for a funeral and his proud mother took great care to ensure he was properly prepared for the ceremony.

3

OF FAME

CHAPTER 13

Weekend at the Waldorf

In the way that a sighted person with the right sensibility might swoon over the visual feast in one of the world's great galleries, Gurrumul relishes the auditory bounty of the Isaac Stern Auditorium. It's his Louvre.

Manhattan in midwinter, 2009, and the hornbeams, chestnuts, elms and dogwoods of Central Park are crusted with snow. New Yorkers bustle down the streets and avenues in overcoats and scarves and the rich assortment of headwear they're attracted to on an icy day like this: fur hats, cloches, berets, contraptions with earmuffs, scarves, knitted snoods and Yankees caps pulled down low. Down at the Waldorf on Park Avenue, Gurrumul and Michael are checking in. The acoustics of the plush Art Deco lobby impress Gurrumul greatly. He turns to Michael and says: 'Good place, *wäwa.*'

'Yeah, good place this one,' replies Michael.

Gurrumul and Michael have come to New York to perform at Carnegie Hall, along with the Adelaide Symphony and other Australian artists including Olivia Newton-John, Jimmy Barnes, David Campbell, Gabriella Cilmi and Ursula Yovich. The concert is part of the annual G'Day USA: Australia Week celebrations but it is unlikely that many New Yorkers have heard a black Australian singing in his own language.

Michael is here to play the double bass and to act as Gurrumul's carer, his guide, his companion and friend. It's easier to look after Gurrumul if the two of them are sharing a room, but the Waldorf, which provides almost everything in the way of sleeping arrangements, does not offer rooms with two double beds. Gurrumul will be required to accept a room of his own. Michael explains the situation to Gurrumul, who is still taking in the rich acoustical reports from the foyer — guests meeting and greeting, piped music, a raised voice calling: 'Hold the lift!'

A journey from the Dreamtime to the city that never sleeps. In the luxurious dining room of the Waldorf Astoria hotel in New York City, Gurrumul gently strums his upside-down guitar and waits for a sound check to begin.

BÄRU

Gaŋgathina ŋolurrŋuru, wäyindja Djambuyma	Eager to leave the nest, ancestor Djambuyma
Mari marrtjina wäyingu, dhärranhana barraka'yu	Off hunting with unwavering determination, ready and poised
Wäyin dhuwalinydja Gaḏumitjpal Gurnyinmurru	That ancestor Djambuyma, Gaḏumitjpal, Gurnyinmurru
Yä dhupuṉdji märiwarra, ya dhupuṉdji warrarrinya	Ah ancestor Djambuyma, ancestor Djambuyma
Djirikitj wa'	Fire explodes
Djirikitj wa'	Fire explodes
Guwaynydja ŋayi giritjina roŋiyina Gukulayu	With feet and arms she dances back to Gukula
Wäŋawuy Gururriŋba Watharrŋawuy Nunungitj	Her country is Gururriŋba, Watharrŋawuy, Nunungitj
Waṉayu mulka Ḻirrtji'ḻirrtji Methuthu Gikawarra	Her arms holding fire, Ḻirrtji'ḻirrtji, Methuthu, Gikawarra
Yä dhupuṉdji märiwarra, ya dhupuṉdji warrarrinya	Ah ancestor Djambuyma, ancestor Djambuyma
'Mari marrtjina wäyingu, gaḏukaḏu gaḏumitjpalwu	'Hunting, focussed, determined for prey
Dhärranana wambalyu, wo mirrwuṉdhu wutthurruna	Djambuyma's tail strong and powerful,
wäyindhu Djambuymayu'	struck by Djambuyma'
Yä dhupuṉdji märiwarra, yä dhupuṉdji warrarrinya	Ah Ancestor Djambuyma, ah Ancestor Djambuyma
Wambalmirri dhumumumirri dhaṉutha dhuwalinydja golirrnydji	Tail quick, dangerous like fire
Bakaṉdjarri ṉulŋuṉulŋu wäŋawuy Rilmitja	Djambuyma of Rilmitja holds fire
Bulapula gurrunhanmina roŋiyina ŋolurrlili	Returns, rests Bulapula (her head) on the nest
Wäŋalili bakulili batali dhuwalinydja Djambuyma	Djambuyma's home, hidden and protected
Ya dhupuṉdji märiwarra, ya dhupuṉdji warrarrinya	Ah Ancestor Djambuyma, ah Ancestor Djambuyma
Djirikitj wa'	Fire explodes
Djirikitj wa'	Fire explodes
Dinyurr..rr wap	

Bäru is the crocodile, Gurrumul's totem. The creature is given a number of names in Yolŋu Matha, reflecting its importance in Gumatj culture. Djambuyma is another Yolŋu name for the crocodile, one that dwells on both the crocodile's role as a fearsome hunter, and as a counsellor of obligation. The female crocodile may wander far and wide in search of food, but she remembers always to return to her nest, to her home. In the same way (as the song tells us) the men and women of the Gumatj clan must remember their home, where they belong. The song includes a ritual exclamation — *Djirikitj wa'* (fire explodes) — that dramatises the fiercely predatory nature of the crocodile. The association of the crocodile with fire may go back to the influence of the Macassan traders, and to the role of the fire-breathing dragon in their culture.

'That's okay, *wäwa*?' asks Michael. 'Two rooms? That's okay?'

'Yeah, yeah,' says Gurrumul, meaning, 'Maybe.' When he wants room service — what happens then? When he needs to use the remote for the telly? 'Yeah, yeah,' he says again. It's worth putting up with minor inconveniences for the sake of playing at Carnegie Hall.

This is Gurrumul's second visit to New York — he was here with Yothu Yindi some years earlier. He takes on the role of seasoned traveller, talking up the city to Michael, a first-timer in New York. It might be thought that one city is like another for Gurrumul, or for any sightless person, but no, he differentiates between cities, towns, even varieties of countryside with as much confidence as the sighted. In his mind's eye he fashions a panorama full of variety and detail. New York excites him. Walking down West 57th Street towards Broadway with Michael, he raises his head and turns it left and right in that characteristic way, pausing when some feature puzzles or delights him. They're on their way to Seventh Avenue to take a look at Carnegie Hall, and put in a little rehearsal time.

The acoustic quality of the Waldorf lobby is one thing; the sound you hear in the Isaac Stern Auditorium at Carnegie Hall is another — rich enough to burnish every note you sing, but at the same time capable of catching nuances that get lost in a lesser venue. In the way that a sighted person with the right sensibility might swoon over the visual feast in one of the world's great galleries, Gurrumul relishes the auditory bounty of the Isaac Stern Auditorium. It's his Louvre.

The rehearsal with Maestro Arvo Volmer and the Adelaide Symphony doesn't pan out well. The arrangement that Gurrumul is supposed to be lending himself to was conceived back in Australia without Volmer's input and, now that he studies it, he sees serious flaws. For one thing, the arrangement only allows for a two-bar intro to Gurrumul's song and he requires four bars. The maestro says: 'No, no, no! Terrible! Terrible!'

Gurrumul says: 'What?'

Michael whispers to his friend: 'Some problem. Beats me.'

Volmer had never heard of Gurrumul until two days ago and when he voices his frustration, it's not to Gurrumul at all but to various members of the orchestral crew. By good fortune, one of the orchestra members knows of Gurrumul, admires his artistry and he's able to talk the maestro into backing off. Volmer is persuaded to return to the problem later.

Back at the Waldorf, Gurrumul asks Michael to read him the menu. Various dishes written up in French fail to exercise much appeal to a man reared on large helpings of no-nonsense lamb and beef. When Michael reaches the monster serving of rib-eye steak with trimmings, Gurrumul says: 'Yeah. That one.'

'*Wäwa*, it's eighty dollars,' says Michael.

'That one.'

'At eighty dollars?'

'No problem.'

Michael calls room service and orders the steak. His own choice is more modest: 'And one Waldorf salad.'

In January 2009, Gurrumul played to a full house at the famous Carnegie Hall, alongside some of Australia's greatest performers in the G'Day USA concert.

Anything to drink? Champagne? Spirits?

'Just water,' says Michael.

It takes a little while, but Arvo Volmer succeeds in structuring a new arrangement for Gurrumul's song. The number is to be 'Wiyathul', a song that the Carnegie acoustics will embrace in all its intimacy. For Gurrumul, the real joy of the rehearsal is not matching the orchestra's strings to the warmth of his voice; it's waiting on the opportunity to meet Olivia. He's a big fan: 'The Banks of the Ohio'; the hits from *Grease*. He has to settle for moments; his rehearsal slot and Olivia's don't allow for much meet-and-greet time. Not to worry, this is New York, and after rehearsal there's pleasure in just walking the sidewalks with Michael, breathing in the aromas of eateries down at Times Square, listening to the racket of the traffic, and the chatter of a thousand voices.

The daydream of musicians everywhere is to live long enough for their names to appear in the bill frame outside Carnegie Hall. Gurrumul is pleased to be told that his name is right there on Seventh Avenue — 'Geoffrey Gurrumul Yunupiŋu'.

Backstage before the performance, Michael and Gurrumul are spotted by David Campbell, Jimmy Barnes' son, and himself an artist featured in tonight's G'day USA line-up. 'Come and say hello to Dad.' It's a crush backstage — the orchestra alone numbers seventy-seven instrumentalists — but David makes a path to his father's dressing room and calls over the heads still in front of him: 'Dad — Gurrumul!' Barnes, only half dressed, waves back: 'Hey, good to see you.' And he adds, to Gurrumul's delight: 'I'm Gumatj, you know!' Barnes had been adopted by Mändawuy Yunupiŋu; he's performed songs in the Gumatj language with Black Arm Band, handling the lyrics with some authority.

Arvo Volmer and the orchestra are on stage when Michael leads his friend out. Many of those in the audience are Australians, but this is only 2009, barely six months into Gurrumul's solo career, and he's something new even to his fellow countrymen. He's in good voice, the new arrangement has restored his four-bar intro, and when he lifts his head and the lyrics flow out into the great cavern of the Isaac Stern Auditorium, it's like a gift. A gift of a special sort. All of the performers here tonight have been chosen as representatives of Australia's musical diversity. The audience is hearing one of Australia's best symphonic orchestras and a number of its most celebrated popular vocalists. And it could be fairly claimed that the G'day USA line-up stands as a broad sample of Australian musical taste. Gurrumul's song 'Wiyathul', in its language and sensibility, offers something uniquely Australian to this New York audience, and the applause is rapturous.

The after-party is held in the Presidential Suite of the Waldorf, reds and whites flowing from bottle to glass, enough food on hand to feed the population of the five boroughs. It's here that Gurrumul hopes to meet Olivia. He's not about to let it go.

He says: 'Michael, Michael, Olivia, find Olivia!'

'I will, *wäwa*. Calm down.'

'Find her. I want a picture, yeah.'

'Okay, she's just arrived. Wait a minute.'

'Don't forget. Better do it now.'

'She's got a hundred people around her, all right? I'm not going to push everyone aside. In a minute. Relax.'

As it turns out, it's Olivia who takes the initiative. She wends her way through the crowd to Gurrumul and greets him with a smile. 'This is a man I want to meet,' she says, and Gurrumul is sixteen again, shy and delighted at the one time, on the tip of his tongue (not that it will go any further): 'I'm your biggest fan!' What he does say, he says to Michael in an urgent whisper: 'Picture! Picture!'

Olivia puts her cheek against Gurrumul's, the camera clicks, and there it is, the culmination of this trip to New York City: Olivia still as pretty as Sandy from Down Under, Gurrumul attempting to satirise himself in this role of avid fan, but unable to disguise his glee.

Hendrix of Elcho

Gurrumul's manner of playing the guitar is generally to pluck the strings with his fingertips and fingernails, with the guitar neck extending to his right. The fingers of his left hand lift and release the strings from beneath, while his left thumb is able to lift and release the strings from both above and below. His right hand, of course, fashions the chords. The guitar given to him as a boy was a right-handed instrument, and in order to play it, the left-handed Gurrumul had to turn it around and upside-down, then teach himself to overcome all the difficulties involved in handling a guitar in this position. His picking is, in fact, unique, creating notes more like an old-fashioned keyboard, in the same mechanical fashion as a harpsichord — plucking, releasing. Superficially, the sound he produces is the same as that of a guitar played in the normal way, but if you listen carefully, the music is a little more poised, with a slightly more distinct timbre than most guitarists.

Family members still take pleasure in talking of the single-minded way in which Gurrumul learned how to play the guitar. His mother, Daisy, recalls his determination to move on from drums to something more demanding. 'He learnt to play when he was only a little boy,' she says. 'Four years old he didn't have a guitar, he didn't have anything. Only a drum, an empty tin cup to play or a flour tin. Milk powder tin, golden syrup tin, everything inside the house. We couldn't go to sleep at night because he used to keep playing from morning till night-time … He said, "Mum, can you buy me a guitar? Any sort — electric or anything." And we went down there to get his guitar at the old shop.'

Gurrumul's brother Andrew was just as avid a would-be musician: 'Michael Jackson, Dire Straits and Neil Diamond and Elvis — this is the music we used to listen to. When we were little kids, we started our own band and we used to play drums. We would go out and cut the fishing lines then we made our own guitar. But it didn't sound good, so we had to wait to buy one from the shop."

Daisy says: 'I used to call him, "Come and have something to eat!" He would say, "Wait, Umala (Mum), I'm still playing."'

Big Frank Djirrimbilpilwuy, the eminence gris of Elcho, recalls Gurrumul as a kid, powering away on his instrument: 'I first saw him he picked up an acoustic guitar … Right-handed guitar he played with his left hand. And everything's got to be back to front. He strummed the string from bottom up because he's playing a right-hand guitar.'

Gurrumul's uncle David Yunupiŋu, gave his nephew advice and encouragement: 'I taught him when he grew up. I taught him only three chords — E, G and D. When he played he picked up other chords that I didn't know.'

What it all amounts to is someone dear to you in the grip of a passion that delights you. The way in which the whole family compensates for lack of money with encouragement and ingenuity seems so old-fashioned now; a scene from an Australia of long ago. Making what was meant for the right-handed work for the left-handed — that's what Gurrumul has been doing all his life, not just when he plays the guitar, but in everything.

Gurrumul's favourite songs

1. Elvis Presley — 'Love Me Tender' (Live, Comedic)
2. Dr Hook — 'Jungle to the Zoo'
3. Dire Straits — 'Sultans of Swing'
4. Cliff Richard — 'Hey Mr Dream Maker'
5. The Eagles — 'Take it Easy'
6. Neil Diamond — 'I am, I said' (Live at the Greek Theatre)
7. Iron Maiden — 'Run to the Hills'
8. Gerry Rafferty — 'Island'
9. Bob Seger — 'Against the Wind'
10. Warumpi Band — 'My Island Home'

The Adelaide Symphony, Michael, Francis and Gurrumul at Carnegie Hall. The acoustics of the Isaac Stern Auditorium were to Gurrumul what the Louvre might be to a sighted person. Carnegie Hall remains one of his favourite venues.

CHAPTER 14

Paris

Sting has heard of Gurrumul, and loves him. Gurrumul has barely heard of Sting, and doesn't know what to think when he learns from Michael that an opportunity to appear with the pop idol has come up.

The Police, with Sting fronting, was never a band that made it big in north-east Arnhem Land; never a band that got under the skin of Indigenous Australians. And Sting's post-Police avatar as a clever and conscientious solo performer with an ear for the unusual hasn't made a great impression on Gurrumul either. Deep into a demanding tour of Europe designed to reveal his power and virtuosity to an international audience, Gurrumul seems to be saying that he can take or leave the Sting thing. The song that's proposed for the duet on the prestigious French television show *Taratata*, is The Police's monster hit of 1983, 'Every Breath You Take', a song with a suggestion of emotional dysfunction in its lyrics. Gurrumul, relishing the swanky hotels booked for the tour (the room service in particular), is having too much of a good time to commit himself to a whispery song with lyrics that deal ambiguously with love and longing. Michael plays the song to him again and again, and always meets with the same response: a shrug of indifference.

Since the prospect of the duet was first raised, Michael has had a dozen conversations with Sting's manager, and each one has moved the project further along. Michael knows exactly how significant this appearance would be; what a compliment to Gurrumul, to be asked to appear with Sting, on *Taratata* no less.

Taratata is a showcase program that attracts highly original artists, and has a following in the millions all over Europe. It's the sort of astute, discriminating audience that Gurrumul has to appeal to if he's to become known internationally. And the foundation of appeal is right there: a fabulous voice from a faraway land. He's on his way, Gurrumul, but he hasn't

Gurrumul takes an out-of-character walk in the Parisian night air to find a friterie or hamburger ... or steak haché.

MARRANDIL

Dhuwala ŋarranha, mulkana warwuyun, ŋäthinana ŋarra, Guṉ
ipunharayu miny'tji ŋarraku gorruŋalana,
Garrumara Baŋgarrari, Galaŋgarri Galathi
maṉaṇ ŋarraku ḏurryurrunana, Wuḻpunduganawirra Gumbaḻkarra,
mali-yolŋuyinana
nhenydja ŋarraku gunbilk ŋorrana, ŋakuna marra-wuḻwuḻ
yäpinanydhu djarrawalwuyu

Here I am, grieving, I'm crying, because of this sunset
My colours across the afternoon sky,
Garrumara Baŋgarrari, Galaŋgarri Galathi
My clouds are rising, Wuḻpunduganawirra Gumbaḻkarra, shapes
like people
Reflections on the calm water for me, shimmering on the water
With this sunset

Yä ŋarra dhuwala yä, yä yolŋu Loli
Yä ŋarra dhuwala yä, yä Galparra yolŋu Gurrumulŋa

O..h I am, oh I am Loli (ancestors)
O..h I am Galparra, Gurrumulŋa (ancestors)

watayu ŋarranha djirripuŋala, waṉayu ḻuŋgurrmayu yiwarryu
dirrmalayu
ga märi'mirrinydja ŋarraku wäŋa, Banguḻŋa Randulkuṉa
Wuḏutjaŋa Gimiyala

The wind caresses me, the arms of the northern winds

And my grandmother country, Banguḻŋa Randulkuṉa Wuḏutjana
Gimiyala

Yä ŋarra dhuwala yä, yä yolŋu Loli
Yä ŋarra dhuwala yä, yä Galparra yolŋu Gurrumulŋa

O..h I am, oh I am Loli
O..h I am Galparra, Gurrumulŋa

Ṉirrpunydja ŋarraku roŋiyinana, Bekuḻḻili Galupayu
dhärriṇḻili Mayaŋ-ŋarakayu
ŋäthinana djotarra maṉḏa Dela Daylulu Dhuwanydjika
warguyurrunana

My mind has gone back, to Bekuḻ, Galupayu, dhärrin
and Mayaŋ-ŋaraka
Those two Gumatj women are crying Dela Daylulu
Dhuwanydjika grieving

Yä ŋarra dhuwala yä, yä yolŋu Loli
Yä ŋarra dhuwala yä, yä Galparra yolŋu Gurrumulŋa, m..m

O..h I am, oh I am Loli
O..h I am Galparra, Gurrumulŋa

Strongly influenced by the gospel dear to Gurrumul, 'Marrandil' is another song of
affirmation, but unlike 'Djärimirri', the affirmation is blended with longing. For Gurrumul
and his people, everything in nature is imbued with spiritual meaning; in 'Marrandil',
the clouds, the sunset, the reflections on the ocean's surface, and the northern winds
are potent with a significance that goes beyond any celebration of their beauty. If the
spiritual narrative of this song-poem were to be compared to anything in Western art, we
would go to the English Romantic poets, especially to Wordsworth, who writes in 'Tintern
Abbey' that he is: '… well pleased to recognise in nature … The anchor of my purest
thoughts, the nurse, / The guide, the guardian of my heart, and soul / Of all my moral
being.' But when Wordsworth speaks metaphorically of nature as the guardian of his
heart, Gurrumul is speaking literally. His ancestors dwell in the clouds and the wind, and
act as nurse and guardian of his moral being.

yet arrived; he's not remotely a superstar. Sting, on the other hand, arrived decades ago and has fashioned a gleaming career as a solo artist, based on heavyweight musical savvy and a widely admired willingness to take risks when he thinks it's important to do so. And in all candour, Gurrumul is a risk. He'll be singing in Gumatj, meaning that the lyrics will have to be translated before he'll show even a cursory interest. And once you get the lyrics translated, fine, but that's only the first obstacle. Gurrumul has to perform the song with real conviction, and that doesn't seem likely.

The tour is a month old at this stage, commencing in Hamburg and followed by performances in Berlin, Stuttgart, Cologne, Zurich and Amsterdam. Still to come: Brussels, London, Paris and Dublin. It's a hefty schedule of dates, hard on Gurrumul, murder on Michael and Mark. Big tours like this, anywhere in the world, are troubleshooting marathons; every new city throws up a dozen potential disasters. If you need to scream, find a quiet, out-of-the-way spot, let it all out, then get back to business. And if an almost ungovernable urge to pack your bags and leave in a huff, find a quiet spot, seek the counsel of your better angels, then get back to business.

Gurrumul is no prima donna, with outrageous demands on the rider, but he has his needs and wants, and it's better for everyone, on any tour, if the star is kept happy. If he's hungry, and he wants to eat a burger with Swiss cheese, no pickles, on a poppy seed bun rather than sesame seed, with Australian tomato sauce and not the rubbish that's called tomato sauce in Europe — where in God's name do you find that, after midnight, on a Sunday, in a city like Zurich, where burger joints are actually torn down to make way for banks?

What you don't need is a problem that shouldn't really be a problem, that has no right to be a problem, but has somehow become a problem. Such as this *Taratata* thing.

In the Brussels apartment, where the Gurrumul entourage is staying for a Belgian gig a week before the Paris appearance, Gurrumul teases Michael with his blasé take on the whole *Taratata* deal. He sings a version of 'Every Breath' as he wanders about the apartment, lampooning the slightly absurd notion of a blind man saying that he'll be 'watching you': 'Every word you say, I'll be listening to you … 'cos I won't be watching you!', finishing with an evil cackle of laughter.

The artist who really matters to Gurrumul is Cliff Richard; *Top of the Pops* Cliff; 'Summer Holiday' Cliff; 'Living Doll' Cliff. Gurrumul is a huge fan, as are a lot of his friends and family back home. It's the gospel version of Sir Cliff that most appeals to Gurrumul's family, growing out of the mission influence in their lives, but Gurrumul is also powerfully attracted to singalong Cliff who can claim fourteen Number 1 hits in the UK and sales of 250 million records worldwide. For anyone under the age of seventy with any claim to musical credibility, Sir Cliff is the boy with a pretty face who went on to become a hit machine. He's often characterised as lightweight but there's none of that sort of snobbery amongst Cliff's Indigenous Australian fans, and not a skerrick of it in Gurrumul. His family rings him from Elcho, urging him to track Cliff down in England and get his picture taken with the man who made it to Number 1 in 2000 with 'The Millennium Prayer' ('Let all the people say Amen/ In every tribe and tongue …').

It's Michael's task to scour the music outlets of European cities trying to dig up some Cliff and, while he's at it, as much live Iron Maiden as he can find. Also Gerry Rafferty and, since he's on the job, maybe some Eric Clapton playing live with Mark Knopfler.

Michael has managed to get an emailed translation of 'Every Breath' out of Gurrumul's sisters on Milingimbi Island, part of the Crocodile Islands group further west on the Arnhem coast than Elcho. It's a very good, painstaking translation, and should have satisfied Gurrumul, except that it didn't. With *Taratata* looming and very little coming out of Gurrumul other than satirical riffs on the 'Every Breath' lyrics, Michael goes to Gurrumul's room in the Brussels apartment to see if he's willing to rehearse the song. 'Because I was worried,' Michael confesses later. 'I know him so well, and one thing I know is when he's ready for something and when he isn't. One week out from *Taratata* and I'm getting nothing from him.'

Gurrumul's strategy when he's cornered with a question he doesn't want to answer is, well, not to answer it. The same with requests that make him uncomfortable. He keeps quiet, goes off into the Gurrumul Zone. He doesn't bother with evasion; just stays silent. It's a strategy he's employed with every journalist who's ever sat with him, notebook in hand, waiting in futile expectation for something to put on a page. This can't really be explained as an Indigenous thing; some sort of rebellion. Plenty of Indigenous performers are prepared to talk their heads off for the media. But they are the extroverts. Gurrumul isn't an extrovert but, at the same time, he certainly doesn't disdain fame and what you might have to do to get some of it.

The real reason for the lack of co-operation, so Michael has come to believe, is that Gurrumul is self-conscious about the way he sounds when he's singing something unfamiliar, or even talking in a language that he hasn't fully mastered, such as English. He doesn't want to be quoted by journalists sounding as if it's a struggle to get the right words out, and he especially doesn't want to be singing something in Gumatj that makes a botch of the English lyrics. Even the translation by his sisters doesn't fully convince him that he can raise his voice with confidence in front of a television camera. On top of all that — well, there's the song itself. If Mark Knopfler had asked Gurrumul to sing 'Walk of Life' with him on the telly, no problem. If Sir Cliff had asked Gurrumul to join him in a Richard/Yunupiŋu rendition of 'The Millennium Prayer' — too easy. But Sting and 'Every Breath You Take'? Awkward.

Touring takes Michael and Gurrumul back to England. In their London hotel the day before *Taratata*, there's still nothing in Gurrumul's manner to suggest he's ready for the Sting duet.

'It's tomorrow, remember,' says Michael.

Nothing.

'How about I help you learn the lyrics? Do you think? You want me to do that?'

Silence.

'I've got time, wäwa. Can we go over the lyrics?'

Not a flicker of interest.

But as Michael heads for the door, anxious now, not knowing what more he can say, Gurrumul stops him: 'It's not in Gumatj. Talk to Djuŋa.'

'It's not in Gumatj?'

'No. Talk to Djuŋa. Get it in Gumatj.'

Gurrumul with Sting (centre) and the presenter of the popular French show Taratata, Nagui Taratata

Gurrumul speaks a number of Yolŋu dialects, but his native tongue of Gumatj is the one that he feels most secure with. The translation that the sisters in Milingimbi have produced is in a version of Yolŋu that Gurrumul speaks, but it's not his language. If he's going to perform this peculiar song with what's-his-name, he apparently needs the security of Gumatj. Michael heads back to his room to ring distant Darwin, hoping that someone at the Skinnyfish office can contact Gurrumul's uncle Djuŋa back on Elcho and arrange a translation. That might work out or it might not. Michael next calls Gurrumul's cousins Johnno and Nigel to see if they can do something. Nigel answers from somewhere out in the bush where he and Johnno are stranded until a car or something comes along. So Michael's left waiting for a Gumatj speaker, who also commands English, to get to work on the lyrics of a late twentieth-century pop song and transmit the translation from the Elcho mulga to a hotel room in London. Bizarre.

It's now eight hours until Gurrumul, Michael, Mark, the musicians and crew leave for Paris, and in that time everyone has to get some sleep. Michael wakes in the morning and leaps straight into a video conversation with Gurrumul's uncle Djuŋa on Elcho. He's recorded a version of 'Every Breath' in Gumatj and is sending it through as an MP3 file; the handwritten lyrics will be scanned and emailed.

Later that day in Paris, Gurrumul remains noncommittal about the duet. He's heard the written version of the Gumatj lyrics, doesn't care for them much, but hasn't ruled out singing them. He has the chance on the two-hour Eurostar trip from London to Paris to listen to the recorded version sent from Galiwin'ku by Djuŋa, but declines.

A radio interview in Paris on a station with a huge audience goes fabulously well, although Gurrumul doesn't say a word; Michael speaks for him. This is normal, but the French station was hoping for a few words from Gurrumul himself, which would have been a first. Just a few words, maybe two sentences, 'Hello France, good to be here in Paris. This is Gurrumul Yunupiŋu from Elcho Island' — something like that? *Non? Tres bien. Pas problem.* But to compensate, Gurrumul allows the station to record him singing 'Bäpa' in his hotel room. And this is a first in itself: one thousand years of Parisian history and never before has a black Australian sung a song in Gumatj of love for a father within its precincts.

Michael has downloaded the MP3 recording from Galiwin'ku of 'Every Breath' onto his laptop and leaves it playing for Gurrumul in the hotel while he attends to chores. When he returns, Gurrumul says: 'Michael, Michael, what am I going to do today?'

'The song! "Every Breath You Take". You do the verses in Gumatj. Didn't you listen to it?'

'Too many words in that song, Michael.'

'Too many words? What do you mean?'

'Too many words, wäwa.'

Michael and Mark, one the adopted brother of Gurrumul, the other the adopted father, love the man. And just as well. Something both Michael and Mark have to recall, when they feel driven to go down to the Metro and jump under a train, is that Gurrumul never pleaded to be made a superstar. He was a man of exceptional talent when Michael first met him and he was glad to have the full range of his gifts revealed by Michael's mentoring and Mark's savvy. But he never said: 'Whatever it takes, make me famous.' Maybe prodding him to lend his talent to this pop song project is asking just too much. He's never liked the idea, never cared for this song with 'too many words', so shouldn't he be allowed to drop it? As far as Mark is concerned, yes, sure — drop it. But Michael has committed to the project, done every tiny thing he can to make it happen, and it would be painful to see the whole thing go down the drain. Worse than losing the opportunity, though, would be losing his temper. Tantrums and adamant demands have never ever been a part of his relationship with Gurrumul. He loves Gurrumul. Mark loves him. Let it go.

Bruno, who's overseeing everything for France 2, the channel producing *Taratata*, is downstairs waiting for Michael.

'Bruno,' says Michael, 'he doesn't know the song. He hasn't learnt it.'

'No?'

'No.'

The blood leaves Bruno's face. He runs his hand through his hair. 'He doesn't know the song?'

'He can sing some of it in English. But the two verses in his own language — no, he hasn't learnt the words.'

Bruno nods but he doesn't say anything more. Michael returns to the hotel room and leads Gurrumul down to the bus that will take them to the studio for the rehearsal. Michael says this: 'Brother, do what you like in the studio. Don't worry about it. Sting is relaxed about it. So, you know, whatever you feel like.'

Michael thought back to a session in the SBS studio in Sydney a year ago. Not much preparation, but when it came to recording Gurrumul produced stuff of extraordinary originality out of nowhere. So maybe, just maybe …

The studios of France 2 are a state-of-the-art wonder, reeking of status, and also a little intimidating. Michael says later: 'I kept telling myself that whatever happens is okay. It was important to remind myself of that. Whatever happens is okay.'

'Wiyathul' was to be released in France as a single, and so the song was chosen for the rehearsal piece. The studio crew is expecting a short version of the song, but the *Taratata* presenter, Nagui, a stylish guy of about fifty, charming in the French way, says, '*Non, non, non absolument!*' He wants the full five-minutes-plus version; he's a Gurrumul fan; he has the album. Nagui is the most popular presenter in France (he's actually an Italo–Egyptian) and if he wants the full version, that's what he gets. The rehearsal goes splendidly.

Waiting for whatever comes next, Michael and Gurrumul are surprised by the arrival of Sting himself who enters the greenroom area with his family and his entourage, and makes a beeline for Gurrumul. He introduces himself, exuding warmth: 'I love your songs. Love them. Play them in my car, in my house. I've been driving all over Paris and that voice of yours is in my ears the whole time. Can't tell you how much I admire what you do. Superb.'

Michael and Mark and Gurrumul retire to the dressing room, Gurrumul high on Sting's praise. Maybe he does like the Sting song after all. Maybe it was all just anxiety, like when you shrug to disguise your unease.

Gurrumul listens to Djuŋa's Gumatj version of 'Every Breath' again, with more focus.

A call comes from the studio downstairs: Everything is ready for the duet rehearsal. Gurrumul stands, Michael takes his hand.

This is as far as you get from singing in front of a small crowd, in a paddock at Galiwin'ku,

Bronwyn, Gurrumul's partner, returns to the hotel after an exhausting day visiting London Zoo.

Gurrumul made one short trip to Paris with just two guitarists, Francis Diatschenko and Craig Pilkington. They spent half their time enjoying cooking for him and the rest chasing phone credit. In fact, he ran up so much credit ringing home to Australia that the mobile phone company put a daily limit on his spend to make sure it was all legitimate.

On tour, more or less. Clockwise from top left: In Covent Garden, London, Michael helping Gurrumul choose a computer for his daughter Jasmine back on Elcho; Mikey 'Yindipuy Pie' Randon, Gurrumul's UK drummer, mugging behind the boss; Mark transformed into a zombie after a marathon search for Gurrumul's all-important phone credit; Gurrumul's punk era look.

with your brothers on stage behind you, someone on clapsticks, moths flying around the stage lights, people eating fried chicken from the Galiwin'ku takeaway. Here, in the plush studios of France 2, the music Gurrumul has played over the years for the sheer joy of it has become art. The Gumatj language, the sacred repository of a culture and history older by far than that of France or of any country in Europe, older than the entirety of Western civilisation, is about to be plaited with the younger, mongrel language of English. Gurrumul is still Gurrumul, yes, but from this point on, he belongs to the world. That's the journey he's travelled since the day his mother Daisy gave birth to him in Galiwin'ku: from the all-encompassing embrace of his Gumatj culture to the embrace of the world. As Gurrumul, led by Michael, makes his way down to the performance stage of the France 2 studios, he is about to commence a new stage of his journey, whether he knows it or not.

Sting is seated on an upholstered stool, his guitar on his lap. Other musicians are seated and waiting. Michael leads Gurrumul to a plain white kitchen chair directly opposite Sting.

'Ah, Michael — you're the double bass player, is that right?' says Sting.

'Yes, that's right.'

Michael has noticed, with a sinking feeling in his stomach, that there's already a double bass player in the ensemble, ready to go; Gurrumul will have to perform without his familiar presence. If it has to be, it has to be. Meanwhile Michael tries to explain the situation with the lyrics, which still hasn't resolved itself. 'He's not that comfortable with the language — the English lyrics. Maybe he could just sing what he can, and we'll see how it works?'

'Okay, we'll try that,' says Sting, perhaps with a hint of reservation.

'And,' says Michael, 'he'd like to hum the tune before he moves into the lyrics.'

'Sure. Sure.'

Michael makes a few further suggestions to Sting, and is accommodated in each. Gurrumul sits waiting on his white kitchen chair as still as graven stone but, as Michael knows, he's listening to every single word, and he understands it all.

The band plays its way through a soft, acoustic version of the song, with Gurrumul contributing small, perfectly judged additions here and there. It works well, and would probably be attractive to the viewers, but it's not what *Taratata* was hoping for. Nagui rushes over to Michael to protest. 'This is not a duet, we said a duet, and this is not a duet, not a collaboration! What can we do?'

Apart from *Taratata*, France 2 is also shooting a documentary on Gurrumul's maiden trip to France. Sting and Gurrumul try 'Every Breath' a second time, for the benefit of the France 2 cameras. But Nagui is right; this version of the song, attractive as it is, is not truly a duet. Nagui knows instinctively that something much more compelling should come out of the session; Sting and Michael know it too. Suddenly everyone's got an opinion — Nagui, Michael, the producer, Bruno, Sting — while Gurrumul remains still and attentive in his chair, registering the lack of satisfaction with what he's provided. Mark, perfectly sanguine about the whole deal up until now, can no longer watch the mayhem of all the 'creative' folk behaving in the time-honoured stuff-up manner of creative folk everywhere and retires to a nook where he can do something practical, like compose emails.

Gurrumul, almost lost in the blizzard of suggestions being generated on the studio floor, suddenly calls to Michael: 'Michael, Michael — listen.'

'What is it?'

'I'll put some language into the song. Okay?'

'Can you do that? You said there were too many words.'

'I'll put some language in. Take me back to the dressing room. Give me time.'

Gurrumul has an hour before *Taratata* goes live to air in front of a studio audience of five hundred. He works rapidly with considerable help from Francis and Bronwyn. In the end Bronwyn, using the lyrics suggested by Djuŋa in Galiwin'ku, creates two verses for the song. Moving from English to Gumatj in this way is demanding. The whole mood of the song, with its power struggle, hint of menace, and the barely disguised warning from boy to girl doesn't fit into the Gumatj sensibility. But something has been achieved that might work. Might.

Gurrumul and Michael are called down to the set.

Sting and the band complete the second of the two opening numbers while Gurrumul and Michael wait off-camera. After the applause, Gurrumul is introduced by Nagui and is led to his white kitchen chair by Michael. In the few moments before the song starts, every breath is held: by the production crew, by Nagui, by Michael and Mark. The whole thing was a risk from the start. It may all fall in a heap.

But it doesn't. Sting, his good looks enhanced by a stylish black snood, faces Gurrumul in his favourite zip-up jacket across a distance of three metres. Gurrumul starts the duet with his gentle, '… Mmm … mmm …' before Sting moves in his effortless way through the first verse. Then Gurrumul brings in the second verse in Gumatj, and all at once this song, so familiar to everyone, seems refreshed, reborn, made new. The entire audience is lifted. In the middle of the song, Sting finds space for Gurrumul to work some acoustic magic with his guitar, then Gurrumul provides a powerful, repeated, 'La la la …' to harmonise with Sting's raised voice in the bridge. Now the outro, and Sting and Gurrumul are swapping hummed phrases and short melodies. The miraculous moments of the duet arrive when Gurrumul croons above the sotto voce loop of Sting's murmurous fade with the backing singers. The crooning makes you think of some bird of astonishing beauty and grace riding invisible currents under a blue sky that extends forever. The soaring bird and Gurrumul's voice have succeeded in transforming this problematic song of capture and torment into a hymn of liberation, right down to the duet's concluding line: 'I'll be watching you.' The audience raises an ecstatic, prolonged applause and standing ovation. 'The voice of a higher being,' says Sting as Gurrumul is led from the stage.

The Black Eyed Peas are also appearing on the show, and backstage will.i.am from the Peas comes quietly up to Gurrumul and introduces himself. He tells Gurrumul that he has his album and loves it. Gurrumul knows The Black Eyed Peas and enjoys their music, so this endorsement means more to him than praise from a stranger. Already lifted high on an updraft of happiness at having brought off the duet with Sting, Gurrumul is now all but chuckling with delight. He finds a seat with Bronwyn at the side of the stage and dances in his chair to the Peas' performance of 'I Gotta Feeling'.

When Gurrumul performed a duet with Sting after a very brief rehearsal, it was fascinating to watch. Sting watched Gurrumul closely to anticipate where Gurrumul would come in. At the same time you could see Gurrumul listening to Sting just as intensely to anticipate Sting. It truly was a moving and beautiful moment.

CHAPTER 15

Duet

NOVEMBER 2011

*Missy up there with Gurrumul — this is reconciliation
unfolding on stage. Even before the duet begins, the two of them
could almost serve as a poster for the solidarity Gurrumul
sings of in 'Gurrumul History'.*

It's Missy Higgins at the piano with a gamine haircut, an attractive sleeveless batik dress, and a look on her face of great concentration. She's about to sing a duet in Gumatj with Gurrumul and, no matter how long you study the lyrics, Gumatj is likely to test you.

This is the Australian Recording Industry Awards (the ARIAs, Australia's most prestigious music industry accolades) of 2011 at Sydney Olympic Park — Kylie being inducted into the ARIA Hall of Fame by Prime Minister Julia Gillard; Gotye and Kimbra together again; band of the moment Boy & Bear on stage; and ginger heart throb David Wenham ready to announce that The Wiggles are now immortal. Also, a live audience in the thousands.

Many of the people in the audience are music professionals, so Missy and Gurrumul want to get it right. Gurrumul with his guitar is seated a little further forward than Missy, towards the front of the round, elevated podium stage.

It means something to him that Missy has taught herself the words to 'Warwu' in Gumatj. It's a compliment to him, and that's how he treats it. This is his language, Gumatj, or one of them, and it's rare for him to speak to any white person, woman or man, who properly understands how much it means to him. Michael and Mark understand; maybe a few other white folk in the world, and that's it. If you have as big a name as Missy Higgins and you're willing to risk looking a bit anxious in front of your colleagues — that deserves respect.

On the higher rear podium, a guy with a mountainous drum kit and another with a piano accordion are readying themselves to support the duet, together with the orchestra. Michael is off to the left in the shadows with his double bass.

Gurrumul and Missy Higgins perform 'Warwu' at the 2011 ARIA Awards. To pay homage to Indigenous Australia, Missy sang in Yolŋu Matha, no easy task, but she sang beautifully.

WARWU

Warwuyu ŋarranha mulkana	Thoughts have taken hold of me
Dhiyala wäŋaŋura Gurrumiya	Of the land Gurrumiya
Dhiyaŋu ŋarranha gadamankuŋala	These have made me think
Rrepayu djäpana galaŋarriyu	This brilliant red sunset: Rrepa, Djäpana, Galaŋarri
Miny'tji ŋarraku gorruŋala	My (Gumatj) colours spread across the sky
Garrumara Bangawarri Marpulwulmirri	Garrumara Bangawarri Marpulwulmirri
Yä märi walala Budalpudal	Oh my grandmother people, Budalpudal
Ŋäthina ŋarra warwuyurruna	I think and weep inside
Yä warwu ŋarra, yä roŋiyina, yä wäŋalili	Oh my thoughts, going back, home
Wanhakana guṉda Gandjitja	Where's the Rock Ganditja
Rirraliny Ṉaŋuypurr Rraywala	Rirraliny, Ṉaŋuypurr, Rraywala
Dhuwalana Buthalumu	Here in the ground, the burial site
Wanygurrkurrwa Dhamuŋurawu Djulwanbirrwu	Wanygurrkurrwa Dhamuŋurawu Djulwanbirrwu
Gu ŋilimurru nhina yarrarra'yun	Come let us sit together and look out, reflect
Djurarr Rräyuŋ Rrakpala	We Gumatj, Djurarr Rräyuŋ Rrakpala
Roŋiyinana ŋarra nhäŋala	I look back
Djerrkŋu ḏurryunara nherranminyara	Gumatj clouds forming themselves in their place
Djerrkŋu dhuwalinydja Wurrpuṉdu	Gumatj clouds Djerrkŋu, Wurrpuṉdu
Gaṉawirra Balaŋu Gumbalkarra	Gaṉawirra Balaŋu Gumbalkarra
Yä warwu ŋarra, yä roŋiyina, yä Gunyaŋarriyu	Oh, I am thinking, anguished by the need to go back to Gunyaŋara

Like 'Djilawurr', this song strips a Saltwater song back to the bones to reveal the beauty of its elements. The Gumatj seize the joy in life as fully as anyone, but it would be true to say that, in their nature, they are a contemplative people who search out what is eternal in life. 'Warwu' is a song of grief and yearning. The initial piano notes, struck with all the intention of a Chopin prelude, announce the sombreness of the emotions about to be engaged. Gurrumul wends his way through a landscape of sorrow, like a man with bowed head who hopes to find his way to eventual peace.

Missy up there with Gurrumul — this is reconciliation unfolding on stage. Even before the duet begins, the two of them could almost serve as a poster for the solidarity Gurrumul sings of in 'Gurrumul History'. No woman in Australia looks whiter than Missy with her fair hair and rose-petal complexion; no man in Australia looks blacker and more Gumatj than Gurrumul. In Missy there resides an acclaimed talent with its roots in an Anglo–Australian musical culture of great distinction; in Gurrumul, another formidable talent with its roots in a culture older than recorded history. This is to be a duet, and it will stand or fall on the quality of the performance. But it's also a political statement.

Inviting Gurrumul on stage tonight was first suggested a couple of weeks earlier. He's a nominated artist, and it was natural enough that he'd be asked. Gurrumul in a vocal solo, that was the original idea, with Michael on double bass and perhaps Francis Diatschenko on another acoustic guitar. Or maybe Gurrumul at the piano for 'Wukun', a song that would likely bring the house down.

The suggestion of a duet came through from the producers only a week before the night of the ARIAs. Of the artists who might have been approached, Missy Higgins, a seven-time ARIA winner, was the singer considered most likely to cope with the technical challenges that a duet of this sort imposes. She's a pop star, yes, but the foundation of her success is terrific musical savvy, an instinctive feel for the way a song works, and what makes it work. The duet might feature Gurrumul singing in his native language with Missy taking a verse or two in English.

It was Missy herself who proposed that she learn the Gumatj words and make it a duet. Now, it's a big ask just to learn Gumatj sentences and speak them aloud with any accuracy, but to sing them and harmonise with a native speaker of the language — that's daunting.

Gurrumul, Michael and Missy met up at Missy's place in Melbourne to try it out. The rapport was there almost immediately — Missy at an old upright piano, Gurrumul's extraordinary hearing picking up every single thing that was happening in the room as accurately as anyone with full vision. Michael had shaped the eight minutes of the song to fit the program for the night, paring it down to under four minutes and giving a song that is really all narrative reflection, something like a verse series.

That was the first of three rehearsals with Missy, the last on the afternoon of the ARIAs. But even with rehearsals that go well, a duet like this remains a risk. In all of Gurrumul's songs there is a patina of mystique. His voice and the Gumatj language of the songs come from a place inside that belongs not only to him, but to his clan. The intimacy he generates has its source in his willingness to open the door to that place — just a little — to the public. He sings as a custodian of Gumatj beliefs. Can a white girl share in this intimacy? Or will it all seem no more than a novelty turn?

Missy Higgins' career as a singer and songwriter has given her experience of risk. Listen to her 2007 hit, 'Scar'. It's a song rendered in the idiom of everyday speech and fashions drama out of lyrics that would still function at the level of intelligent monologue. It's very hard to do this — maintaining the integrity of your own voice, while still producing an attractive pop song. But the risk goes further than that. Her lyrics are candid without being confessional, working with emotions that never get away from her; never overwhelm the narrative. The sincerity and intimacy isn't manufactured. And she retains her own accent in her vocals in preference to widely adopted mid-Pacific popspeak.

Backstage at the 2011 ARIAs — Michael,
Gurrumul and Missy. Opposite: Bronwym, Terepai
Richmond, Francis and Stephen Teakle (in front).

She also has the credentials for a song in Gumatj. At the peak of her acclaim, she took time off from her career (although not from music) to study Indigenous cultures at Melbourne University. She came away from that period with a distinction in her field of study and an even greater maturity in her songwriting, seen everywhere in her third album.

'Warwu' is the quintessential Gurrumul song. Far from home, the singer finds consolation for the heartache of absence by picturing a sunset spread across the sky like sheets of flame. The colours of the sunset are the clan colours of his Gumatj people. The singer recalls his beloved grandmother, no longer amongst the living but, at the same time, eternal. The only escape from the grief of remembering is for the Gumatj to come together in sympathy and contemplation.

Missy commences at the piano, gaze locked on the music sheet like an apprehensive student under the scrutiny of a demanding teacher. Just for the moment, she looks about sixteen. Gurrumul picks up the opening chords on his guitar and moves into the song so quietly, so gently that he could almost be rocking a cradle and crooning a lullaby. He's more relaxed than Missy, as you'd expect, singing in a language that he's lived with since he was born.

The lullaby quality fades as Missy comes in on the second verse, and all at once we're listening to a love song. Missy's mid-teens look vanishes; as soon as she lifts her voice, all of her accomplishment as a singer, as a performer, floods into her face. Michael's abridgement and refashioning of the song to suit the television audience gives Missy a verse to herself, followed by the two of them, harmonising superbly. The melody becomes a type of garland handed from one to the other and back again and, in this passing back and forth, reconciliation is enacted. It is as if the words Missy sings and those sung by Gurrumul have transcended their immediate meaning and become messages of esteem, each for the other.

The ARIAs is a sit-down event; you and your friends form a seated circle around a table covered in a white cloth and chat and gossip over your drinks. There are many, many tables. Your drink is refreshed regularly by the busy waiters. It is expected that at the end of the night, a number of those seated upright at the commencement of festivities will have to be retrieved from under the table. The gossip, the glib and the genuine compliments, the banter — they don't stop for anything. But they stopped for Gurrumul and Missy. Everyone knew what was happening.

Sarah Blasko with Michael Hohnen (foreground) and Gurrumul. Sarah had quite a spiritual influence on Michael and Gurrumul's collaboration, with her classical, delicate and heartfelt harmonies and overtones on 'Bayini'. Below: Gurrumul, Bronwyn and Fredrik Kinbom with Sarah Blasko in Zurich.

Patience

The guitarist Francis Daitschenko has toured with Gurrumul a dozen times and knows his music and his temperament as well as anyone. At the time of this interview, he's keeping Gurrumul company in a Sydney hotel after the 2012 ARIAs presentation.

He can be extremely stubborn. Stubborn and persistent. One time on a European tour, we'd missed the plane to Poland. This was a really busy tour — stressful. And at one place and another during the tour, we'd been trying to get this Cliff Richard Live CD for Gurrumul. This happens all the time — he wants a particular CD and no matter what else's happening, like missing the flight to Poland, we have to find that CD. One time he wanted this Abba Gold CD. It's not easy finding a particular CD. You can't just run into a servo and grab an Abba CD. When he wants it, you have to find that one. And it happens at the weirdest times. We could be half an hour late for a gig, and he suddenly wants that CD, he wants Abba Gold, or this time when we missed the flight, he wants Cliff Richard Live. We had people looking for it everywhere, we were looking online, everywhere. It was out of print. We finally found it on Amazon, it was a DVD, not a CD, but the only person who had a UK credit card at that time was Andrew, the A & R guy who was head of Dramatica Records, and he purchased it. But then we had to wait for it to arrive in the post. Gurrumul was phoning Andrew, who was in Brighton, phoning him over and over to find out if it had come. 'Andrew, yo, it's Gurrumul, you got that Cliff Richard?' The last time was eleven o'clock at night, and we were in London, and Andrew says, 'Yeah, it's come.' It was such a big issue, this Cliff Richard CD, and Gurrumul says to Andrew, 'You should bring it down here now, yeah.' This is, like, drive from Brighton to London with the CD at eleven o'clock at night, as if Brighton was just next door. Andrew says, 'No, no, I can't do that, I'll post it to you.' A couple of days later the DVD came, and we had to rip the audio off the DVD and put it on Gurrumul's iPod. But the program ripped the audio off as one track, an hour and a half long, no breaks. So then we had to break the audio up into tracks, and we ended up missing the flight. We took a taxi back to the hotel, and then we're looking for something to eat, which for Gurrumul means a variation on steak and chips or chicken and rice. And Gurrumul gets Michael back to work breaking the audio up into tracks for his iPod, and it's late at night, everyone's upset about missing the flight, everyone's exhausted, and I'm like, 'Gurrumul, please, let Michael sleep, he hasn't even had anything to eat.' And Gurrumul's a really sweet guy, but he needs that CD, and he says, 'Yaka, yaka'. I went out somewhere and came back later, and Gurrumul still won't let Michael go. And why? Michael was recharging Gurrumul's iPod and he won't let Michael out of the room until the light on the iPod turns green, to show it's completely recharged. And Michael, who's utterly exhausted, could've said, 'Yeah, it's green', because Gurrumul wouldn't have known. But Michael would never do that. And Gurrumul knew he wouldn't do that.

*Gurrumul often asks prior to a concert if
there is a big or small crowd in attendance,
and when he is told it is a full house, he often
lets out a quiet exclamation of joy.*

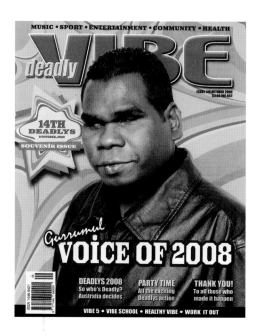

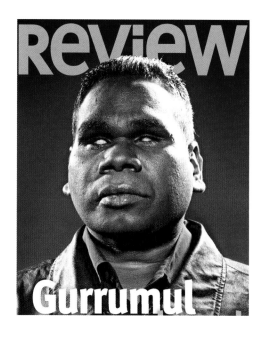

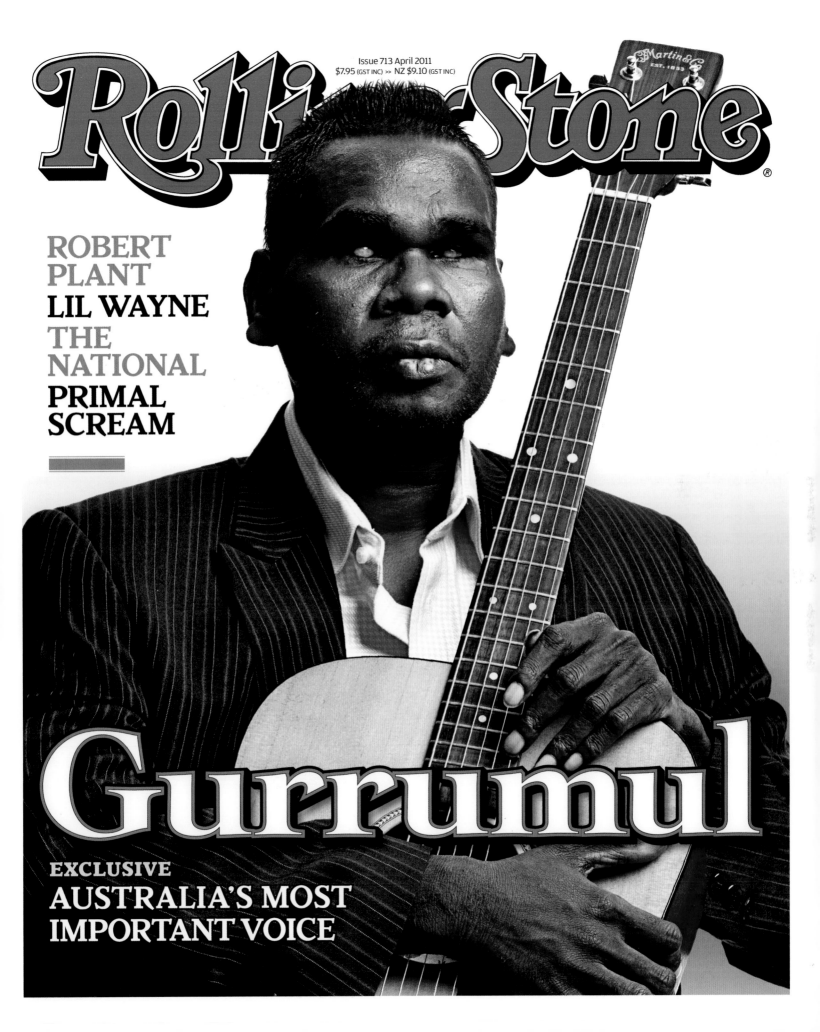

Issue 713 April 2011
$7.95 (GST INC) >> NZ $9.10 (GST INC)

Rolling Stone

ROBERT PLANT
LIL WAYNE
THE NATIONAL
PRIMAL SCREAM

Gurrumul

EXCLUSIVE
AUSTRALIA'S MOST
IMPORTANT VOICE

One of the great successes of Gurrumul has been the pride generated by his family and clan in the knowledge that their songs and their language are now heard and respected around the world.

CHAPTER 16

'Who's that Guy?'

The Presidential charisma reaches out to Gurrumul

and he responds as fully to the President's warmth

as his shyness on such occasions permits.

It's been arranged. Mark will put Gurrumul on the late morning flight from Galiwin'ku to Darwin, where he'll be met by Michael and Francis. The three of them will then travel by bus to an airfield outside Darwin, and there, in a huge aircraft hangar — not sure about the acoustics; might be great, might be awful — he and Michael and Francis will perform a couple of songs for fifteen hundred military personnel — American and Australian — and three hundred guests. Then Gurrumul will be introduced to the VIP, shake his hand, maybe enjoy a glass of juice and a couple of sandwiches, shake the hands of a few other people, themselves VIPs, although not as VI as the main VIP. And that's it.

Gurrumul says to Mark: 'Okay *bäpa.*'

'You shake hands, he says something, "Nice to meet you", something like that, then you say — whatever. That's all good?'

'All good, Marky.'

But late on the evening before the flight, Mark's mobile rings, and it's his son, his *gäthu;* it's Gurrumul.

'*Bäpa,* who's this fella we meet tomorrow?'

'Who are we meeting? *Gäthu,* you're not serious.'

'*Bäpa,* what's his name? I forgot.'

Mark mutters something to himself, 'Unbelievable …' and shakes his head in wonder.

'Obama,' he says. 'President Obama.'

'Obama?'

'President Obama. Barack Obama. He's the president of the United States of America. The USA.'

'Okay *bäpa.* Obama. Thanks.'

Next morning, the flight from Galiwin'ku arrives in Darwin; Michael, Francis and Gurrumul

GOPURU

Ŋoy-ŋupara gunbilk Marrawuḻwuḻ	Underneath, following the reflecting sea surface Marrawulwul
Ŋoy-ŋupara Golulaŋu	Underneath following the north-west winds Golula
Gopuru gopuru wapthurra Yiwarrwu Yäŋaywu	Gopuru, Gopuru leap for the north-west winds, Yiwarr, Yäŋay
Gopuru gopuru wapthurra Yiwarrwu Yäŋaywu	Gopuru, Gopuru leap for the north-west winds, Yiwarr, Yäŋay
Wapthurruna Ḏirrmalawu	Leaping for the north-west wind, Ḏirrmala
Gopuru wapthurra, ŋurukuna Yiwarrwu	Gopuru leaping, for that north-west wind, Yiwarr
Wapthurra djimdhurra, dhä-watjurra ŋoywu Waŋatjpalwu	Leaping and diving, nose in the deep, heading towards the clouds on the horizon
Wapthurra djimdhurra, dhä-watjurra ŋoywu Waŋatjpalwu	Leaping and diving, nose in the deep, heading towards the clouds on the horizon
Buḻarrwuḻarr balanata, ŋoy-ŋupara Marruṉdutjŋa	Chasing from below, the ocean currents Marruṉdutjŋa
Ŋoywu wapthurra, Balalŋu Gumbalkarra	Chasing from below, the clouds above
Gopuru gopuru wapthurra Yiwarrwu Yäŋaywu	Gopuru, Gopuru leap for the north-west winds, Yiwarr, Yäŋay
Gopuru gopuru wapthurra Yiwarrwu Yäŋaywu	Gopuru, Gopuru leap for the north-west winds, Yiwarr, Yäŋay
Wapthurruna Ḏirrmalawu	Leaping for the north-west wind, Ḏirrmala
Gopuru wapthurra, ŋurukuna Yiwarrwu	Gopuru leaping for that north-west wind, Yiwarr
Wapthurra djimdhurra, dhä-watjurra ŋoywu Waŋatjpalwu	Leaping and diving, nose in the deep, heading towards the clouds on the horizon
Wapthurra djimdhurra, dhä-watjurra ŋoywu Waŋatjpalwu	Leaping and diving, nose in the deep, heading towards the clouds on the horizon
Ḏi ḏi ḏi, ḏi ḏi ḏi, ḏi ḏi ḏi, ḏi ḏi, ḏi ḏi	Ḏi ḏi ḏi, ḏi ḏi ḏi, ḏi ḏi ḏi, ḏi ḏi, ḏi ḏi
Ḏi ḏi ḏi, ḏi ḏi ḏi, ḏi ḏi ḏi, ḏi ḏi, ḏi ḏi	Ḏi ḏi ḏi, ḏi ḏi ḏi, ḏi ḏi ḏi, ḏi ḏi, ḏi ḏi

A relaxed version of 'Gopuru' on the first Saltwater album, *Gapu Damurruŋ*, featured playful keyboard and the contribution of a half-dozen happy voices. The meditative piano notes before the entry on the *Rrakala* version underscore the altered musical agenda of Gurrumul's solo career. For the Saltwater boys, the Gopuru figure was just about one of the gang. In this version, Gopuru is revered in his vigour, honoured in his omnipotence. When you watch Gurrumul on stage singing this version, lifting his head, leaning forward, it's as if he's calling to the wind, courting it.

are shown onto the shuttle bus with their instruments, but only after the instruments have been examined and x-rayed and probed. Gurrumul, Michael and Francis have also been examined and x-rayed. Their backgrounds, their demeanours, their prejudices, their politics, their ancestry, their employment history, their friendships, their periods of foreign travel, their wives and girlfriends and pals and uncles and aunts — they've all been subjected to the sort of exhaustive search and analysis that must be endured if you are to be granted a Homeland Security Meet-and-Greet Security Clearance. By the time Gurrumul, Michael and Francis step aboard the shuttle bus to the bomb-proof aircraft hangar, as much detail on their lives has been gathered as might be found — well, in a thick book devoted to the subject of Gurrumul's music and relationships.

Jessica Mauboy, the Indigenous pop artist will also be performing at the hangar, following Gurrumul. It's to be an Indigenous double act, at the request of the President. It's unlikely that all but a few of those listening have ever heard a black Australian singing in his own language. So this audience of the unitiated will be a further test of Michael's musical judgment. He's the guy who influenced the Gurrumul sound in such a way that listeners raised on Western musical structures became engaged enough to listen to songs out of Arnhem Land rendered in versions of Yolŋu. But there is no need to worry, the audience listens to 'Wiyathul' and 'Djärimirri' with something of the spellbound awe that Gurrumul's more conventional audiences offer up.

And now the meeting with the President, and with Prime Minister Julia Gillard. Gurrumul has met Julia Gillard in the past, just as he's met John Howard (of whom he asked, famously: 'Rupiah ga' which means, 'Please can I have some money?') but he's never met a US President before, and now that he's actually aware of who the current US President is, it would be a shame not to say a few words.

Only around a dozen of the invited guests are shown into the secure area where President Obama is waiting to meet-and-greet. Michael takes Gurrumul's hand under his arm, leads him forward. Prime Minister Gillard introduces Michael and Gurrumul to the president. President Obama is wearing a tailored grey flannel suit, white shirt and a tie in mid-blue. Gurrumul is wearing black jeans and his favourite zip-up jacket that advertises his allegiance to rock'n'roll. The Presidential charisma, potent if you're sighted, a little diminished if you're blind, nevertheless reaches out to Gurrumul and he responds as fully to the President's warmth as his shyness on such occasions permits, very few words of course but both men very sincere. In the photo op Gurrumul turned away from the camera and towards the man who's holding his hand, the President, as if the immediate source of the warmth he's experiencing commands much more of his interest than the way he might look in an image preserved for posterity.

American visitors

Jimmy the Monkey was not in fact a monkey but a chimpanzee with a great deal of showbiz flair and a much-admired knack for comedy. He was the first and only chimpanzee ever to visit Elcho Island and lives on in the memory of those who met him as a bizarre example of whitefella perfidy. Jimmy was, after all, owned by a white man, and eventually abandoned by him on Elcho when the chimp became a burden. Questionable conduct, considering that Jimmy had paid his way for a number of years and had once graced the silver screen in three Tarzan films with Johnny Weissmuller as his co-star.

Jimmy came to Elcho Island in 1959 on the *Sea Fox*, a motor yacht owned by John Calvert, master magician, movie star and raconteur, born 5 August 1911 and still alive when this book was being written. After more than forty Hollywood movies, Calvert had returned to his trade of magician, touring the world, first in his own Douglas DC-3, then in the *Sea Fox*. Wherever he docked, he'd put on a show. And what a show! Astonishing feats of illusion: folk made to float three metres above the stage; his beautiful assistant Pilita pierced with swords yet smiling and unharmed a minute later. Jimmy the Monkey was introduced to the audience as a novelty and for being Tarzan's pet.

Elcho was an unscheduled stop for the *Sea Fox*. The yacht was leaking and had to be beached before she sank. Gurrumul's mother and father, and some of his uncles and aunts were at this time no more than teenagers. The only white men they had ever seen had been missionaries, and the occasional government functionary. What on earth would the Yolŋu of Elcho have made of Jimmy? How would they have placed him in their scheme of things? Certainly he made an impression, remembered as he is after all these years. And Calvert is remembered, too, not only for his dramatic, Errol Flynn-like looks, but also for producing gold coins from his ears and making birds disappear in mid-air.

The *Sea Fox* was towed to another port on the Arnhem coast for repairs. Calvert, Pilita and the crew left Elcho to stage their extravaganza of illusion to paying customers all over Australia. But Jimmy the Monkey was left behind. He wandered about in desolation for a month before being sent south, eventually finding a home in Perth Zoo.

Jimmy lives on as a reference in the spirited banter that's played out between Mark and Gurrumul; between father and son. Thus Mark calls Gurrumul on his mobile to tell him that he's met a mutual friend down on the beach at Elcho.

'Who's that?' asks Gurrumul.

'You'll never guess. Very famous fella.'

'Famous fella? Who's that?'

'Jimmy the Monkey.'

The Gumatj sense of humour, always close to the surface, relishes the element of the absurd in the Jimmy the Monkey story.

Stars and Stripes — Gurrumul performs for Obama in Darwin.

Gurrumul and Michael flanked by US President Barack Obama and Prime Minister Julia Gillard. The warmth of the President's greeting moved Gurrumul.

CHAPTER 17

Crisis

The ambush that was waiting for Gurrumul

was bound to result in his early death but for the love

and concern of those around him.

Mark says, despairingly: 'It's no good. It's no good. He can't go.'

It's May 2010, Mark, Michael and Gurrumul are in Darwin and it's time to go to the airport. The person who can't go is Gurrumul; the place he can't go to is America, and the reason he can't go is that he's ill and dying.

This was to be a triumphal tour through venues all over the US, coming in the wake of the triumphal progress of Gurrumul's first album to the top of the charts, not only in Australia but elsewhere in the world. If you're an Aboriginal Australian singing in a language that nobody has ever heard of, and yet you somehow manage to attract promoters in the biggest market in the world, you don't want to lose the opportunity to shine on stage. But Gurrumul can't get out of bed. He has a work ethic and a sense of obligation that would compel him to rouse himself and get on the plane even if he'd had a leg taken off at the thigh, so if he's bedridden at a time like this, it's serious.

Any black Australian who becomes seriously ill in his late thirties has a very remote chance of reaching his late forties. A frightening number of black Australians — both men and women — lose their lives to renal failure, heart disease and liver disorders at about the age Gurrumul is now — almost thirty-nine — and many who are spared succumb ten or twenty years later. Any other Australian, in most cases, will live to blow out eighty candles on a birthday cake; most Indigenous Australians will be lucky to blow out fifty-five.

Michael is in the midst of the worst few days of his life. The missed opportunity in America is of little consequence compared to the distress he's experiencing at his friend's struggle to stay alive. He knows that Gurrumul needs a doctor desperately, but here's the problem: Gurrumul is no more likely to permit a doctor to examine him and conduct tests than he is

Gurrumul plays 'Wukun' on piano.

WIRRPAŊU

Y..i, y..i, y..i, y..i
Wirrpaŋu dhäya yaka, ŋarru ŋunha Bawuḏuwuḏu
Ŋaypinyayu
Dhaŋurryuna nhanany ḏupthuwan, bäpiyu Garrawanaŋu
Liḻipiyana
y..i, y..i, y..i, y..i

Bäpa, bäpawuḻi, nhätha ŋalma ŋarru ḏitjunma
Dhamdhamli?
bili dhawalnydja dhaŋu wirrpa ŋoya
go ŋalma ḏitjuna Mawiyu

Wirrpaŋu dhäya yaka, ŋarru ŋunha Bawuḏuwuḏu
Ŋaypinyayu
Dhaŋurryu nhänany ḏupthuwan, bäpiyu Garrawanaŋu
Liḻipiyana

Yi, yi, yi, yi
The thunder has formed, there at Bawuḏuwuḏu
Ŋaypinya
Dhaŋurryuna threw it, the python Garrawanaŋu
Liḻipiyana
Yi, yi, yi, yi

Dad, to dad, when will we return to Dhamdham
(Goulburn)
Because the time for thunder is here
Come let's return to Mäwi

The thunder has formed, there at Bawuḏuwuḏu
Ŋaypinya
the thunder sent his mind back, the python Garrawanaŋu
Liḻipiyan

Straight from church. The strumming entry to 'Wirrpaŋu' could be handed over to the guitarist who's leading the congregation in any slow-tempo hymn from the Methodist songbook — 'O What Their Joy and Their Glory Might Be'; 'Alas! And Did My Spirit Bleed'. The lyrics place 'Wirrpaŋu' amongst what might be termed Gurrumul's heart songs — those that speak of desired destinations, in this case the Goulburn Islands (Dhamdham) off the Arnhem Land coast east of the Coburg Peninsula, but it would have come as no surprise if the English translation had read: 'Let our vesper hymn be blending with the Holy Calm around.' White gospel relates Gurrumul's Christian heritage to Michael Hohnen's own Uniting Church experience as a child, and both Michael and Gurrumul have a soft spot for this song, even though it's amongst Gurrumul's less important compositions.

to fly to the moon. His aversion — it amounts to a phobia — dates from childhood, when he was ferried about to doctors in places distant from his home. Blind as he is, he couldn't see what was being prepared for him, what instruments were being readied.

In addition to his dread of being handled and probed and pierced, he had been raised according to the rites of a culture in which medical procedures of the sort that were now being urged on him played no part. Because of the dire state of Indigenous health in Australia, friends and relatives who had been compelled to hospitalise themselves had often waited too long, and died while in care. The postponement of medical care — and sometimes its simple unavailability — has led to identifying hospitalisation with decline and death.

But Michael and Mark and Mark's wife, Michelle, attempt again and again to persuade him to see a doctor. Gurrumul says: '*Yaka*!' ('No!')

Then Michael sits beside his bed and pleads again: '*Wäwa*, listen to me. It's important. Very important. I want you to let the doctor look at you.'

Gurrumul says: '*Yaka*!'

A number of Gurrumul's family members live on Elcho, and that's where he should be right now, back on Elcho. But for complex cultural reasons all to do with the chaos that ensues when Yolŋu live away from their homeland (Elcho is not, strictly speaking, the country of Gurrumul and his family), it is difficult for him to return to Elcho with Bronwyn, and he is not about to go home without her.

So it's '*Yaka*!', and Michael and Mark have to endure it. Gurrumul's illness hasn't even been diagnosed. Educated conjecture based on the evident symptoms suggests something renal, or if not renal then hepatic, or possibly cardiac, or a wicked alliance of pathologies associated with all three — kidneys, liver and heart. Gurrumul is lethargic, prone to long periods of unrefreshing sleep; his belly is bloated; his complexion greyish. He has been ill before with symptoms very like those he's exhibiting now, but never as pronounced. Many Indigenous Australians find a way to 'normalise' feeling ill; to accommodate enervation within the structure of everyday life. GPs in the field of Aboriginal health meet patients in their fifties who have only just conceded that things aren't right after half a lifetime of feeling crook.

Days pass and the news from the house at which Gurrumul is living in Darwin remains dire: 'He's very sick. He stays in bed.' Michael and Mark, both in Darwin, not far from the communal house where Gurrumul is living, are reduced to an impotent wishing and hoping. Gurrumul refuses to see them when they attempt to intervene. It's agonising. If he were flown down to Sydney or Melbourne, Gurrumul could be hooked into the most sophisticated treatments available for whatever it is that ails him. And he can afford them. But he has withdrawn into himself and adopts a sullen obstinacy.

Michelle, with her years of experience in Indigenous healthcare, sends a doctor to see him on her own initiative, but Gurrumul won't allow the doctor to enter the house. Michelle tells him: 'If you don't do something, you'll die. Do you know that? Let the doctor look at you.'

Gurrumul says: '*Yaka*!'

As if his situation is not grim enough, Gurrumul's place of residence in Darwin leaves him prey to exploitation by local itinerants, both black and white. The success he's enjoyed allows him to extend a helping hand to those around him; to pay for a flight from here to there; to cover moving expenses; to meet the cost of repairs on a car. This is expected of him, as it would be expected of any member of his clan with means. But now he's being badgered by people on the fringe of his life who seem to care more about what he can provide for them than about his suffering. Those who do care tell Mark and Michael: 'No good. Better get him out of there.'

Weeks into the crisis, Mark and Michael remove Gurrumul from the fraught situation in which he's been living, dismissing all objections. They've found a house for him and for Bronwyn, with some privacy, some respite. Bronwyn now has the opportunity to minister to Gurrumul unimpeded by the many people who interfered with the care she was attempting to provide back at the communal house, and her care makes a difference. No doctors, no proper medicine, but at least he's improving. Still, he keeps himself at a physical distance from Mark, Michael and Michelle, unwilling to listen to their pleading. When he does communicate, it's by phone, and it's to urge Mark and Michael to accept appearances for him here and there, including the Byron Bay Blues Festival a few months off. Kidney disease, liver disease — it's possible to experience a period of feeling a bit better, but you're not better; it's just a hiatus in the progress of the disease.

When Mark asks Gurrumul if he can do the Byron gig, Gurrumul replies: 'It's good, Marky.'

'You're sure about that?'

'Yeah, yeah. Byron is good.'

Gurrumul doesn't look 'good' at all when Michael sees him in the flesh; he's as bloated as a poisoned pup. But Gurrumul insists on flying down to Byron — no no, don't cancel, no no, don't need a doctor, it's good, it's good. And as it turns out, the performance is fabulous, one of his best; he precedes Bob Dylan on stage and seems to revel in the billing he's been given. After the performance, though, he's in a wretched state. A woman who knows Mark well and is widely respected in the Indigenous community, takes one look at Gurrumul and draws Mark aside.

'Mark, what the hell? What's happening? He's going to die, can't you see that?'

Mark explains that Gurrumul won't see a doctor, won't accept treatment. He tells her, too, of the situation that prevents Gurrumul from returning to Elcho.

'You fix it, Mark. You do it. He'll die, I can see it. Fix it, Mark.'

Gurrumul doesn't hear any of this, but it is nonetheless the turning point of his adult life. Mark can't go on any longer listening to Gurrumul say: '*Yaka*!' Back in Darwin, he tells Gurrumul that he's taking him back to Elcho. He talks to Gurrumul's close kin in Darwin, then in Elcho. He says to Gurrumul's mother: 'This is it, Daisy. He comes back to Elcho and Michelle gets him to the clinic, or you bury him.'

Within twenty-four hours, Daisy gets back to Mark: 'You bring him here.'

'And Bronwyn?'

'You bring them both back here.'

Gurrumul returns to Elcho, with Bronwyn. Between Gurrumul and his family, there's business to attend to. Between Bronwyn and Daisy and Daisy's sisters, more business. It concludes with reconciliation, as it must if Gurrumul is to live.

The next day, Michelle sits with Gurrumul and explains everything he can expect when he's in the hands of the doctors. 'They'll take off your shirt and examine you,' she says. 'They have to touch you. They want to see if your liver is enlarged. They'll ask you questions. They want to know where you feel pain. They'll take your blood pressure — of course they will. And they'll take some blood. They have to test your blood. Not much. They'll take some urine, too. For testing. And they have to test your cardiac function — your heart. They'll use a machine, but it doesn't hurt you at all. Not at all. They have to test your pulmonary efficiency — that's to see how your lungs are working.'

Michelle goes into even more detail about what lies ahead for Gurrumul. He listens quietly; whatever his distress, he controls it. He says: 'I don't want to die.'

The treatment, including the medications that result from the diagnosis of a chronic and complex disorder, does Gurrumul the world of good. He enjoys equal relief, equal benefit from the reconciliation with his family. Mark and Michelle impress on him the importance of diet, of limiting his smoking. And Mark and Michelle are there to oversee Gurrumul's new regime of vegies, followed by vegies, a little chicken, the occasional barbecued chop, more vegies, bulk bananas. But it is Bronwyn who takes on the greatest share of responsibility for keeping Gurrumul on track. Without her, the entire program of recovery would have wobbled along a very bumpy road.

This health crisis of Gurrumul's had been waiting on the road ahead to ambush him for years and years. Gurrumul's diet had never been egregiously awful; he had never been a really heavy boozer; never puffed away on cigarettes one after the other; never had to endure homelessness, depression, poverty. Nevertheless, by the time he'd reached his late twenties and his early thirties, a constitution perfectly adapted to the age-old tribal regime of the Gumatj had begun to struggle with the saturated fats and refined sugars of the European diet. If you walk thirty kilometres a day with a handful of spears then sit down in the evening to a serving of lean wallaby stew, you're going to be a thinner and nimbler adult than the guy who drives two kilometres to the KFC outlet.

The ambush that was waiting for Gurrumul was bound to result in his early death but for the love and concern of those around him — something that not every forty-year-old black Australian can count on. As it is, we should be grateful that his family and friends were there for Gurrumul. Grateful that Gurrumul could record his second album and work towards the completion of his third album; grateful that he had the chance — and so many black Australians never get this chance — to fulfil his manifest destiny; that he could continue to enrich the National Cultural Estate. Oh, and simply grateful that a bloke like Gurrumul is still with us, even if he were to hang up his guitar and take up fly-fishing. We're a better country with him amongst us.

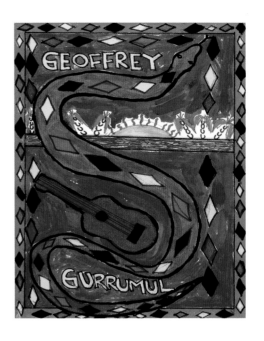

When Gurrumul's first album Gurrumul *went Platinum,*
Skinnyfish thought it a nice idea to get the community involved in
designing the artwork for the Platinum sales plaque, so the kids from
Shepherdson College on Galiwin'ku were invited to come up with
some paintings Skinnyfish could choose from. They were overwhelmed
with artworks. The Sony ATV office in Sydney now has a Gurrumul
Platinum plaque with artwork from the children of Elcho Island
sitting next to plaques for Silverchair and Angus and Julia Stone.
Here is a selection from those artworks done by the children of
Shepherdson College.

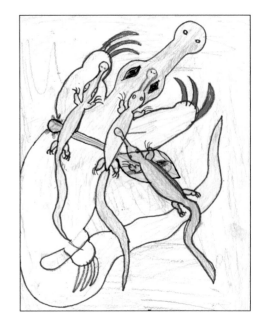

CHAPTER 18

Blue Mountains to London

The film clip for 'Sing' takes in locations up and down the Commonwealth, and even though Gurrumul could have produced a ravishing vocal if he'd been recorded in a coal cellar, the Blue Mountains provide a visual that viewers will swoon over.

The suggestion of Gurrumul's inclusion in the concert comes from the Palace. Gurrumul must have made an impression on the Queen when he met her in October 2011. He was the sole performer at a reception for her and Prince Phillip at Parliament House in Canberra. The invitation isn't conveyed by the Palace, however, but by the Prime Minister's Department in Canberra. The man who will soon be in touch is the organiser of the whole concert extravaganza, Gary Barlow, one of the go-to guys of the British pop industry. He's a warm and generous fellow, Gary Barlow, and apart from these attractive qualities, he brings an almost boyish zeal to the job.

It's that zeal that entices Michael and Gurrumul down from the tropics to the Blue Mountains west of Sydney for a recording session with Barlow. Picture Gurrumul sitting on a peak near the Three Sisters with a shawl around his shoulders (it's testingly chilly for a Territorian at any altitude above fifty metres) and a fabulous vista before him. A camera crew from the BBC is filming Barlow for a documentary that follows him to all sorts of latitudes as he gathers together the voices for the 'Sing' anthem he's composed with Andrew Lloyd Webber. This is to be the song that will feature as the centrepiece of the Diamond Jubilee Concert, and Barlow is here today with the BBC crew to capture Gurrumul's contribution for the single that will go on sale before the concert. He's brimming with enthusiasm for this thrilling voice of Gurrumul's.

Gurrumul is perfectly content with his accomplishments as an artist and doesn't suffer from the insecurity that plagues so many performers, forever craving endorsement.

WUKUN

Y..o Wukuṉ ŋal'ŋalyunmin. dharayirryirryuwan Dharapinda
Dhawal mukthuwan Gayku Mawuymana Watharrakarr
Djunuuŋguṉu

Waywayyuwan Djarraraṉ Milbuṉpuṉ, Yarawarrtji Yarrawarṉura
Gaḻtjurrwanŋu Wurrumba, Ṉukuṉuku Mäminŋu

Wukuṉ ŋal'ŋalyunmin, wukuŋdhu dhawal galmuwan
Mayawungarri Mayawuku Galapunbarri mala-wuḻkthuwan
wukuṉ

Yä mäḻuwana, yä märiwana,
nhalpiyan wukuṉ mala-wuḻkthuwan. dharayirryirryuwan
Dharapinda

Waywayyuwan wukuŋdhu wirilgalapuwan
dhawal rakaran Gaḏapaltjiwa
Gaḏapalŋura Yiwurṉa, Gawunŋura Ḏambawili

Waywayyuwan Mali-Wotjawuynha, Gapinynha Dharrapaŋannha
Bulurruma Galthaḏikpa. Milmari Ganambarrnha

Yä mäḻuwana, yä märiwana
nhalpiyan wukuṉ mala-wuḻkthuwan. Dharayirryirryuwan
Dharapinda
Yä

Y..o Storm clouds rising, storm clouds forming*
The country is still, Gayku Mawuymana Watharrakarr
Djunuŋguṉu

Heading to Djarraraṉ Milbuṉpuṉ, Yarawarrtji Yarrawarṉura**
Gaḻtjurrwanŋu Wurrumba, Ṉukuṉuku Mäminŋu

Storm clouds rising, storm clouds covering the land
Storm clouds Mayawungarri Mayawuku Galapunbarri
separating

Oh my fathers, oh my grandparents
storm clouds why do you separate, why do you form?

Storm clouds covering the country, heading towards
saying, to the country of Gaḏapaltji
Gaḏapalŋura Yiwurṉa, Gawunŋura Ḏambawili

Heading towards the Mali-Wotjawuy, Gapiny Dharrapaŋan
Bulurruma Galthaḏikpa. Milmari Ganambarr nations

Oh my father, oh my grandparents
storm clouds why do you separate, why do you form?
o..h

*The Wukuṉ storm clouds are images of Gurrumul's
mother, the Gälpu people.
** Gälpu nation seas

Michael Hohnen: 'Ten years ago Gurrumul came into the Skinnyfish office really excited
to play me this song. He sat at the keyboard until he found the beat, then he found some
piano chords. But he first presented "Wukun" to me as a really groovy, cool thing, and he
had this beat going, like dum, dum, pow, dum, dum — and he had this piano riff going,
very modern and groovy, sort of funky, and then he sang those "Wukun" lyrics over the
top. Not at all the version we put on the solo album.'
      This is the definitive Gurrumul heart-song, and the album's greatest individual
accomplishment. The drama and passion of the singing perfectly enacts the drama
of the lyrics, which tell of the massing of storm clouds, themselves embodying the
mother-spirits of the Gumatj people, on their journey over land and sea.
The mother-clouds bring generation. The song celebrates their power and,
one might also say, their law.

Nonetheless, it's touching to him that Barlow, in a trip that's taken him all over the globe, has made this day in the mountains a priority. Gurrumul isn't likely, ever, to signal with a high five and a broad smile that he enjoys your company; it's not his way, and he is, in any case, subtle with signals of any sort. But he likes Gary Barlow and he shows it, quietly.

Barlow has been fashioning what will unfold on the day of the Jubilee Concert for almost two years, working closely with Buckingham Palace. In the planning of the Diamond Jubilee celebrations and tours — the hundreds of events that go into the behemoth roadshow — nothing is left to chance; the planning rivals the preparations for D-Day. Before this session in the mountains, Barlow would have listened to Gurrumul's albums, studied film clips, and sketched in the role that Gurrumul will play on the day. 'Sing' is to be a panorama of the Commonwealth, with vernacular voices such as Gurrumul's blending with the polished sound of the Military Wives choristers and the pop contributions of the great and near-great. The film clip for 'Sing' takes in locations up and down the Commonwealth, and even though Gurrumul could have produced a ravishing vocal if he'd been recorded in a coal cellar, the Blue Mountains provide a visual that viewers will swoon over.

Gurrumul, seated maybe a little precariously on the lip of a cliff, sings a verse of 'Bäpa' just to test the acoustics of his mountain perch. Barlow, hunched over his laptop as the images come through, speaks to the off-camera mic: 'It's not a big voice, fairly high, but oh so passionate!' Now Gurrumul tries out the lines he's devised for his 'Sing' contribution, and yes, they work perfectly. This fair-haired fellow from Cheshire with a string of singable hits behind him is shaking his head in time to the Gumatj lyrics, even trying out phrases himself. Then: 'Yes, yes, that's good, it's good!'

The day's filming and recording comes to a close with the forested peaks of the Blue Mountains — the traditional home of the Gundungurra people — throwing a blurry silhouette against the autumn sky. It's a day that yields rewards for everyone. Gary Barlow is confirmed in his decision to give Gurrumul more to do on concert day than simply strum his guitar; Gurrumul has spent hours in company he enjoys, and Michael has been spared the awkwardness of playing the double bass on the edge of a precipice. The film clip will show Gurrumul, solo, sending his voice out over the valley.

The Skinnyfish contingent of Michael, Gurrumul, Bronwyn and Skinnyfish's new general manager, Penny Arrow, arrives in London five days before the Jubilee Concert and takes up a billet at The Gore, a boutique hotel on Queen's Gate just down from Kensington Gardens and Hyde Park. It's in the heart of the museum precinct, with the Victoria and Albert Museum, the Museum of Instruments, the Science Museum and the Natural History Museum a couple of minutes' walk away. Handy for sightseers, of course; not of much benefit to Gurrumul, unless he visits with Bronwyn. The concert site itself, outside Buckingham Palace, is a short hike down Kensington Road past the Royal Albert Hall, along Knightsbridge to Constitution Hill.

Penny Arrow, the Skinnyfish chatelaine, in charge of a hundred things at any given time, has made sure that Gurrumul and Michael understand the protocols of address for the people they're about to meet: 'The Queen — always "Your Majesty" on first meeting, and thereafter, "Ma'am" (and "Ma'am" is spoken as if it rhymes with "jam" and not, as some people imagine, with "farm"); the Duke of Edinburgh: "Your Royal Highness" on first meeting, and thereafter, "Sir"; other members of the Royal Family (Prince Charles, maybe; Princess Anne) "Your Royal Highness"; the Governor-General: "Your Excellency" on first meeting, then, "Governor-

Two national icons.

Warming up in the studio.
Above: The reading room at the Gore Hotel
(Gurrumul's favourite hotel in London).

General"; and the Governor-General's husband, that's Mr Bryce: "Your Excellency" on first meeting, then, "Mr Bryce". Finally, the High Commissioner in London — "Your Excellency" — the same as the Governor-General and her husband, then, "John" or "Mr Dauth".'

Penny also has a printed sheet of polite advice for the dignitaries Gurrumul will meet — actually, it's polite advice for everyone, whether they've been born great, achieved greatness, or had greatness thrust upon them:

Gurrumul is very shy and has a limited command of English. He may not say much at all — feel free to converse but it may be Michael Hohnen who 'speaks for him'. Bronwyn is also very shy and may not say much. Both Gurrumul and Bronwyn will listen to you, take it all in and enjoy the opportunity to meet. One further point: as Gurrumul is blind, he can't see a hand that is put out to shake his. His carers are usually there to facilitate handshakes. It may seem very obvious but it is extraordinary how many times people know he is blind but forget that he can't see a hand to shake — which can cause a moment of awkwardness for the person meeting Gurrumul.

Gurrumul's hair and fingernails are clipped and snipped, but there is a need for a new smart suit. At his most recent meeting with Queen Elizabeth in Canberra last year, he and Michael hired identical dark suits. Now he wants something even more handsomely tailored.

'Same colour,' he tells Michael, Penny and Bronwyn, who have taken his measurements and will handle the shopping while he waits at The Gore.

'Same colour as the other suit?' says Michael.

'Same colour.'

'Yellow shirt?'

'Yellow shirt, yeah.'

'Yellow tie?'

'Yellow shirt, yellow tie.'

Gurrumul is not able to 'see' colours at all. But he does. And he has a special place in his heart for yellow, since it's his clan colour.

'Handkerchief?' says Gurrumul.

'Pocket handkerchief to go with the suit?'

'Yeah, yellow one,' says Gurrumul.

Michael and Penny have the option of strolling down to Jermyn Street, where the suits start at about two thousand sterling, or popping into Marks and Spencer on High Street Kensington, where the suits start at … well, less than two thousand. Marks and Sparks it is.

Or isn't. Amongst the many fine suits at Marks and Sparks, there's not one that would be guaranteed to please Gurrumul. But further down High Street, an Italian tailor has just the thing — conservative, but suave. Bronwyn locates the requisite pocket handkerchief, ties and shirts in the requisite Gumatj yellow, and everybody's happy.

Except that Gurrumul's suit, once tried on at the hotel, is a fraction too long in the leg. Gurrumul expresses doubts about appearing in public in such a garment. The trousers must be altered, and right now, because the whole of London will close down for the four-day Jubilee in maybe thirty minutes.

It's Penny's mission to dash down to the Italian tailor's shop and have the trousers shortened. Taxi or sprint? Sprint. Only there's a hiccup, as there must be — the tailor has gone home. Penny is directed to a second shop, further up High Street, but the duty tailor there has also departed. A very poor work ethic amongst the tailors of London on this particular day. A third shop is suggested, this one in Gloucester Road, back down Queen's Gate. Penny sprints to the door of the third shop, where she's told that the trousers can indeed be altered, but only in the fullness of time.

'But it's for the Queen!' says Penny.

'For the Queen?'

'For Gurrumul! He's singing for the Queen!'

The tailor of Gloucester Road is a patriot. Without a further word, he sets to work with needle and thread.

All's well that ends well, or what you will.

Gurrumul's relish of bananas plays a crucial role in his satisfaction when he's touring. In London, it becomes Penny's task — one of a great number — to keep Gurrumul in bananas, and the banana must be the Cavendish. Lady Fingers, Mysores, Red Daccas, Williams Hybrids, Ducasses, Goldfingers, Senoritas — no. Only Cavendish. As for the stage of ripeness, Michael has educated himself to judge the prescribed degree of banana maturity by smell. Penny, a novice when it comes to establishing the aromatic status of a Cavendish banana, does the best she can.

In London you have the Underground, and you need it if you're schlepping for Gurrumul. The hotel is close to High Street Kensington, shops everywhere, but can any of these shops be relied on to stock the hair oil and body oil favoured by Gurrumul? Penny and Michael are in and out of the shops along High Street and Gloucester Road, pleading for understanding. No, no, didn't I make myself clear? — it must be such-and-such hair oil and such-and-such body oil! But there's no such-and-such hair or body oil in London, and Michael is a worried man. Without this particular hair oil, Gurrumul will be reluctant to leave the hotel room. This isn't fussiness; it's just Gurrumul's thing. Michael purchases a product that is as close in gorgeousness to Gurrumul's favourite oil as he can find, and keeps his fingers crossed.

'I looked everywhere, *wäwa*. Everywhere. This one is very close to your favourite. Very, very close.'

With misgivings, Gurrumul applies the substitute product, and what do you know? He approves. He more than approves; he sends Michael back to the shop to purchase the entire stock of this new product to take back to Elcho. That old product, such-and-such — rubbish. Forget it.

The people who danced attendance on Maria Callas in her glory days knew what it meant to displease a diva. Tantrums, threats, shrieks — you had to suck it up, and postpone to a more convenient time your urgent desire to end your life. Gurrumul might test the patience of Michael, Penny and Mark at times, but he's no Maria Callas. He doesn't think of himself as a superstar and what ego he has is kept for his art. Many of the errands that are run for him are explained by his blindness. He can't cruise High Street Kensington looking for body oil or hair oil. In his relationship with Michael, Mark and Penny, he has been allowed to develop a dependency on his friends. His whole life has a theme of dependency — how could it be otherwise? Michael, Mark and Penny are not lackeys, and

*The intense concentration on Gurrumul's
face reveals a capacity to be minutely aware of
everything that is going on around him.*

Gurrumul isn't a tyrant, but a humble man with needs he cannot service himself.

That said, Gurrumul does possess an almost supernatural knack for anticipating the moment at which his friends will have a free moment between tasks, and for filling up the free moment with requests:

'Penny, Penny, souvenirs — London things. Okay? Maybe a hat and a T-shirt. Yellow ones, flag of England on them, "London" here across the front.'

And Penny: 'No problem. But I'll just finish what I'm doing first. That's okay? When I finish this?'

'Maybe go now, Penny. I'll forget. Go now.'

'Now? Right now? This very minute?'

'Yeah, better go now, Penny.'

And Penny goes, as she must. Until she has that hat and T-shirt, Gurrumul won't be able to concentrate on a damned thing, and he needs to concentrate. London is the Jubilee Concert, yes, but there are a number of other events and appearances to negotiate before Buckingham Palace. Michael and Gurrumul have to get themselves up to BBC Manchester for a breakfast show, then there's the sound check at the concert site, another television date, and an invitation to Stoke Lodge, the Governor-General's residence.

The Governor-General's invitation has a significance that goes beyond vice-regal courtesy. Quentin Bryce has visited Elcho a number of times over the years. She requests a personal few minutes with Gurrumul before the reception at Stoke, during which she tells him about her close relationships with many of the older women on Elcho, most of whom have passed away now. A bond is formed. Gurrumul offers to sing for her; she is touched and delighted. As Penny goes over the schedule with Gurrumul in the hotel room, filling him in on the Governor-General's vice-regal role in the Australian political system, he remarks that women ('*miyalk*' in Yolŋu) have scored all the high-status positions in the Wide Brown Land: Elizabeth II is Queen of Australia; Quentin Bryce is Governor-General, and Julia Gillard is Prime Minister. Any roles left for blokes? 'Me and the Pope, we have to busk on the street to go make some money,' he says.

The minute you step out of your hotel in London, you're sightseeing. London, like Elcho and Arnhem Land, seethes with spirits and stories and sites of wonder. No songlines, but narrative threads that wend their way from Tower Hill to Hyde Park, down through Westminster to the Thames, across the river to Lambeth. If Gurrumul wished to, he could visit any number of sites in London that have as much relevance for his people as they would for a British tourist, including the Museum of Mankind down at Burlington Gardens and the British Museum up in Bloomsbury where items crafted by Indigenous Australians are kept on display.

But sightseeing is not for Gurrumul. What he does enjoy is sitting on the floor of his hotel room with Bronwyn, up close to the telly, listening to the BBC presenters describing the pageantry of the Jubilee celebrations; the vast armada of boats and barges powering down the Thames. When we say that Gurrumul is sightless, it's true, of course, but at the same time it's not. A drama of a sort we could not possibly understand is unfolding in his mind as he sits turning his head left and right, up and down, fashioning from what he can hear images that are perhaps not really images but which satisfy him maybe more than any image could.

Another viewing highlight is Gary Barlow's documentary *On Her Majesty's Service*. The clip of Gurrumul in the Blue Mountains is right there in the short montage that plays over the song in the promo video, and stills from the promo have made it into all the British newspapers. Gurrumul's part in the promo is brief, but compelling: a charismatic black Australian singing his heart out for the Queen with the mountains and the blue sky all around him. People adore it. At one point in the doco, Gary Barlow is at the palace chatting about the concert with the Queen and happens to mention Gurrumul. 'Oh yes,' says Her Majesty, 'I know that man.' That's the part that most moves Gurrumul. When the doco comes out on DVD, that little byte is bound to go into high rotation on Elcho Island.

Gurrumul is content and happy. Penny and Michael have noticed from the very start of this Jubilee journey that his smiles linger longer; he gives out little yelps of pleasure; he jokes and japes; and there's vitality in his demeanour. When he's healthy and well, Gurrumul's a contented man, not given to brooding and, here in London, carried along by the current of Jubilee glee that runs all through the great city, he's the healthiest he's been in years; bubbling with it. It does Penny and Michael a lot of good to be with him when he's up in this way. He's a loveable man at any time but especially so when he's happy.

The Australian media is all over the Jubilee, and in particular demand is the Aussie contingent of Kylie Minogue, Rolf Harris and Gurrumul. The Channel 10 folk seize on Gurrumul and Michael wandering about outside Kensington Palace, the humble London home, at one time, of Princess Di. Gurrumul, no sightseer, nevertheless wanted to stand outside Kensington Palace; Princess Di was his favourite member of the royal family. Gurrumul's dressed in his woolly winter overcoat, notwithstanding the season in London being summer. Michael tells the camera of Gurrumul's devotion to the Queen and to Princess Di, a devotion shared by his family back on Elcho. After the interview, an American tourist who'd seen Gurrumul on the BBC a day earlier hurries over to say howdy. Gurrumul gives a big smile in response. His pleasure has nothing at all to do with the gratification of ego; he's simply touched by the American's good manners in approaching him. It's what the people he knows on Elcho would do; shake the hand of someone they saw on the telly.

Michael and Gurrumul have two BBC dates to honour before the concert. The first takes them way up the M6 to BBC Manchester for a *Breakfast* interview with Charlie Stayt and Louise Minchin on the much-satirised red sofa. Gurrumul sits impassive throughout the interview, while Michael, extended along the sofa, either highly relaxed or in excruciating discomfort, answers all the questions. This way in which Michael takes on the role of psychic amanuensis for Gurrumul can seem a little peculiar to some people, as if he's listening to his friend's thoughts and summarising them aloud. But it is, in fact, the most natural continuation of their relationship. Gurrumul's interest in talking about himself, his motives, even his music to a broadcaster is so slight as to barely exist at all. There's an unspoken agreement between Michael and his friend that all public tasks (and some private ones) thought of as tedious by Gurrumul will be handled by Michael. Everything Gurrumul has to say about himself and his music is expressed in his songs. Think of Beethoven who, when once asked by a patron to explain what a newly composed piece he was playing on the piano meant, replied: 'Oh did you not understand it? Here, I'll play it again.'

The second telly appearance is on the BBC's *Andrew Marr Show*, a Sunday morning gig the day before the concert. Andew Marr is the baritone BBC presenter who hosted the four-part

BBC series on the reign of the Queen, a chap who plays a good, straight bat. To obviate any lengthy explanation of why it is that Michael does all the talking, he simply announces: 'Gurrumul doesn't speak English.' Gurrumul has chosen to perform for the BBC Sunday audience two verses of 'Mala Rrakala', a song from his second album, *Rrakala*. It's a contemplative song, easy to embrace, and goes down well with the studio audience. Gurrumul is wearing his venerable zip-up vinyl jacket, saving his new suit's first outing for Her Majesty's Eyes Only.

The final dress rehearsal and sound check for the Jubilee Concert brings all of the performers together in a relaxed, chattering way. The small army of performers is supported by a second small army of technicians; both armies crossing paths backstage. Michael keeps Gurrumul's hand under his arm as he negotiates the crowded, off-stage areas of this wondrous construction around the Queen Victoria Memorial. Tents and marquees that serve as auxiliary dressing rooms and catering sites spill over into the precincts of Green Park and St James's Park, the whole assemblage so like a fairground that you expect to see tumblers and jugglers and fire-eaters rehearsing around every corner. Instead, you see the kids of the African Children's Choir giggling and grinning; the thirteen members of the Kenyan Slum Drummers band, with their vernacular instruments, preparing for the biggest gig of their lives; the ladies of the Military Wives choir dissolving into OMGs and gasps of delight whenever they catch sight of a star like Elton or Tom Jones.

Gurrumul hopes to meet some of the stars himself, Stevie Wonder above all, another blind, black musical genius. Gurrumul is twenty years younger than his hero, so he's been responding to Stevie Wonder as a mature, acclaimed performer for the whole of his life. It's Stevie Wonder's music that means the most to Gurrumul, but the fact that a man blind almost from birth could achieve so much has been an inspiration. It won't be until concert day itself that he'll have the chance to meet a few of his idols.

Meanwhile, he's relaxed. He's used to people hurrying about with an event to organise. Maybe he's also picking up on the vibe of ceremony at the venue. Because what he's taking part in tomorrow is in fact a ceremony, not a concert, a protracted outpouring of praise for a tribal elder with a dynastic link to other elders going back two hundred years, concluding with a ritual chant: 'God Save the Queen'. It's this honouring of ceremony that attracts Indigenous Australians to the Queen. Gurrumul sees past all the hoopla to the familiar features of ritual beyond.

Andrew Lloyd Webber's grand piano is hoisted onto the stage, then the strange and wonderful building-site timpani of the Slum Drummers, and now Gary Barlow's keyboard. Gary himself makes his appearance once all those on stage are settled in their chorus positions. This is the first time many of the performers have seen him since the filming of the promo for 'Sing', but everyone remembers his warmth and his charm. Gary wends his way to Gurrumul seated amongst the legion of performers and thanks him for being here — a gesture that in its intimacy elates Gurrumul. Cheering breaks out as Gary turns to face the performers. He acknowledges the applause, then raises his hands for shush. He has an announcement to make: 'Sing' has just taken the number one spot on the charts. And the cheers are renewed.

London is sound, motion and aroma to Gurrumul, but for Bronwyn, it has the additional visual dimension to enjoy when she strolls out with Penny for a tour of the city's attractions. It's vital

Only a phone call away

Gurrumul has to be in a position to talk with everyone on Elcho at any hour of the day or night. Michael has made it a priority, over the years of touring, to purchase a local SIM card immediately on arrival in a city, and to seek out sites at which it can be topped up. Connections to Gurrumul's family on Elcho can run for hours, almost as if he had invited his mother and father, his aunties, uncles and brothers into the hotel room and were sitting with them discussing family matters. Or if not family matters, making arrangements for charter flights to and from Elcho or Darwin. It's not uncommon for a family member to call him up in Beijing or Paris at some insane hour of the night needing a taxi from Nightcliff to Stuart Park, and Gurrumul then arranges the cab with the help of Mark or Michael or Penny. None of this is thought of as an imposition on Gurrumul; for him, it's a deeply honoured obligation. When Gurrumul travels, he travels with his family, with his clan, with his tribe, with his culture. He needs that comfort, and his family needs the reassurance of his voice. The culture of the Gumati has its foundation in the intimacy of physical presence. A man alone, isolated from his family, from his that Bronwyn is not left to languish in a hotel room, because if she becomes bored, Gurrumul loses focus, loses enthusiasm, and can't think of anything but sweetening Bronwyn's mood. It's not that Bronwyn is especially temperamental; any partner of either gender would begin to fray on tour if she or he felt underemployed. No man is a hero to his valet, so it's said; and in something of the same way, no performer is a god to his partner or her partner. Bronwyn has seen Gurrumul in performance countless times and is happy to miss the rehearsal at the concert site in favour of … well, the London Eye, for starters, then Hyde Park. The ducks on The Serpentine attract Bronwyn's attention especially, because, as she tells Penny, 'On Elcho, we eat them.' Later, in the Aquarium, Bronwyn homes in on the stingrays and octopuses, special mealtime favourites of coastal-dwelling Indigenous folk. 'Oh yes, we love them on Elcho.'

You can't help thinking when you look at Bronwyn's responses to London that what we see is what our culture teaches us to see. Mark Grose tells a story of some Gumatj friends he accompanied to the art gallery in Darwin. His friends barely spared a glance for anything in the gallery, but stood transfixed and delighted before two bark paintings from Elcho. Later, Mark's friends spoke in an animated way of the bark paintings in all their detail but had no memory of anything else in the gallery.

Michael and Gurrumul turn up at Stoke Lodge in their identical suits, yellow shirts and ties, looking like members of a most unlikely Temptations cover band. The Governor-General has asked for a few minutes in private with Gurrumul and Michael before the ceremony. A little later, Gurrumul and Michael perform two songs, 'Bäpa' and 'Djilawurr', for the small gathering of twenty-five. If Gurrumul can move an audience of three or four thousand to tears in a cavernous concert hall, imagine the impact of these two songs in a drawing room. For most of those attending, this is the first experience of Gurrumul's way with a song; a revelation, of sorts.

The Governor-General's short speech at the end of the performance is, in its essence, a personal and deeply felt endorsement of the reconciliation of black and white Australians, underway for some time now. She speaks of the Jubilee celebrations all across Britain, but moves quickly to the 'uplifting, haunting, beautiful music' that Gurrumul and Michael have just provided, '… music that reaches into our souls … He brings us great pride in our nation's Indigenous culture and heritage.' At the conclusion of the Governor-General's speech, Gurrumul shows his thanks and appreciation in a way that is very rare for him: he applauds.

CHAPTER 19

Jubilee

'Yes,' says the Queen. 'I've already met this man.
He played for me in Australia.'

Andrew Lloyd Webber at the piano; a stage constructed along the lines of an Art Deco starship; maybe two hundred voices raised in a hymn of praise for Queen Elizabeth. Yes, 'extravagant' will describe it. Gurrumul is at the heart of it all, a vision of elegance in his new black suit, yellow shirt and tie. His guitar across his lap, he raises his head to contribute his lines of Gumatj to the tribute, looking as if there's nowhere in the wide world he'd rather be at this moment, wrapped in the joy of the event. He can't see the countless thousands of Union Jacks held aloft, and he can't see how far the crowd reaches — all the way down The Mall to Admiralty Arch, seventy thousand people in total. But he knows exactly how big an occasion this is, the Jubilee Concert, and that his family back on Elcho are watching, maybe at this instant shrieking: 'It's him!' Rolf is on the bill, and Kylie, but Gurrumul is the only other Australian. This concert crowns a year of achievement for him, but he's well aware that today's date could so easily have marked the first anniversary of his death, so dire was the state of his health this time last year in 2011. Now he's fit and well, and must feel that the spirits that minister to his people have rallied to reprieve him. Perhaps more than at any other time in his life, he has reason to feel blessed. On top of everything, he's on the bill with Cliff Richard, the great favourite of his family, and with Stevie Wonder, whom he adores. Does it get any better than this?

It's a concert evening request: would Stevie Wonder in a moment of leisure be prepared to say hello to Geoffrey Gurrumul Yunupiŋu, because Gurrumul would love to meet him? In the meantime, Gurrumul gets to have his picture taken with Cliff Richard, the idol of his family back on Elcho. Here's the performer will.i.am, a Gurrumul fan and himself a favourite of Gurrumul's, with kind words to say. More kind words come from other performers who know of Gurrumul even if they haven't met him before. Gurrumul sits in one of the many

BAYWARA

I heard my mother
from the long distance
making me cry yä ŋänd..i

Mother dreaming
storm clouds building across the sky
wo..o, murryun wäŋa ŋupan

The place was changing
for the new season
yambaṯthun dhawalyu wirrpaŋuya

Yä my mother, Baywara
you are creator, yä ŋänḏi

Ḻikandja ŋänḏi walala, Guṉdjuḻpurr
Buliyaŋu Dhawu-Minydjalpi
m..m

Wiripunydja ḻikan ŋänḏi Guwarruku
Baḻpaḻuna, Mämbila, m..m
Wiripunydja ḻikan ŋänḏi Wandjuḏupa
Gapu-waḻkaḻmirri, Nuŋguritjmarra,
m..m

Wiripunydja ḻikan, ŋänḏi Dhämayi
Waŋarrthuḻa mala Birritjama
M..m

Yä my mother, Baywara
You are creator, yä ŋänḏi
Yä my mother, Baywara
You are Creator, yä ŋänḏi

I heard my mother
from the long distance
making me cry oh mother

Mother dreaming
storm clouds building across the sky
W..o thunder spreading across the land

The place was changing
for the new season
spreading to the ancestral places

Yä my mother, Baywara
You are creator, oh mother

Connection to all my mothers, to
Guṉdjuḻpurr, and Buliyaŋu Dhawu-Minydjalpi
m..m

And connections to more mothers
Guwarruku Baḻpaḻuna, Mämbila m..m
Other mother connections, to
Wandjuḏupa Gapu-waḻkaḻmirri, Nuŋguritjmarra
m..m

And other connections to mothers at Dhämayi
Waŋarrthuḻa mala Birritjama
m..m

Yä my mother, Baywara
You are creator, oh mother
Yä my mother, Baywara
You are Creator, oh mother

A tribute song, not honouring Gurrumul's biological mother alone, but everything maternal, including mother ancestors, and the spirit of generation. Traditionally it's a very important song, with many references to what is held sacred amongst the Gumatj. It's co-written by Manuel Ŋulupani Dhurrkay, the jaunty lead vocalist from Saltwater. 'Baywara' departs from the other songs on the album in its embrace of pop, which perhaps explains its great appeal to listeners out in the bush, who relish the sentiment and the rhythm.

greenrooms, waiting for the Wonder summons, and when it comes he's out of his chair as if ejected from the cockpit of a jet.

Stevie's at a keyboard in his dressing room, doodling and sketching in the way an artist would if he worked with pencils and crayons rather than musical notes. Stevie, nudging into his sixties now, a man of ample physique, his head crowned with braids, continues to amuse himself at the keyboard while he chats amicably with Gurrumul. You might think after all this anticipation that our guy has a hundred questions ready, but no — not a one. Stevie chatters on, accompanying himself, perfectly aware that Gurrumul is standing there too shy to speak. So strange! — these two blind men of seething creativity, neither able to see the other, each contented with a rapport that goes beyond anything that sight would have provided.

On the way out of the dressing room, Michael and Gurrumul walk into the warm embrace of Elton John, who knows Gurrumul and his music, and remembers him from a concert in Darwin a few years earlier when Gurrumul played between the support act and Elton's own appearance. Elton says: 'I'm a big fan of yours, Gurrumul. That first album of yours — I have it. You're amazing — really an amazing musician.' Now Paul McCartney finds his way through the milling throng to add his praise, and by this time, Gurrumul must be floating — or maybe not.

His culture doesn't fashion heroes in the manner of many other cultures. You may build a tower to heaven stone by stone, but you'll still be thought of as one man in a clan, one man in a family. Gurrumul's shyness is partly explained by this lack of a praise structure in his culture. A quiet word of affirmation from his mother, from his aunties — yes, that he can place. He enjoys meeting the musicians he admires, but he never fishes for endorsement from them; never hopes or expects to get a boost to his ego through association. It's a personal thing, as if he were saying something as simple and sincere as: 'I like what you do.'

Robbie Williams and the Coldstream Guards; will.i.am and Jessie J; Lang Lang tickling the ivories; Sir Cliff still brisk at seventy; Alfie Boe hitting the high notes; and Gary Barlow, as if he didn't have enough on his plate, in a love duet with Cheryl Cole. Then Grace Jones takes centre stage in a crimson headdress, looking like the consort of Ming the Merciless in the Flash Gordon comics. The deco-influenced art of Flash Gordon's creator, Alex Raymond, could well have been the inspiration for the entire space-age Jubilee stage. Grace is swinging a circus-grade hoop around her waist while she sings, and she intends to keep it up for the duration of her number. The performers who preceded Grace regaled the audience in a like way (save for the hoop), and those who follow her will keep it up. Fireworks, acrobatics and dynamic dance steps will take the place of hoops, but essentially the concert fare for the evening is defined by Grace's act: a lot of razzle, a lot of dazzle and a certain amount of just plain exuberance.

But as was suggested, this is more a ceremony of tribute replete with ritual elements than a concert. Gurrumul's role this evening is to represent the native genius of Australia's Indigenous people. He's a serious musician, and so are the other performers appearing tonight, but it isn't intended that the audience should go away thinking of individual triumphs; the underlying message of the spectacle is the thing.

The Queen arrives and takes her place in the Royal Box in time for the central anthem of the evening's performance — 'Sing'. Any anthem is, in its essence, an oath of loyalty set to music.

But to suit our times, Gary Barlow's lyrics substitute an avowal of love in place of any promise to obey and serve. And this suits a twenty-first-century audience just fine. When the chorus sings, 'So hear a thousand voices shouting love ...', everyone knows that the love is intended for the Queen, while at the same time the song celebrates 'love' as the universal medium of human sympathy. In the climate of the concert, Elizabeth II is both monarch and neo-hippy Earth Mother.

When Gurrumul raises his voice to sing 'Sing', the joy on his face is that of gladness in being part of this huge celebration. The ceremony two years earlier on Elcho Island, attended by fewer people and all of them Yolŋu, Gurrumul sitting still and proud while his mother painted his face and forehead with a substance made from talc and clay — that ceremony took him to a place too remote, too mysterious, for us ever to follow. But we can be sure that Gurrumul is happy to lend himself to the message of goodwill and unity that braces today's Buckingham Palace ceremony.

That suntanned Welshman, Tom Jones, one of the cohort of knights ornamenting the festivities this evening ('Sir Tom, meet Sir Cliff, Sir Cliff, this is Sir Elton, Sir Paul, say hello to Sir Cliff, Sir Tom, Sir Elton and Sir Andrew'), has brought his cheerful song about a murder committed in a jealous rage to a rousing conclusion. Paul McCartney has honoured Commander James Bond, if not the Queen, with 'Live and Let Die'. And now the Queen and Prince Charles have been ushered to the stage by Gary Barlow and Kylie (the Pearly Queen of London an hour earlier). Prince Charles and the Queen take up a position on the stage just in front of Gurrumul and Michael while Charles makes his fine speech of thanks on behalf of Her Majesty. The BBC vision gives us a good long look at Gurrumul appearing about as happy as anyone can recall, and Michael smiling in an ecstacy of pride.

Later, in the backstage area, the Queen is introduced to the performers by Gary Barlow and Kylie. Gary has taken pains to see that Kylie remembers to include Gurrumul on her list. 'Your Majesty,' says Kylie, 'this is Gurrumul, a special voice from Australia ...'

'Yes,' says the Queen. 'I've already met this man. He played for me in Australia.'

So he did. If you've heard that 'special voice from Australia' you're unlikely to forget it. Perhaps the Jubilee Concert will enhance the respect in the rest of the world for Gurrumul and for all Indigenous Australians. Few things make people more curious about a race they know so little about than the art of these strangers. The paintings of Indigenous Australians have excited wonder and enchantment for decades, now Gurrumul's music is poised to reveal more widely a further dimension of Indigenous genius.

THE DIAMON

The Diamond Jubilee kiss, with Gurrumul in the background 'jealousing' Her Majesty's gold coat.

Another interview. This time in front of Kensington Palace.

Celebrity time with Sir Cliff Richard backstage after his Brisbane concert.
Opposite: Stevie Wonder backstage at the Queen's Diamond Jubilee in London; Sir Elton John and Rolf Harris backstage at the Queen's Diamond Jubilee in London; Olivia Newton-John at the Waldorf Astoria.

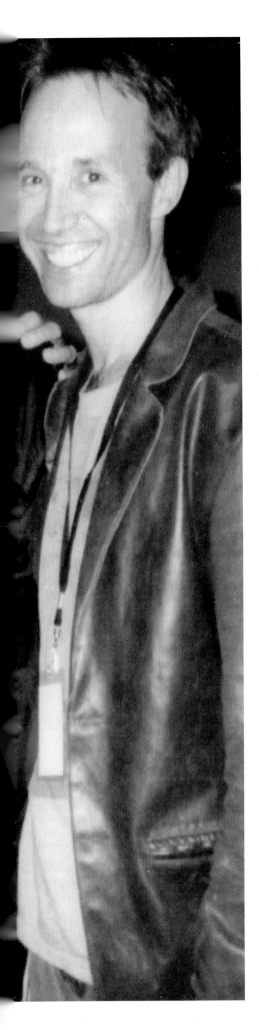

4

ON RECORD

CHAPTER 20

Yothu Yindi

This was the first time the people of north-east Arnhem Land had seen their brothers, cousins, sons and daughters illuminated on the big stage.

Gurrumul had just turned eighteen when Alan James came to the door of his mother's house in Galiwin'ku, introduced himself as the manager of Yothu Yindi, and asked him if he'd like to join the band at very short notice — in fact, immediately. Gurrumul said: 'I'll ask Mum.'

The reason for the haste was that Yothu Yindi's regular drummer had gone AWOL in the middle of a tour. Gurrumul's name was mentioned as a possible replacement; fabulous drummer, lovely bloke. This was opportunity come calling, but if James hadn't found his way to Galiwin'ku on that day in 1989, somebody else would have knocked on the door. Gurrumul had been beating out rhythms on makeshift timpani since childhood, teaching himself chords on a ramshackle guitar and simple tunes on a toy piano. Little by little, he'd mastered better quality versions of each of these instruments. The whole community of Galiwin'ku came to believe that the boy was something special. And Yothu Yindi was family.

When Gurrumul told James, 'I'll ask Mum', he knew that his family's approval couldn't be taken for granted. Vulnerable in his blindness, he relied at that age on those near to him to make all important decisions. The knock on the door had been, in its way, expected, but this wasn't a tour with a gospel band; this was Yothu Yindi. How would a blind boy cope with all that rush and racket? Nobody wanted to hold Gurrumul back, and the family's answer was, 'Yes, go.' But it was an approval hemmed about with misgivings. Rock'n'roll? It was a worry.

Yothu Yindi grew by stages from a happy-go-lucky outfit to a band with a lively political agenda. The Yolŋu wanted to be heard on issues of importance to them — land rights for black Australians, a treaty that acknowledged the reality of Indigenous occupation of the Australian continent going back tens of thousands of years, cultural respect. All of these issues had been spoken of in a politely insistent way for a long time, but the Yothu Yindi people were different

Slim Dusty's early success was based on his popularity amongst Aboriginal people. Who would have guessed then, that the quiet, shy, blind musician in this photo would go on himself to become a successful artist due largely to the support of non-Indigenous Australia.

DJOTARRA

Djotarra warwuyurruna, ŋäthinana	Djotarra thinks, cries
Yumalildja, Guywuyun, djoliŋdhina	Thoughts like the wail of a harmonica
Roŋiyina ŋäthina, Bothalili	Thoughts of departed relatives
Ŋuruŋuna yapinanydhu	Reminded by this setting sun
Wäluŋdhuna, yä ganuru	from this sunset, sad, caring emotions
Djotarra, ... Yumalildja, Guywuyun	Djotarra, thinks, cries inside
Yä ŋäthina Djotarra	Oh, weeping Djotarra

(Ŋäthina warwuyun), ga ŋäthina	(anguishing inside), and crying
(Ŋuruŋuna yapinanydhu), djoliŋdhina	(because of that harmonica), like a harmonica

(Yumalildja guywuyun), Djotarra	(wail of a harmonica), Djotarra
(Djotarra warwuyun), warwuyurruna	(Djotarra, consumed by sadness), worries

Roŋiyina ŋäthina Makarrlili	Crying thinking of home
Dhundhuŋa Djarrimiliyu, Gunyaŋarayu	Dhundhuŋa, Djarrimiliyu, Gunyaŋara
Nhepina, waku ŋäthiya, makarr waltjaṉdhina	You, my mother's grandmother people cry for, remember, your country

Läpurruŋu, Guriniŋu, Wuḻandjarra	
Wu..u, yä ganaru, Djotarra	Land-ancestor-people called Läpurruŋu, Guriniŋu, Wuḻandjarra
Yä Yumalildja, guywuyun	

(ŋäthinana), Djotarra	Oh, thoughts, worrying inside Djotarra
	Oh thoughts like the wails of a mouth organ

(Ŋäthina warwuyurr) ŋäthina	
(Ŋuruŋuna djoliŋdhu) Djoliŋlilnha	Crying, Djotarra

(Ŋäthina Djotarra) yä Djotarra	(anguishing inside), and crying
(Warwuyurr) Warwuyurruna	(because of that), like a mouth organ

Nhepina waku ŋäthiya Guṉitjpirr	(Gumatj woman crying), oh Djotarra
Ŋarakuwu, Guyuḻungu, Baḻmanymirriwu	(Thinking), thinking

Makarrlili Ḏawu-makarr, Wurrwiḏilili	You, my great grandmother's people, cry for your country at Guṉitjpirr
Ŋarranydja Djotarra, ŋäthina	For your soul, your country's soul, Guyuḻun, Baḻmanymirri
(W..o) Ya ganaru, Djotarra (wo..o)	
Yumalildja, Guywuyun	The shade and sheltering place Ḏawumakarr, Wurrwiḏilili
(Wo..o) yä ŋäthina, Djotarra	I, Djotarra cry and worry
	Oh the thoughts, Djotarra
	Thoughts like the cries of a mouth organ
	Oh crying Djotarra

For the Gumatj, home is not only the land they walk but the teeming life buried in the soil. Absent from home, a Gumatj woman ('Djotarra' in Gumatj) pines for the land that sustains her soul. The lyrics of Gurrumul's songs, in keeping with tradition, are not hothouses of invention; it is rare to find metaphoric illustration. But in this song, Gurrumul has compared the woman's thoughts of home with 'the wail of a harmonica'. Whenever he employs metaphors, they are usually drawn from the drama of sound in his life.

— louder, ruder and more exuberant than anyone who'd come before them.

The driving force behind the band's creation was Yolŋu Mändawuy Yunupiŋu, from Yirrkala on the Gove Peninsula. Mändawuy drew together Indigenous and white musicians with enough wherewithal to take contemporary rock hostage and hound it into a marriage with Indigenous music. Keyboard, electric guitars and a four-piece drum kit shared the stage with *bilma* (ironwood clapsticks) and *yidaki*, or didgeridoo, an instrument that hailed from north-east Arnhem Land, where its greatest exponents lived.

Yolŋu men, painted up as if for ceremony, joined the musicians on stage, together with young black women in hip-hugging mini-skirts. This marked the first time that the widely recognised imagery of black Australian culture — painted bodies, a seated figure holding a didgeridoo to his lips, the staccato dance steps of traditional ceremony — had been adapted to suit a stage rock act. Mändawuy and his friends had seized on the inexhaustible resource of rock'n'roll, with all its energy and liberty of expression, and made it the medium of their message. What might have once struck non-Indigenous Australians as vestiges of the primitive — painted black men engaged in some ritual of animal mimicry — suddenly took on the force of revolutionary metaphor. It all amounted to a type of rocket-fuelled corroboree of raucous sound and black agitprop.

Gurrumul's place in all this noise and joy and in-your-face politics was innocent enough. He played the drums when he was on stage (changing to keyboards and guitar later on) and partied without becoming a madman; sometimes he sat about in his motel room listening to the television. His niece Merrkiyawuy (later Dhalulu Ganambarr-Stubbs), who danced with the band but disdained all the extracurricular hedonism, guided Gurrumul about in the way Michael Hohnen would later, and kept him company away from the stage whenever she could. Merrkiyawuy was not the only member of the band who kept Gurrumul close; it was just that she had the greater persistence.

But it was impossible for Gurrumul to remain uninfluenced by the band's leading figures. Mändawuy later confessed that he was regularly putting away two dozen stubbies of beer each day in those early Yothu Yindi years. ('I didn't know what harm it did to my body,' he wrote. 'Before I knew, it was too late.') Other members of the band partied as hard as anyone could while retaining the ability to function up on stage. A big, loud rock band upholds a creed of heroic hedonism; it's an expectation, never more so than in the eighties and nineties. Drink life down to the lees and die pretty. Gurrumul, without much of a taste for grog, nevertheless accepted what was offered. Word filtered back to his family. His mother and his aunties worried that he was being exposed to influences that contradicted their abstemious Methodist beliefs. They had been aware of the danger from the beginning, but they chose to accept the greater benefit of Mändawuy's overarching ambition: to reveal Yolŋu culture to the world, and to demonstrate, with this union of Indigenous and Western music, the bounty of co-operation.

Yothu Yindi travelled all over Australia, playing rousing gigs to audiences of cheering Indigenous kids proud of what they were witnessing, and to white audiences eager to embrace the cause. But not only the cause. Rock'n'roll can never be an essay; it must entertain. Even amidst all the earnest slogans, the Yothu Yindi folk were having the time of their lives. It's no stretch to imagine a Yothu Yindi cover of 'The Times They Are A-Changing', as a blast of coloured smoke and flashing lights with the whole crew coming through on the refrain with an exuberant leap into the air.

Overseas tours took Gurrumul even further from home; first to Papua New Guinea and Hong Kong, which required the approval of his uncle David, his champion in the family. 'He said to me, "Uncle, what do you think? Can I go? What do you think?" I told him to go. I told him to see the world. Of course! Why not?'

The Hong Kong date in 1989 was followed by tours to New Zealand and Europe. This was the Motelville experience: a steady diet of burgers, chips, extra-large soda pop, beers, chocolates, cigarettes — a regime likely to leave you on a respirator within a decade or so. He was rarely neglected in his blindness, but there were periods of loneliness, of homesickness. When Merrkiyawuy wasn't on hand to keep him company, Witiyana Marika, one of the male traditional dancers, sometimes took a turn watching over him. On occasions, though, he sat solitary in a hotel armchair with his guitar on his lap, picking out chords for the sake of it or listening to Dire Straits tapes. When his solo career bloomed many years later, Gurrumul would use up hours of time chatting on his mobile with his family back on Elcho, but there were no mobile phones in 1989, and even if there had been, the budget for a tour that had to provide an income for a dozen people wouldn't have accommodated runaway mobile bills.

Yothu Yindi's emergence as a cultural force in Australian music and politics handily coincided with Australia's 1988 Bicentennial celebrations. Two hundred years of white settlement was not a landmark that a dispossessed people could be expected to embrace. Prime Minister Bob Hawke's visit to the Northern Territory in 1988 included a meeting with Mändawuy and Arrernte artist Wenten Rubuntja, who asked him to accept a carefully written document detailing the grievances and broad political aspirations of Indigenous Australians. One of the Prime Minister's objectives in coming to the Territory was to demonstrate the government's sympathy for the Indigenous cause in the Bicentennial year, but he went further and promised publicly that a comprehensive treaty covering every aspect of black–white relations would be negotiated with Indigenous Australians by 1990. When Gurrumul joined Yothu Yindi in 1989, the loud hosannas of the Bicentennial celebrations were still echoing around the country, and the Prime Minister's treaty promise proved to be more a rush of blood to the head than a considered commitment. Yothu Yindi was the standard bearer of Indigenous protest at the lack of any progress on the treaty.

The personal political beliefs that Gurrumul brought with him to the band were never expressed as forcefully as those of Mändawuy. It was not in his nature to raise his fist in defiance, and slogans bored him. Gurrumul was the most gifted musician in the band and his contribution to the Indigenous cause was to give Yothu Yindi's songs of protest musical clout.

Mark Moffatt, who produced Yothu Yindi's breakthrough *Tribal Voice* of 1991, recalls working closely with Gurrumul on the album at a studio in Balmain, Sydney: 'We spent endless days together doing guitars, vocals, keyboards ... No one knew how great his contribution really was.' Yothu Yindi's big leap forward came with the remix of the 'Treaty' track on *Tribal Voice* — a song that was to become to Indigenous aspiration what Archie Roach's 'Took the Children Away' became to the Stolen Generations. 'I very much doubt that the remix would have been possible without the basic piano sequence I did with Gurrumul,' says Moffatt. Gurrumul's bias is always towards the practical; as a blind man, working within sane limitations is a matter of survival. He couldn't stand at the front of the stage like Mändawuy and hammer out vocals,

Top: Yothu Yindi 'performing' for a promotional photo.
Bottom: Mändawuy Yunupiŋu.

Merrkiyawuy Ganambarr speaking

Gurrumul and I, we joined the band later than most of the others. It was 1989 before we joined. Yothu Yindi was a family band. We were all part of a family. Gumatj are all one family. That's where the name of Yothu Yindi comes from. Mother and child. All of us in the band were 'yindi' — we were the children. That's how Gurrumul and I became part of the band — through family. And we weren't just singing for entertainment. We were singing to educate people, not just nationally but internationally. And we did. But touring was hard work. Hard, hard work. People in Europe, they were interested in us. We were on television in Germany, in a little studio. They'd researched us really well. They wanted to know more, I think. It's true that Yothu Yindi made it easier for Gurrumul's music to be accepted later on. They were interested in the instruments. The didgeridoo — yidaki. Some of the young men in Europe, they took up the didgeridoo, started learning it. Particularly in Germany.

When that second album came out, Tribal Voice, Gurrumul was on that album, we knew that it was going to be really big, and not just for Indigenous people — for non-Indigenous people, too. But I just got the feeling that the federal government, that song 'Treaty' on Tribal Voice put them right on the edge. I got the feeling that they wanted to do something along the lines of stopping it. You know, one year before that song, the federal government was promising a treaty, but then I think they wanted to stop it after that song, 'Treaty'. And we still haven't got a treaty. I don't think we ever will have one, not in my lifetime.

I went to New Zealand on tour with Tracy Chapman, and that was a good experience, but I didn't go to America and Canada. About that time, after two years with Yothu Yindi, I had to think of other things. It's not a very good job in a big band like that, you can't do it forever, touring with ten or eleven people and you're living out of a suitcase and in and out of hotel rooms. I was homesick, too, I missed home and country, I missed going hunting, all that stuff.

I knew Gurrumul before Yothu Yindi, of course. He's my uncle. In the band, I thought he was my responsibility. I was always by his side, helping him onto planes and into taxis, many, many things, always with him. It was a maternal instinct, to look after him, tell him things about where we were when we were touring.

In the band, Gurrumul's role was the drums, and guitar, too, also keyboards. I knew he was an extraordinary musician mostly by listening to his voice. Sometimes he would sing in the hotel, or at the parties after the show. There were always parties after the show, but he was quiet, he was mostly a non-drinker like me, so we would sit and he would play his guitar and sing songs by other artists. Beautiful. Just the voice. So beautiful.

When that first solo album of his came out, I cried. He sings the songs a little bit up, a little bit more contemporary, and that makes them appeal to a white audience. But the expressions he uses in those songs, they're the expressions we use in traditional songs, they're genuine. Those very same words and tunes that Gurrumul uses in his album, they're our traditional songs. People don't have to know what the words mean. All that they listen to is the voice, and the impression that the voice conveys. And when Yolŋu listen to it, we understand every word, and the meaning of every word. It's so powerful, so powerful. Even adults when they listen, they're in tears. And in those songs, there's healing. Healing. You know, we say in our traditional songs, the healing comes when you cry. When you cry. Everyone in the family, they all gather for singing, and the women cry. They cry. And healing comes when you cry. That keening sound that women make is both sorrow and healing. Even white people, balanda, listening to those songs, they cry and they heal.

The 1999 Garma Festival saw Saltwater Band and Yothu Yindi perform on the same stage; it was a milestone event. Gurrumul performed in both bands; even though he had been out of Yothu Yindi for a couple of years he would join the band on special occasions. This was to be Gurrumul's last performance with Yothu Yindi as he moved onto concentrating on Saltwater Band. A changing of the guard moment.

but he could make sure the vocals were supported by something more subtle. His nickname at this time was 'the Guru'.

Back on Elcho the Yothu Yindi experience made Gurrumul a local hero; all of the Yothu Yindi people were heroes. A life on the margins can be demoralising, but it's amazing how quickly morale recovered when Yolŋu people heard voices in their own language listened to with such respect by the Australian community. This was the first time the people of north-east Arnhem Land had seen their brothers, cousins, sons and daughters illuminated on the big stage; the first time that the Yolŋu had enjoyed the flow of culture going the other way, out into the *balanda* community. It was like witnessing the slow awakening of Australia.

The popular and critical success of *Tribal Voice* in 1991 and 1992, taken together with the High Court's Mabo decision in 1992, marked the acceptance of Indigenous rights as a mature political cause in Australian public life. The acclaim for *Tribal Voice* won the band an invitation to New York in 1991 for a performance at the New Music Seminar and drew enough international attention to take Yothu Yindi to Europe in 1992 for an extensive tour. Mändawuy negotiated leave from his position as principal of the Yirrkala School in north-east Arnhem Land to devote himself full-time to music and, although the band's members were likely to number as many as a dozen performers at any given time, the Yothu Yindi creative core, including Gurrumul, seemed settled.

And then it wasn't. Throughout 1992, Gurrumul came under increasing pressure from his family to quit Yothu Yindi. Merrkiyawuy had given up her role as dancer with the band and without her care and company, some of Gurrumul's family members felt that their boy was left lonely on these tours that took him so far from home. Their concern was probably out of proportion to any pangs Gurrumul may have experienced, magnified by the special position he held in the hearts of those who'd cared for him since he was born, but for one reason or another, the family wanted him back in Galiwin'ku. Gurrumul doesn't talk about the crisis at all, but what can be said is that his family's wishes take precedence in any and all decisions he is required to make.

North-east Arnhem Land is infected with a genius that has endured for thousands of years. It is one of those regions of the earth where something potent slumbers and awakens, and at those times of awakening, a spell is cast. In one of Gurrumul's songs, he speaks of a wind that blows and 'makes you clever'. Yothu Yindi might have emerged from anywhere in Australia where Indigenous people congregate — the central deserts, the western cape, the riverine, even from Redfern — but it happened in north-east Arnhem Land, where the wind blows.

If Gurrumul's career had ended when he left Yothu Yindi, he would only be recalled when scholars, studying Indigenous music and politics of the time, shone a light on the contributions of all the individual members. The wind blew, and as of New Year's Day, 1993, Gurrumul was three years and seven months from his first sight of Michael Hohnen, and sixteen years from his own triumphal progress up the charts, his own ARIAs, his own landmark contribution to Australian music. But to Gurrumul, everything that has happened in his life is part of a single, coherent journey. There are no snakes, no ladders, no moments of overwhelming triumph, no setbacks, no ideal destination. Just the wind.

*Yothu Yindi performing on stage in Darwin, June 1995.
Below: During a music concert at Sydney's Domain, September 2000.*

*Gurrumul and Mändawuy playing at the NT
Indigenous Music Awards in Darwin, 2010.*

Witiyana Marika speaking

Mändawuy had the vision. It was Mändawuy who made that band, Yothu Yindi. He is a great man, Mändawuy. We were making a political statement to this nation and to the world. *Balanda* — we had *balanda* in the band, too. Stu, Cal. But it was the traditional music that made us strong enough to tell about the rights of our people. We wanted mainstream people to understand. Mainstream people. We wanted to say, different cultures, but one people. When *Tribal Voice* came out, and that song, that 'Treaty' song, we felt this was a powerful song for the nation to listen to. A powerful, powerful song, 'Treaty'. We combined traditional singing and modern singing. Traditional singing is called '*manikay*'. I danced Yolŋu traditional dances and sang *manikay*. That was my job in Yothu Yindi.

When we toured, it was something else. We went to Europe and people there hadn't seen Indigenous people before. They loved it. They loved it. Before Europe, Yothu Yindi toured with Midnight Oil in Canada, in America. That was the first tour. Incredible. That was before the Bicentenary. We were starting the protest, the Bicentenary protest. It was a powerful time then, a very powerful time. North American Indians sang, too. They sang with us on that tour with Midnight Oil. John Trudell, he sang with us. It made me really, really proud, that tour. Really proud.

I've known Gurrumul before Yothu Yindi. I've known he was a special man. A really special man. In his mind, what he thought, and in his spirituality — awesome. He was so special. And his music — so awesome. He was the drummer, he was on keyboards, he was on guitar — everything. The best. After Yothu Yindi started, Gurrumul wasn't in the band then. Not for a few years after we started. Then we needed someone, a drummer, and I said to Mändawuy, 'We should get Gurrumul.' That's what I said. 'We should get Gurrumul.' And they asked me, 'Why?' I said, 'Okay, believe me, he's the most fantastic person for this band.' And Mändawuy heard Gurrumul and he had this big smile right across his face because he knew the sound that Gurrumul could create. He knew.

You know, when Gurrumul's record came out, that solo record, we Yolŋu knew that this is the real voice of our traditions and our culture. The real voice. And everyone who heard it — Indigenous people, white people — they knew this is something special. Really special. That's what they think when they listen to that record. Special.

Mändawuy Yunupiŋu, with Gurrumul accompanying. Two Gumatj lead singers who have contributed so much to Australian's musical history.

CHAPTER 21

Saltwater Band

All of the Saltwater boys have thrown their arms around Indigenous culture and given it a big group hug. You can't help but delight in what's been achieved.

If not Yothu Yindi, then who?

When Gurrumul withdrew from Yothu Yindi in 1992 there was nowhere to go other than to improvised groups of Elcho boys — a bit of reggae, a bit of traditional, four or five Yolŋu guys amusing themselves harmlessly. If he were a white musician in any of the continent's big cities, he would have been spoiled for choice with his musical credentials. But north-east Arnhem Land in the early nineties, even in the midst of the Indigenous Spring, didn't offer that sort of bounty.

It wasn't until Michael Hohnen and Cal Williams were sent to Elcho in 1996 with instruments and amps and speakers that a way forward after Yothu Yindi appeared for Gurrumul. Michael's TAFE in Darwin was sponsoring an outreach program designed to draw young Indigenous men and women into a more organised engagement with music that had not been possible up until then. Music thrived on Elcho — it was the dominant creative outlet on the island — but it came together in a ramshackle way. Gurrumul, though, was a standout; a multi-instrumentalist with something like genius in his uptake. But what he might achieve as a solo artist was years away when Michael and his music first came to Elcho. Michael thought, 'Exceptional', and left it at that.

The acknowledged livewire of the Island was Manuel Dhurrkay, a guy with robust schemes of fame and fortune, but nothing at this stage to bring to Michael's workshops other than his good looks and his voice. Michael said: 'Sure, you can sing, but you have to find a band to front.' Manuel said: 'Hold on!' and raced away to gather the instrumentalists he'd need. He plundered the Yunupiŋu households of the island and brought back Gurrumul, Andrew, Nigel and Johnathon, as well as his own cousin Joshua, and a brace of Garawirrtja: Lloyd and Adrian.

BLOKE'S.

Manuel Dhurrkay was the outgoing
energetic lead singer of Saltwater and writer
of many of Saltwater's songs; Gurrumul
was its quiet engine, driving the music.

YA YAWIRRINY (YOUNG MEN)

Napurrdja dhuwal ŋoywuy gapuwuy	We're salt water people
Ŋayiny marrtji gukunattja dhärra'tharra	Coconuts abound
Ŋayiny ga gapuny ŋorra wapurarrnha	The seas are calm
Dhiyali wäŋaŋur Galiwin'ku	Here at Galiwin'ku
Yä, yä, yawirriny	Oh, oh, young men
Yä, yä, yawirriny	Oh, oh, young men
Bala walal marrtjina marthaŋayyun	They went off by boat
Larruŋal marrtjin miyapunuw	Looking for turtles
Ŋayiny ga Rrepa ŋorran ŋurukunmirr maŋanmirr	The sunset clouds are brilliant red for them
Ŋunhal runu'ŋur Dalmana	over the island Dalmana
Yä, yä, yawirriny	Oh, oh, young men
Yä, yä, yawirriny	Oh, oh, young men
Yä, yä, yawirriny	Oh, oh, young men
Yä, yä, yawirriny	Oh, oh, young men
Bala walalaŋ wata do'yurr, ŋunhili gapuŋur dhulmuŋur	Strong wind arrived, there at the deep water
Yä, yawirriny, gurrupuruŋumirr	Oh, you poor young men
Yolnha walalaŋ dhu gumurr'yundja?	Who will help them?

In traditional Indigenous cultures, there was no news cycle. So much emphasis was placed on continuity, on the unchanging, that extraordinary events — taking in good news, such as the arrival off the coast of coveted fish in great numbers, and bad news, such as ferocious storms that catch people in boats at sea unaware — had to be given a generalising gloss in the tribal narrative. Nobody is about to refer to the monster typhoon of 1722, for example. The message of monster typhoons has to be spread over eternity. 'Ya Yawirriny' celebrates the pluck, even the bravado, of the tribes' young men who are off looking for turtles, and laments what can happen on such an enterprise.

They came together, all of these Yunupiŋus, Dhurrkays and Garawirrtja, as if they were born to shine. Their instrumental skills (after some tutelage from Michael) were not too bad at all, and it must be said that Manuel, with his vocals, was living out a fabulous destiny, all over the stage like Jumping Jack Flash. The band's sound was a fiesta of roots, reggae, ska, folk, rock and folk-rock, with a complement of the traditional, all of it in a willy-nilly cascade but likely to result in something more original than anything Elcho pick-up bands had fashioned before then. Not only more orginal, but better. Michael could see that Manuel would have to keep his crowd-pleaser thing going, since it released so much of his energy, but he could also see that the boys might fashion something uniquely Elcho out of the as yet rough-hewn sound.

Gurrumul sat in his chair as tranquil as a buddha while all this guerrilla stuff went on around him, handling his guitar with casual mastery, like Doc Watson sitting in with a round-up of enthusiastic amateurs. This was the sort of thing that came naturally to him; the sort of thing he loved — he, his family and friends taking almost every song in an upward trajectory, the atmosphere thick with rasta theatrics. What he'd find in himself in years to come would eclipse his achievements with the Elcho band, but building up to Saltwater, and then Saltwater itself in the early years — it wasn't the great art of *Gurrumul* and *Rrakala*, but it wasn't that far behind, and probably gave him as much joy, maybe more.

The life of people in a band is very like that of people who are not in a band; a lot of gazing about absently, imagining the next meal that will come your way, wishing you were home, or if you are home, wishing that you weren't, flicking through magazines, staring out the window. The music only occupies a few hours out of the twenty-four in which you're all together every day when touring. Tensions develop. The rapport of the Saltwater members was potent from the beginning, and yet the instinctive musical understanding didn't rule out grief. The social rules of engagement between different Indigenous clans are so complex that coming together is often fraught. Saltwater is made up of three clans — the Gumatj, Wanguri and Birrkili — so there were spats, and stand-offs, episodes of mild resentment. It was only the music that made this intimate mingling possible.

Most of the songs were in language, most were written by Manuel and many have the Manuel bounce. Gurrumul was the musical genius of the band, certainly, but when it came to spectacle, Manuel was master. Born in another place at another time, Manuel would have made his name in the rock'n'roll milieu. His voice doesn't have the range, subtlety and emotional clout of Gurrumul's, but it would be true to say that Manuel was more important to the success of Saltwater than Gurrumul. What Michael and the Saltwater boys created was a good, solid outfit, highly flexible, and above all, cheerful. It's on stage that Manuel's contribution becomes most apparent. He's everywhere; he dominates the performance and, although Saltwater's greatest artistic achievements came in the studio, it's essentially a performance band. Manuel could sing the Lord's Prayer and give it a genial quality; he can't help it. Making it all work musically — Gurrumul is crucial there. Making it carry over the footlights — that's Manuel.

The first twelve-track Saltwater album, *Gapu Damurruŋ*, came out in 1999 and began to pick up rotation on radio stations, thanks to the energetic spruiking of Mark Grose. *Gapu Damurruŋ* gave Mark a lot to work with; it may not have been a masterpiece, but it was head and shoulders above anything that had come out of the north since *Tribal Voice*. The production of the songs — and this was Craig Pilkington's big contribution — was professionally astute from beginning to end. Nothing self-indulgent made it into the final cut; just well-made music, robust and engaging, with a confident glow about it. Gurrumul's musical savvy helped create cohesion from track to track, and Manuel provided the bounce and brio.

The album starts with the sound of surf running up the sand, followed by a bit of cheerful, off-the-cuff Jamaican biff, then finds its way through a good-natured version of 'Gopuru'; an evocative Manuel song in English, 'Arafura Sea'; and on through the blended voices of 'Ya Yawirriny', performed with something like a Polynesian lilt that almost conjures ukeleles and hibiscus blooms worn behind the ear. Didgeridoo and ironwood clapsticks introduce 'Bäru', which jumps from the traditional into a jaunty rhythm out of Trinidad, Tobago and Elcho. The same thing carries through into 'Yanguna', but the next track, 'Bakitju', slows the tempo and gives us subtle strings before the beat kicks in. 'Gela Boy' is a hectic dance tune, although certainly not the dancing of ceremony; then follows the infectious beat of 'Djomula', and 'Galuku' with a nicely judged string complement; next a version of 'Gurrumul History' with strings behind a steady beat giving it a ballad quality; and so on to the concluding track, 'Baŋadi', where you begin to get an idea of what Gurrumul's miracle of a voice will deliver in years to come.

Djarridjarri, the second Saltwater album, was released in 2004. Between *Gapu Damurruŋ* and *Djarridjarri*, Saltwater had played gigs all over, establishing, as you'd expect, a reputation for giving an audience a good time. Aboriginal audiences adored the band; in footage shot at this time, you see Indigenous girls, young women, boys, all with huge smiles and shining eyes clamouring down by the stage. Mark Grose claims that Indigenous people are always ready to be happy, if only something comes along, and Saltwater came along. It wasn't as though they'd have smiled in that way for just anyone. Some years ago, Paul Kelly went to Arnhem Land to sing for Indigenous audiences, and he had a great deal to offer, but the audiences didn't turn out even for the co-writer of 'Treaty'. Saltwater was hometown and happy, and that was the foundation of its appeal. Second albums that seek to build on the success of a first album can surprise or disappoint. Often the first album clears out the cupboard and all that's left second time around are the ingredients for a thin gruel. Or maybe you just do the first album again, and hope nobody notices. But *Djarridjarri* is a follow-up album that exceeds the achievements of the first. The band members had become a little more ambitious in the years between *Gapu Damurruŋ* and *Djarridjarri*, but Michael Hohnen's imagination was the wellspring of the real development. He'd recognised more fully the potential of a band in which Gurrumul's gifts were on offer.

The 'portrait' strategy that would be employed on the Gurrumul solo albums was given its pilot outing on *Djarridjarri*. Rather than the ear-to-ear Saltwater smile, an expression is captured in which a greater variety of moods might dwell. What was created in Craig Pilkington's Audrey Studios in Melbourne was an album of flourishing variety, produced to world standards, every note distinctive in its clarity. And that embrace of Gurrumul's gifts is announced on the first track, 'Djilawurr', a song of transporting beauty, then and now the most radiant three minutes and forty-one seconds of sound. 'Warwu' is not quite Saltwater Land either; it's heading towards a quieter place where solitude and sorrow are more tolerated. And

'Bäpa' too, the tenth track, is suggestive of what will be wrought in the same studio three years later. Not that Manuel himself doesn't enjoy periods of reflection every now and again. His song, 'Let's Work Together' is a simple, sincere sermon promoting cross-cultural respect and understanding, but listening to it makes you wish with all your heart he'd instead reprised his 'Reggae Music'. The final track, 'Wata' (Healing Wind), a traditional arrangement rendered by Kevin Djamina Gurruwiwi, is welcome at the end of the album, but at the same time it makes you realise that unmediated traditional songs are not, in fact, very accessible.

The third Saltwater album, *Malk* ('Our Skin'), was recorded in 2006, before Gurrumul's first solo album, but not released until 2009, well after the release of *Gurrumul*. *Malk* is a work of art; one of the most sophisticated albums by an Indigenous band ever produced. *Djarridjarri* showed what a painstaking (and inspired) approach to production could be achieved by the Saltwater members; *Malk* goes further, but not only in the polish applied. It's a thought-out album, each track matched for mood and message to every other track. The first track, 'Martjanba', rendered half in English, half in Yolŋu Matha, is a type of paradise-postponed song, pleasant enough, but light. Then the title track, 'Malk', takes on board Natalie Pa'apa'a (from Blue King Brown) as a guest performer, and once again the result is pleasant, but light:

> *Our skin name is called Malk,*
> *This is your name,*
> *This is your skin forever,*
> *They unite us together,*
> *Come on everybody,*
> *Come on and dance tonight,*
> *Come on and dance tonight.*

A few tracks further on, a remix of *Malk* ready for the nightclub startles you even as you smile. Muted versions of a chirrupy ditty called 'Gapu Gapu' helps overcome any resistance you have left to the breeziness of the album: 'Listen to the sound of the Elcho Island music, Yeah Yeah Yeah!' This is Saltwater Land in the twenty-first century. Michael, Craig Pilkington and all of the Saltwater boys have thrown their arms around Indigenous culture and given it a big group hug. You can't help but delight in what's been achieved.

But where could Saltwater travel after *Malk*, which probably takes the band as far as it can go in that dance-y, carefree vein? If, for the sake of a new direction, Saltwater were suddenly to get serious and earnest, the zest would be lost. Perhaps the Saltwater project and the Gurrumul project should be looked at as a single accomplishment that reveals two equally valid dimensions of Indigenous experience. One dimension is suggested by Mark Grose's comment about the willingness of Indigenous Australians to be happy when something that can make them happy comes along. That's Saltwater. The other is the mystery and wonder of an ancient culture. That's Gurrumul, solo.

Saltwater Band preparing for a gig on tour. The band members hated the idea of separate rooms and always insisted on sharing, regardless of the bedding configuration. (Note the mattress on the floor.)
Right top: Old and young and everyone in between came along to Saltwater concerts. Community elders were only too pleased to welcome visiting bands and witness the way in which they inspired young people.
Bottom: Any Saltwater concert away from Elcho commenced with the audience sitting quietly to show respect for the visitors, but after three or four songs, everyone was up and dancing, cheering and laughing.

Gapu Damurruŋ album

Geoffrey Gurrumul Yunupiŋu, lead singer & lead guitar
Manuel Nulupani Dhurrkay, lead singer
Andrew Djanarri Yunupiŋu, backing vocals
Jonathan Manirri Yunupiŋu , backing vocals
Nigel Barrakuwuy Yunupiŋu, didgeridoo & vocals
Adrian Rrupanda Garawirrtja, bass guitar
Lloyd Malalun Garawirrtja, keyboard
Joshua Mungula Dhurrkay, drums
Frank Gonmalwa Wununumurra, rhythm guitar
Barry Garrawitja, traditional singer

Additional Live Performers

Mario Dean, bongos
Tiras Dhurrkay, keyboard

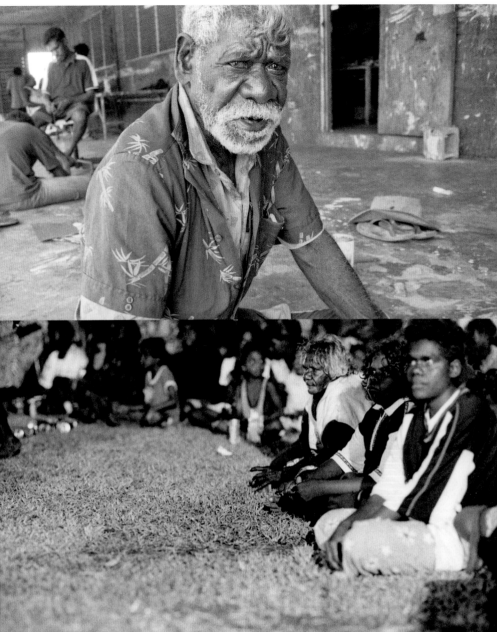

Djarridjarri/Blue Flag album

Geoffrey Gurrumul Yunupiŋu, lead singer & lead guitar
Manuel Nulupani Dhurrkay, lead singer
Lloyd Malalun Garawirrtja, keyboard
Luke Bukultjipi, keyboard
Andrew Djanarri Yunupiŋu, backing vocals
Nigel Barrakuwuy Yunupiŋu, didgeridoo & Vvocals
Jonathan Manirri Yunupiŋu, backing vocals
Adrian Rrupanda Garawirrtja, bass guitar
Joshua Mungula Dhurrkay, drums
Kevin Djamina Gurruwiwi, vocals
Barry Garrawitja, traditional singer

Malk album

Geoffrey Gurrumul Yunupiŋu, lead singer & lead guitar
Manuel Nulupani Dhurrkay, lead singer
Lloyd Malalun Garawirrtja, keyboard
Luke Bukultjipi, keyboard
Joshua Mungula Dhurrkay, drums
Andrew Dhamarrantji, bass
Jason Dhamarrantji, guitar & keyboard
Nigel Barrakuwuy Yunupiŋu, didgeridoo & vocals
Jonathan Manirri Yunupiŋu, backing vocals
Adrian Rrupanda Garawirrtja, bass guitar
Marcus Dhurrkay, vocals & keyboard
Barry Garrawitja, traditional singer

Ours

Outdoors in Darwin, big stage, magenta spotlights, midnight-blue backdrop with a Starry Night motif imitating the starry night over the city. The boys are up for this; they're in front of what's fairly close to a home crowd. Manuel, in loose dark slacks, black shirt and shimmering gold-and-black waistcoat, calls over a hand-held mic: 'Ladies and gentleman, I'd like to introduce you to the members of the Saltwater Band! Our lead singer Geoffrey Gurrumul!'

And Gurrumul calls back: 'Yo!'

'Over on my left Nigel Yunupiŋu! Yeah, yeah, on keyboard, Lloyd Malaluŋ Garawirrtja! On drums …'

Everyone on stage is either leaping or bopping by the time the intros are completed, including two traditional dancers in vivid garments, their bodies painted and patterned in traditional designs. Out in the audience the giddy-up beat of the band has people smiling and clapping and whistling and throwing peace signs to the cameras. In the glow of the arc lights, frenzied moths mimic the excitement of the crowd below.

'Once again ladies and gentlemen, Saltwater, *Gapu Damurruŋ*!'

People who have lived in north-east Arnhem Land long enough to know, say that the Yolŋu have survived by being adaptable. A feature of this adaptability is embracing that which seems worthwhile in white culture. This concert tonight is something the Yolŋu have borrowed from the *balanda*: amplified music driven along by rapid percussion, paying customers, atmospheric lighting, a nine-item song sheet, and last but far from least, north-east Arnhem sex appeal.

'This one is a special request, this one is for you, all you girls up there,' Manuel shouts into the mike, throwing his arm out in the direction of a cohort of women shrieking with delight under an arc light. And the band launches itself headlong into one of Manuel's favourites, 'Wurrapa' (Ocean Woman). The sexiness is further adapted to suit the more strait-laced culture of the Yolŋu: no pelvic thrusts, just a type of low-level gettin' jiggy suggestiveness. Gurrumul meanwhile, seated centre stage with his guitar, allows a quiet smile to play at the corners of his mouth. Without sight, he can't do what Manuel does, but it's apparent that he gets a type of vicarious enjoyment out of the sass and energy Manuel puts into his work.

This next song is Gurrumul's — 'Gäthu Mawula' — and like Manuel's 'Wurrapa' it's written to honour a woman, but a woman he speaks of as 'daughter'. The song comes from the heart. The woman it honours once devoted herself to caring for Gurrumul in Darwin. He sings of her country and her people, of the beauty of sky and sea that nourished her as a child.

Witnessing the performance of these two songs throws into relief the distinction of each performer. 'Wurrapa' defines Manuel in his artistic maturity; 'Gäthu Mawula' defines Gurrumul. It's that creative maturity of its two songwriters that powers Saltwater and gives the band its thrilling versatility.

The two painted dancers fashion traditional movements to the beat of the music. Neither is lean in the least and they're sweating with the effort. Sweating, but loving what they're doing, loving being a part of the whole extravaganza.

Nigel Yunupiŋu up at the front of the stage keeps up a demanding schedule of off-the-floor dance leaps even as he's sharing vocals with Manuel and Gurrumul. On 'Djomula' he dances closer to Gurrumul and makes some private comment, maybe a joke, and Gurrumul in the midst of the song provides a brief smile. Then Lloyd at the keyboard smiles, Andrew grins and shakes his head, and just for a few seconds, everyone on stage is grinning mightily. It's a minor moment in the performance, but it throws a bright light back to the gleeful smiles of the audience, as if the band and the crowd formed a single community. Whatever has been borrowed and adapted by the Saltwater people, the music is theirs, and that's what so thrills the Indigenous audience. It's ours.

*Saltwater were a typical
'Arnhem Land trio' with nine
or more people on stage.*

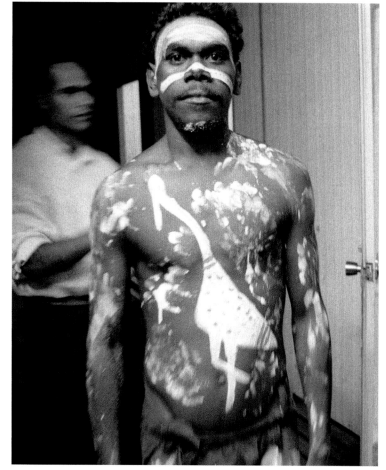

Clockwise from above: Big Frank and Kevin Djamina Gurruwiwi (sunglasses); Nigel Yunupiŋu is ready; Manuel Dhurrkay (McCartney); Big Frank, lead singer from Soft Sands Band, never missed an opportunity to tour with Saltwater.

At Skinnyfish we call Manuel and Gurrumul Lennon and McCartney. Manuel's pop style tied with Gurrumul's more serious ballad style which set Saltwater Band apart from all other bands.

George Rrurrambu, lead singer of Warumpi Band, performed with Saltwater on their first community tour. George is an Australian music legend and was responsible for the new wave of Australian music that saw Indigenous artists sing in their own languages and draw on their own cultural experiences.

Saltwater Band on tour. The Saltwater Band was evenly split down the middle: half the band were Gumatj (Yellow Flag) and half were Gupapuyŋu (Blue Flag).

Tony Hillier on *Malk*

Collectively, the Elcho Islanders are the most exciting Aboriginal act to have emerged from the Top End since Yothu Yindi … Saltwater Band blends ancient Yolŋu culture with pop and roots influences at least as effectively as their trail-blazing predecessors, if a little less vigorously. The songs centre on traditional stories and culturally important places in the band's homelands off the coast of north-eastern Arnhem Land, more than 500 kilometres from Darwin. The snappy title track, though delivered predominantly in English, dwells on the essence of Yolŋu identity … The set starts with a pop ballad, 'Martjanba', also in English and language, that waxes lyrical about one of the uninhabited islands in the Wessel group. Contrary to the title, 'Compass' is sung exclusively in language and talks about the ancestors setting directions for future generations. 'Marwurrumburr', a bright, up-tempo number with reggae backbeat and horns, and the starkly contrasting 'Djilawurr' incorporate ceremonial songs. The latter has Gurrumul's dulcet tones set to string quartet and piano, and is utterly sublime … If *Malk* is afforded the requisite airplay, Saltwater Band will be in danger of losing its status as one of the country's best-kept secrets.

Gurrumul with Lloyd Malaluŋ Garawirrtja. Lloyd's mother's mother is Gurrumul's aunt. Lloyd was the youngest member of Saltwater Band and was Gurrumul's official carer while on tour.

Joshua Dhurrkay. At the first Garma Festival, Lindy Morrison was asked to run some drumming workshops. She saw Joshua in action just once and said, 'Nothing to teach that boy'. Joshua is another product of the 'flour drum' school of drumming.

Tyranny of distance

Saltwater Band is one of the very best bands this country has produced, but its popularity is largely restricted to Indigenous audiences. It has never broken out in the way Gurrumul's solo albums have reached right into the mainstream. The reasons are not to do with intrinsic appeal, or even commercial savvy; the songs are right in there, and the band would be delighted to be thought of as chart-toppers. No, the issue is travel. The eight regular members of the band are usually joined by at least two dancers and maybe another brother jumping in with clapsticks or didge. Just to get the band and a couple of crew to a performance site in any of the big capitals costs twenty-thousand dollars before fees. After *Gapu Damurruŋ*, requests for performances came in thick and fast to Skinnyfish, but only appearances local to the Territory could be realistically contemplated. Without a certain level of visibility on the concert and festival circuit, bands looking for recognition struggle for airplay, and sales tend to plateau.

But there's another obstacle to mainstream success for Saltwater Band. Any band or individual performer sooner or later has to fashion a tale to put over to the public. The Yothu Yindi story was one of red-earth politics and racial justice. All that Saltwater Band could offer was quality and a broad smile. Nine or ten guys you'd never heard of from a place you'd never heard of? That's an awkward story to sell. An important feature of Gurrumul's success is an appealing narrative: the blind genius with a voice from heaven.

Saltwater Band performing at their peak with their two lead singers Gurrumul Yunupiŋu and Manuel Dhurrkay in full voice.

CHAPTER 22
Solo

He's not thinking about how famous he must be, nothing like that.

He likes it when it happens — it pleases him at a certain level.

But it's not important.

It's February 2007, eight months out from a federal election that will yield, amongst other things, a Prime Ministerial apology to the Indigenous people of Australia. That will be one landmark; another smaller one is in the making. Gurrumul is flying down to Melbourne from Darwin to begin recording the songs of his debut album as a solo artist.

The recording venue is to be Craig Pilkington's Audrey Studios in Sydney Road, Coburg, or Little Istanbul as the area is known; the Turkish ghetto of Melbourne. Craig is a producer and engineer of high reputation, a masterful musician and a founder of The Killjoys, the band Michael played with in his pre-Darwin days. Michael wants a place where Gurrumul can feel relaxed and happy, which is what he'll find at Craig's studio.

Craig is a friend of Gurrumul's, and has been given his own Yolŋu name of 'Djanda', or 'Goanna', an honorific he came by a few years earlier when the Saltwater boys were recording with Craig at Mount Bundy Station, south of Darwin. Mount Bundy is a tourist resort with a wildlife park attached where goannas roam about in a leisurely way, under the smug impression that they are protected creatures. Gurrumul's friends caught one of these goannas, bashed its brains out and cooked it, as any self-respecting black man from Arnhem Land would. There was trouble, not too serious and a certain amount of screaming and shouting when the half-eaten goanna was found in the refrigerator. Somehow, Craig became honoured with the name, Jenda.

Gurrumul's friendship with Michael allows him to exercise trust in whatever is about to unfold at Audrey Studios, but if he were put in a studio with only himself and his friends to please, he would not make the album that Michael has in mind. If it were up to him, the tracks would be flavoured with the reggae of his Saltwater songs. But Michael is very aware of what Gurrumul

Gurrumul is a multi-instrumentalist, playing guitar, piano, yidaki (didgeridoo) and drums.

GALUPA

Wuyupthurrunana dhawal Galupaŋu
ŋirrpunydja ŋarraku ŋäthinana
nhenydja ŋarraku djirrmiḻyurruna
manhanhayurra bäyma Bekuḻŋura
ŋirrpuŋura dhuwalinydja, bäpawala Banunydjiwala

Go ŋilimurru nhina yarrarrayun
yolŋu Bandirriya dharwulŋurana
wäŋa marrkapmirri wäŋa marrkapmirri
ŋarrakuŋu boṉal nherranhara gapany gopulu

Dhuwalana dhawal Nhalilaŋu Gunyaŋara, Gunyaŋarriyu
Gawupu Butjumurru, Lepa-Bandirriya Guymaḻamurru
nhenydja ŋarraku miḻn'miḻnthurruna Nambaŋura Bandirriya

Y..ä Djarrami, y..ä Batumaŋ
ŋirrpuŋura dhuwalinydja wäwawala

Wanhakana guṉda Yunupuyŋu, Birayŋu Ḻuku-mangamirri?
wäŋawuy Dhamuŋura, Garrabaḻaŋu Djingupaŋu
yä guṉda Yunupuyŋu, yä guṉda Birayŋu
yä guṉda Marrulayŋu, wäŋawuy Dhamuŋura
ḻuku-nherraṉmina
ḻuku-nherraṉmina, ḻuku-nherraṉmina

The country Galupa disappearing from sight
My mind is crying
You stand there for me
Standing, stay there at Bekuḻŋura
In the mind, of aunty Banunydji

Come let's all sit lined together
ancestors at Bandirriya under the dharwul shade tree
beloved country, beloved country
on Gumatj ground a site cleared by me

Here is the places Nhalilaŋu Gunyaŋara, Gunyaŋarri
Gawupu Butjumurru, Lepa-Bandirriya Guymaḻamurru
You my (country) are bright in my eyes

O..h Djarrami, o..h Batumaŋ
in the mind of my brother

Where is the rock called Yunupuyŋu,
Birayŋu Ḻuku-mangamirri?
of that place Dhamuŋura, Garrabaḻaŋu Djingupaŋu
o..h Rock Yunupuyŋu, o..h Rock Birayŋu
o..h Rock Marrulayŋu, put down its feet at Dhamuŋura
put down its feet, put down its feet

'Galupa' was first recorded for a Saltwater album, but this version retains none of the
Saltwater tang. It has been slowed down and rebuilt to suit the tempo and mood of the
album. Michael Hohnen says that 'Gurrumul likes to do this very up and dancey, but that
funky, groovy thing never quite worked for me'. The change from the Saltwater version is
emphasised in the mid-track acoustic guitar solo.

can do with his voice; knows that its range and temper eclipses anything that Saltwater has ever attempted. He's looking for a level of sophistication in the production of the songs that will bring into play features of Gurrumul's vocal talent that have barely been expressed before.

Michael isn't carrying any great burden of expectation to the studio or any fear of failure — he doesn't suffer from lack of self-confidence. What he wants to explore at Audrey Studios is the classical, acoustic sound that will emerge from a stripped-back production of acoustic guitar and vocals. He also has in mind some harpsichord here and there to more fully exploit the fragile quality of Gurrumul's voice. Over the years of their friendship, Gurrumul has played song after song for Michael, simply for the pleasure of it, and almost every song was presented in that acoustic guitar and vocal style. 'Michael, Michael … listen, Michael …' That's where the vision of what the album should be comes from: Gurrumul in an excited state seeking Michael out with a song to play in a simple way. And at this time of musing over possible strategies, it happened that Michael heard the Swedish–Argentinian artist José González's record *Veneer*, gorgeous acoustic guitar and gentle, intimate vocals, a lot of the voice double-tracked to give it a more contemporary sound. Michael thought: 'Yeah, that's acceptable, we can put something out like that.' The Gonzalez album helped to give him the confidence that a beautiful, stripped-down album would amount to something.

Gurrumul enjoys the chance to rock a song along as much as anyone, and reggae is a sort of default setting for him. He does it well. But the mood of the first album has been carefully judged for its emotional cohesiveness. No song is permitted to stray too far from the elemental reverence for land and ancestors that dominates Gurrumul's creative make-up. From the first song on the album, 'Wiyathul', to the last, 'Wukun', he provides a portrait of the spiritual estate of his own Gumatj people and that of his mother's people, adjusted to suit his temperament. If the album had included some Indigenous rock, a flourish of reggae, a little more gospel, it would have indexed Gurrumul's creative life as fully as a work of art can. But it would also have surrendered its cohesiveness.

At Audrey Studios, things went right from the beginning. Gurrumul relaxed and happy; Michael brimming with purpose.

It's usually a priority when putting an album together to cast about for light and shade, bounce and ballad. But neither Michael nor Gurrumul give much thought to creating distinction between tracks in the conventional way. 'We thought about the album as an across-the-board thing,' says Michael later:

> A cohesive mood that bound the album together. Anything that was too up, we stripped back. So whether it was 'Wiyathul', 'Djärimirri', we were after that one mood. As soon as Gurrumul goes up, as soon as he goes reggae, he's in Saltwater land. He grew up with Yothu Yindi, and as soon as he wants to be entertaining, he goes up — it's the legacy of Yothu Yindi. The tracks are different, yes, but we didn't sit down and think how we could do that. We went after mood, and let the rest take care of itself.
>
> You know, the guy in our local record store in Darwin listened to the album and he said, 'It's terrible, you need more reggae, it's too much the same.' And the album became the best-

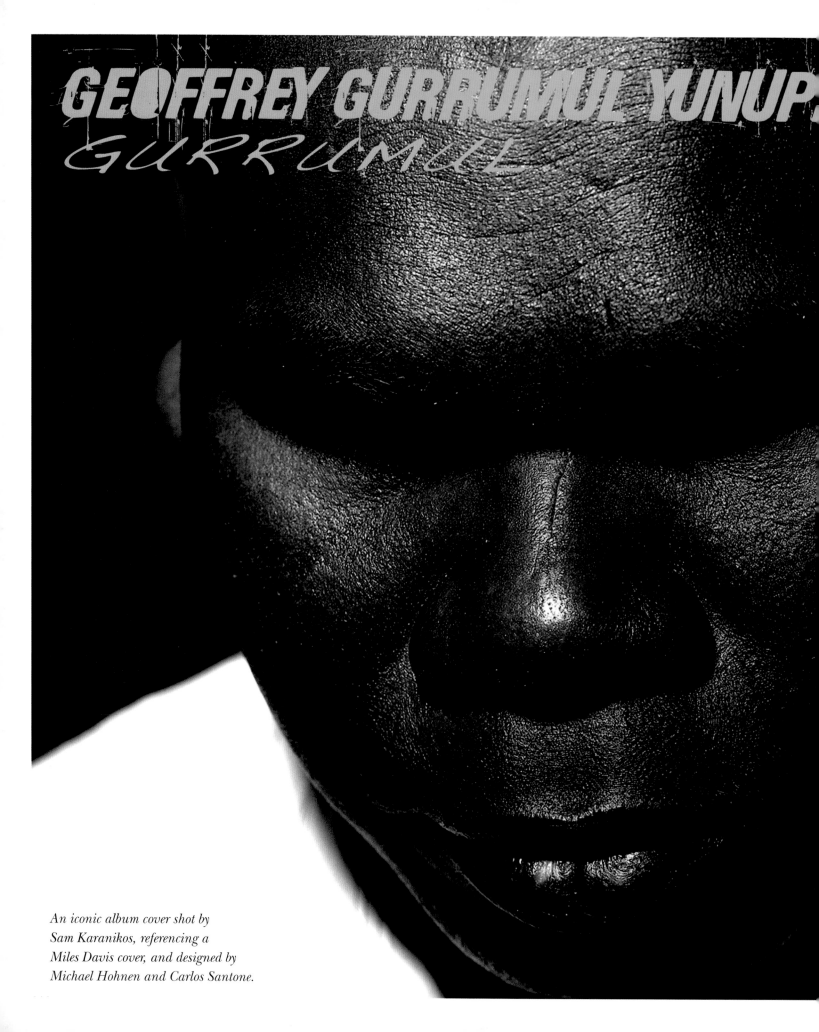

GEOFFREY GURRUMUL YUNUP,
GURRUMUL

*An iconic album cover shot by
Sam Karanikos, referencing a
Miles Davis cover, and designed by
Michael Hohnen and Carlos Santone.*

Gurrumul on stage at the launch of his first album. He had no idea at that time of how successful and influential his music would become.

Archibald Portrait by Guy Maestri

This is the idea: Gurrumul sits himself comfortably in a chair for an hour or two while the artist Guy Maestri crafts a dozen sketch references for a full-scale Archibald portrait. But how likely is it that Gurrumul will sit about doing nothing while Guy gets busy with charcoal and crayons? Not likely at all. Gurrumul doesn't enjoy being studied in that way and has little interest in being hung in the Archibald. That said, it has to be conceded that a portrait by such an accomplished artist as Guy Maestri would be a wonderful thing for posterity. And Guy is an admirer of Gurrumul. He saw him performing live at a concert to welcome in the 2009 New Year, just two months before — 'an inspiring, amazing man' — and wants to get the face that goes with the voice down on linen. Maybe it could be managed this way: Gurrumul is off to perform in Beijing in March and will be subjected to an hour or so of enforced leisure at the Sydney airport departure lounge. If Guy scoots out to the airport, he can fashion his sketches while Gurrumul idles away the time in an armchair — a captive subject.

Guy takes up the offer without a moment's hesitation. On the day of the Beijing departure, there he is, rapidly rendering the distinctive Yunupiŋu physiognomy as the current of thought works changes in Gurrumul's expression. It's not all about what Guy gets down on cartridge; he's learning as he sketches, taking in the quiet charisma of the man, envisioning the portrait to come, imagining what he can convey. To the accompaniment of announcements declaring arrivals and departures and the wickedness of leaving bags unattended, he builds up the foundation of his portrait. By the time Michael Hohnen tells his friend that it's time to board — 'Wäwa, that's us' — Guy has exactly what he needs. 'I got a sense of his presence, and this determined the nature of the portrait: quiet and strong.'

A portrait can never act as a catalogue. The artist is compelled to seek out that which is most revealing and find some way of suggesting the sum of a great many parts in a single expression. What that expression might be requires intuition. Gurrumul is not an extrovert; almost everything that is crucial to understanding him is kept private.

Intuition also plays a part in setting the scale of the portrait. Maestri is working large — 200 by 168 centimetres. Any misjudgement of scale can be fatal, particularly when only the face and neck is depicted, as Maestri intends. To devote such a large area of linen to the face alone calls for great technical skill. The drama of the picture has to extend to every corner. The danger is that a face rendered on this scale will not be able to sustain the artist's narrative — the story that whispers to the viewer.

To the sound of Gurrumul's voice singing his way through the tracks of his first solo album, Maestri begins to transform what he has imagined into something that can be shared. It's an intellectually demanding process; the brain sweats with effort. In the space of an hour, a hundred individual judgments are made. 'I usually work in a very liberal, gestural way,' says Maestri, 'but this time I built up the image quietly and slowly with many glazes in an attempt to capture the beautiful quality of his skin. I worked on it for over a month … The whole process became quite an emotional experience.'

What emerges from that month's work is an image that emphasises the mystique of black Australia. Nothing in the picture suggests that the man depicted is a musician. It's as if Maestri has said to the viewer: 'Everything you are ever going to know about this man is what stands in front of you. Figure it out.' The two revealing areas of the portrait are the dark caves of the eyes, and the mouth, illuminated from above. The eyes are left in darkness not to dramatise Gurrumul's sightlessness, but to suggest the mystery of what he sees in his mind's eye. Sensitivity is concentrated in the lips. It takes a little time before the viewer is able to distinguish that the image is of a poet but once the idea catches hold, all you can see is the poetry. It's there in the lustre of the skin, the introspection conveyed by the concealed eyes. It's a portrait of a particular man, but also of all that we wonder about when we stand face to face with a black Australian.

When Gurrumul's portrait by Guy Maestri won the 2009 Archibald Prize, he issued a public press statement through Skinnyfish letting his family know that he didn't actually win the money for the prize, someone else did.

*selling album the shop had ever had. It outsold Kylie, Madonna, Prince, and now when I go
into that store, we laugh.*

*From the start, we didn't want a jazzy, vibey record, we wanted a fragile, emotional record.
If you listen closely, then yeah, lots of variation. Gurrumul changes his voice, he sings in
two voices, and then there's the change in languages, he sounds different depending on what
language he's using.*

The choice of songs in the studio is fairly casual.

Gurrumul says: 'Let's do "Baywara".'

Michael says: 'Maybe "Marrandil".'

Gurrumul says: 'A rock one, Michael. "Galupa".'

Michael says: 'I like "Galupa", but it just doesn't move me. Let's slow it down.'

So 'Galupa' is slowed down to preserve the overall mood, and it's slowed down perhaps
more than Gurrumul cares for, but he says: 'Michael we do your idea, okay, we go with that.'

Gurrumul and his then-partner Shirley are guests of Michael's parents in Sandringham.
Every morning Gurrumul and Shirley rise in what is, in fact, the afternoon, and drive with
Michael down Beach Road to The Esplanade, down Queens Road to the back of the city and
up Royal Parade and Sydney Road to Audrey. Four hours late, but it's okay; Gurrumul and
punctuality have never been on speaking terms.

This switched-on Gurrumul stands in vivid contrast to the phased-out Gurrumul of the
months leading up to Audrey, when he seemed to have lost interest in almost everything.
Saltwater was having some internal problems, maybe terminal, so that outlet was denied him.
And he was living in Darwin with Shirley for complex cultural reasons, and not on Elcho.

But more recently, this solo project has begun to feed a little tonic into a previously
torpid bloodstream. If you look at Gurrumul's life, he's reaped praise and endorsement from
the time he was a kid — a lot of praise — but it was as if it had all lost meaning. And then this.
He'd never expected to feature as a solo artist, and now he finds pleasure in the experience.
It's new — that's important. Repetition leeches the life out of him. Further down the track,
Gurrumul will confide in Michael that he had very big doubts about anyone actually liking
the album he was making, but creating the album itself — that he loved. And he will confide
something else: his pride in his achievement; his delight that something that should have had
next to no chance of success found hundreds of thousands of ecstatic listeners. Michael says:

*Recording that album was a return to life for Gurrumul, if I can put it that way. You
know, people are often waiting for something that makes them feel more … more complete,
that completes them in some way, and that might be a child — it often is a child. And
even though Gurrumul wouldn't say this, I think that the album was like that for him
— something was lacking and it made him feel complete. I might be seeing this all in too
romantic a way, that's possible, but I really believe that it meant something special to him,
gave him that feeling of being complete. Other things came into it, but I think what he did
with that album, psychologically, was incredibly important for him and for his family.*

A work of art is a jigsaw of judgments and, at Audrey Studios, the puzzling is Michael's
responsibility. Within his own culture, Gurrumul makes his own way, but when it comes to the
white world, he's prepared to let Michael make the call. He doesn't want the grief. Everything
that comes naturally to Gurrumul has to be considered before it's acted on, as if the foreign

language he's required to speak extends to the whole of white culture: a foreign language of manners and customs, of things that are acceptable and things that are not. When he appears shy, it is often a shyness of not knowing the way ahead; of unsureness. Michael will take Gurrumul's hand during their public appearances and guide him to his chair on stage, and he guides him in just the same way in all negotiations with the white world. This album tells of people and places either dear or sacred to Gurrumul's clan — it is nonetheless a whitefella thing. When Gurrumul's uncle Djuŋa speaks of bridges between cultures, he's not talking of two groups of people separated by a chasm, each struggling to reach the other. No, he's talking of Indigenous people, with so little prospect of reward, reaching over the chasm to those on the other side, offering everything they've got. Gurrumul is not chasing fame or riches, he doesn't need to be here; he's acting out the generous impulse of a generous people. Part of that generosity is saying to Michael: 'I'm here with my voice, you know how to achieve this thing, make it happen.'

To Craig at the studio, Michael says: 'Maybe some strings. What do you think?'

Craig shakes his head. 'I don't think it needs it.'

'No?'

'No.'

Much later, Michael says: 'There was a sort of epiphany for me when we'd finished the recording. I thought we had something extraordinary. I left the studio, rang Mark and all I said was "Got it!" Can you imagine going back before Gurrumul's time and releasing an album in Australia in language, all acoustic, and thinking it's going to go great?'

Those halcyon days at Audrey will translate into the twelve-track *Gurrumul* album, but only after months of mixing and tweaking. Michael, Gurrumul and Shirley will fly home to Darwin and immerse themselves in the lives they led before Sydney Road. The journey that Gurrumul will soon commence — the journey he knows nothing about, as yet — will take him all over the world. He will spend more time away from home, from country, than ever before in his life. Australians who have never heard any of Gurrumul's languages are about to listen to its syllables for an hour or more, enchanted. The monochrome image of Gurrumul with his blind eyes downcast and the light reflecting from his forehead and cheekbones will appear in magazines all over Australia. The success that will come — and it will fulfil him in certain ways — is not going to make nearly as much difference to the fundamentals of his life as an equivalent success would make in the life of a non-Indigenous artist. His family, his clan, will forever mean infinitely more to him than platinum albums, than acclaim.

Michael says: 'He doesn't think of sales. He never thinks of the market. He never thinks of the half a million copies that the album sold. It doesn't amaze him. He doesn't know what it means. He's constantly amazed by people recognising him, or knowing him, and coming up to him and saying, "I know your music, I love your music, I love what you do." All that sort of stuff. But he's not thinking about how famous he must be, nothing like that. He likes it when it happens — it pleases him at a certain level. But it's not important.'

Going for a mark —w football and music rule supreme at Galiwin'ku.

CHAPTER 23

More Piano

The second album, like the first, is determined to provide a largely non-Indigenous audience with the opportunity to embrace the music.

The single most important thing to be said about the collaboration between Gurrumul, Michael Hohnen, Mark Grose and Skinnyfish Music is that it has produced superb music. It's a point worth making, even if it seems obvious, because the artistic accomplishment of the partnership is sometimes overwhelmed by the cultural and political implications of Gurrumul's emergence. Any benefit the songs provide to our understanding of Indigenous culture; any deepening of our sympathy for the Indigenous cause is to be welcomed, but the music comes first.

What the two Gurrumul albums provide is a series of daring experiments that succeeded against the odds. The languages in which the songs are sung — Gälpu, Gumatj, Gupapuyŋu — should be alienating, but instead they enhance the impact of each song; the narratives should be baffling, but instead we seem to follow them with growing intimacy; the rhythms should reach our ears only to have us baulk, but instead we welcome them. Even the beauty and fine temper of the Gurrumul voice could become cloying in certain songs, and yet we never tire of its subtlety. In other words, what we should be listening to is World Music at its most indulgent; instead, we hear something that conjures the mystery of a continent we thought we knew completely.

When Bruce Elder famously wrote in the *Sydney Morning Herald* (11 April 2008) that Gurrumul's voice was the finest Australia had ever produced, he might have qualified his claim by saying it was the finest vernacular voice. Or need he have bothered?

A voice highly trained for art music has some advantages over an untrained vernacular voice, and a lot of disadvantages. An art voice is of little benefit when it comes to dramatising what happens in the real world of living people; our lives, after all, are lived in the vernacular. Sinatra's voice worked with the vernacular, superbly, and so did Bob Dylan's. The crucial question is: can the voice carry passion to its destination? And how many destinations can it reach? Gurrumul's voice carries that freight of passion to almost every point on the emotional

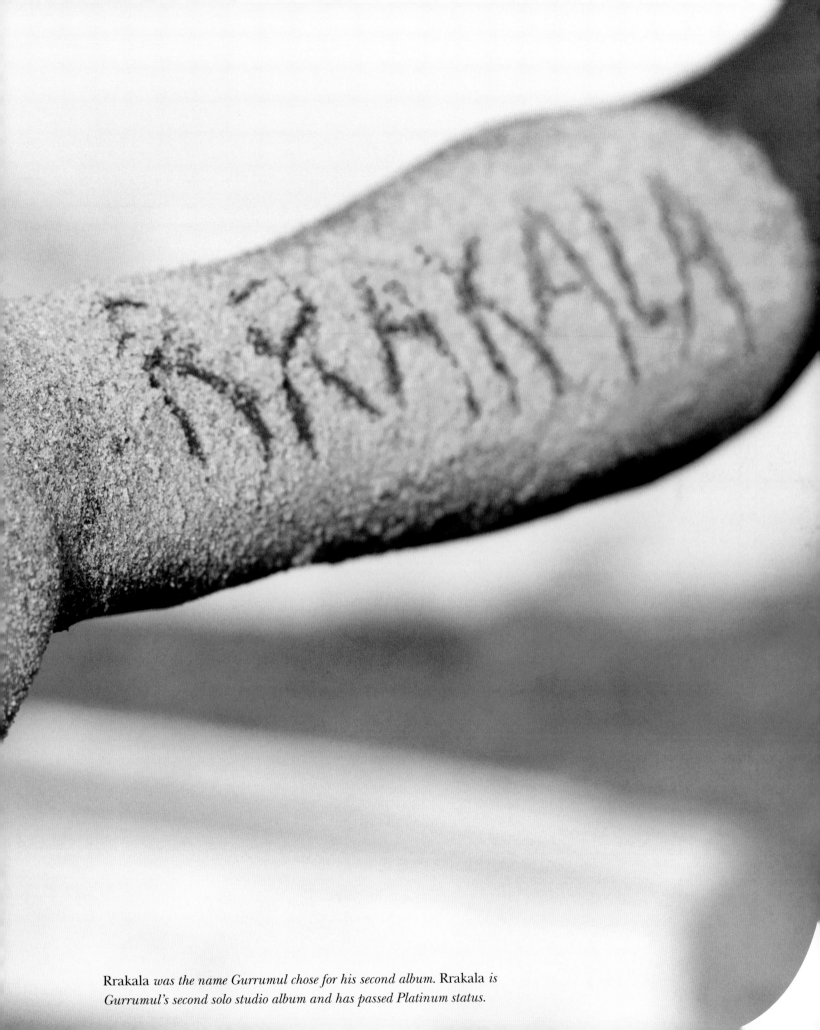

Rrakala *was the name Gurrumul chose for his second album.* Rrakala *is Gurrumul's second solo studio album and has passed Platinum status.*

WUL̲MINDA

Ya nhalpiyan nyäku Wul̲minda

Oh how my thoughts are focussing

Munhakuyin yä gärulwarul

Like night closing in, like the darkness of jungle

Dhawal-mukthuwan, Gayku Mawuymana

Country falls away, the path lies ahead Gayku, Manuymana

Watharraŋarr Djunuŋuŋu

Watharraŋarr Djunuŋuwu

Yakurr-wätjuwan, Yolŋuwa dhawalmiŋuwa

Sleep descends upon the elder-ancestor

Muluymuluyyin ya Dhorupurra

Lying, resting, elder-ancestor Dhorupurra

Ŋaya gunyanmin, barrpa wakumid̲il̲i

I give myself, to the earth

Gunyanminan Yolŋu Gurruwiwi

Placing myself, elder-ancestor Gurruwiwi

Warraw'wilyuwan nyäku Minitjpurr

Afternoon approaches, the shade of the shelter shifts

Ŋayiŋa ya Mulakala

Country Mulakala

Ŋayiŋa Gamurramburr

Country Gamurramburr

Yakurr-watjuwan nyäku gärulwarul

Sleep descends, like the darkness of the jungle

Yakurr-watjuwan nyäku gärulwarul

Sleep descends, like the darkness of the jungle

Munyakuyin nyäku Wul̲minda

My mind and thoughts sleep

A tender song of oneness with those who have given the Gumatj their wisdom and lore. Wulminda is a name of honour for an ancestor of his mother's. The sorrow of the song is so mixed with esteem that it can't be spoken of as a song of mourning, or even of the mourning to come. The extremely spare piano and double-bass accompaniment complements the mood of calm and quiet acceptance of all that will come.

compass of his people. (It would have to be conceded that his temperament doesn't take in much on the anger spectrum.)

The opening to 'Wiyathul', a wistful song of memories from the *Gurrumul* album, is a sigh set to music, and Gurrumul weaves that sigh all through the song. In 'Djärimirri', a song of gladness also from *Gurrumul*, Gurrumul manages to control the sentiment of quiet affirmation so that we are left with something as tender as a cradle song. In other songs, he is capable of not only conjuring poignance, but of varying the poignance with a deft modulation of tone.

The album has also been carefully judged to appeal to mainstream listeners. It's not an album of traditional songs and sounds; no ritual chanting, no clapsticks, no *yidaki* (didgeridoo), no imitative bird cries. True Indigenous music is so alien to Western ears in its rhythms and structures that it would have a hard time attracting any non-Indigenous listeners other than collectors of exotic music.

Michael Hohnen goes further: 'It's not an Indigenous album at all,' he says, meaning that it hasn't attempted the rough-hewn quality that Yothu Yindi or Warumpi perfected on certain tracks. If the album is to be a portrayal of a black Australian raising his voice on an Elcho Island beach, it's probably better to concede that a lot of influences have made their way to that shoreline. Nothing matters more to Gurrumul than his heritage, but it would be false to pretend that he is his heritage and nothing more. He's also 'Jailhouse Rock', 'I Shot the Sheriff', 'Amazing Grace', 'The Name of the Beast', 'Walk of Life', 'No Woman, No Cry', 'Summer Holiday', 'Ticket to Ride', 'Hallowed Be Thy Name', 'You Are the Sunshine of My Life'. An album of strictly traditional songs out of East Arnhem Land would no more convey the vigour and variety of Gurrumul's musical being than would a record of Beatles hits. This follow-up album, neither traditional nor truly Indigenous, is the honest testament of a black Australian whose sources of delight take in the creativity of people from all over the world.

That said, the songs, even when sung in their winning way, are unlike anything recorded before them. Gurrumul's uncle David (Djuŋa), taking on a role like Michael's and saying what Gurrumul himself leaves unsaid, tells us that the songs are all from the soul; 'From his spirit, in here,' he says, putting his hand on his heart. All sorts of claims of singing from the soul are made by all sorts of people, but in the case of Gurrumul, it's actual. The fabulous, nuanced voice and the brilliant settings wrought by Michael do not give us the most telling feature of Gurrumul's singing, which is its complete loyalty to its origins. Gurrumul is not a tourist in the culture of his people; he lives it and breathes it. The identity he carries with him everywhere is Gumatj, and that's where the passion in his voice that so impressed Gary Barlow comes from: the riches of his heritage. Michael has the talent to get something bigger and better out of almost anyone with a good voice and some musical wherewithal, but he cannot give Gurrumul the passion that carries the songs to their destination.

What Gurrumul sings about does not stray far from country, ancestors, his family, his people. He sings of love and longing, of sorrows to be acknowledged, of the exultation of being a proud man amongst the proud men of his clan, of his mother and his mothers, of the life-giving rituals of the Gumatj. There are no love songs in the age-old tradition of Western songwriting; no songs of sexual conquest, of erotic engagement; no songs in the tradition of black American blues; no songs of political protest; nothing especially wry or comic.

We think of song lyrics as the poetry of everyday life, but the lyrics of Gurrumul's songs are not conceived as poetry in the Western sense. Poetry is an attempt at original language; at saying things that haven't been said in exactly that way before. Its freshness is honoured, as is its brilliance in illustration; its freedom from cliché.

The emphasis in the cultures of Indigenous Australians has not always fallen on originality, for its own sake; originality has to demonstrate its compatability with custom and tradition. There are no clichés in Indigenous languages. Nor do Indigenous stories and songs employ symbols and metaphors in the manner of Western writers. A rock is an ancestor, and the ancestor is celebrated for his strength and wisdom, but the rock doesn't symbolise the strong and wise ancestor; it is the ancestor. If we wish to, we can convert figures in Gurrumul's lyrics to metaphors and symbols, and say of the storm clouds, 'They express generation and regeneration'. But that's not what Gurrumul thinks. The storm clouds of 'Wukun' are the Gälpu people and have no metaphoric function at all.

Gurrumul's lyrics are made up of the traditional names of people and places, linked by the idioms of Yolŋu Matha: 'Storm clouds rising, storm clouds forming … heading to Djarraraŋ, Milbunbun, Yarawarrtji, Yarrawaŋu, Galtjurrwanŋu, Wurrumba, Nukunuku, Maminŋu …' A complex network of lore governs the use of traditional names, and it is in the observance of that lore that the poetry of the songs lives. Gurrumul is approved by his people for knowing what to say and how to say it. It's for this reason that he has no need to preserve the lyrics of his songs in writing because the lyrics already exist in the vast archive of Yolŋu idioms.

Gurrumul, as Michael maintains, is not truly an Indigenous album at all. He distinguishes three categories of songs on the album. The first is the contemporary Western folk-style ballad, and in this category Michael places 'Djärimirri'. The second is traditional/contemporary, and 'Wukun' would be an example. The third is traditional ambient — songs which include improvisation around a traditional theme, such as 'Gäthu Mawula', a song Gurrumul wrote for the woman who cared for him in Darwin. The songs in each of these categories, even when improvised, still employ basic Yolŋu Matha idioms, but in 'Gäthu Mawula', when Gurrumul sings '… the breeze will make you clever, make you clever …' he leaves the template behind. That is as far as he can depart from traditional idioms, and probably as far as he would wish to.

Manhattan, winter 2011. Gurrumul has been here twice before — with Yothu Yindi back in 1999, and as a solo performer of growing fame in 2010, when he performed with Olivia and Jimmy Barnes at Carnegie Hall. The mission of this third visit is to lay down tracks for a new solo album.

Gurrumul adores New York; his favourite city of all. It's partly the distinctive New York soundscape, which he picks up with his subtle hearing and builds into shapes and forms, and partly what he's been told about New York, and what every visit confirms: that this is the place in the world where the best of everything in music has its home. As the 747 begins its approach to New York City, he suddenly calls to Michael: 'Stevie Wonder!' — a fragment of thought that has escaped the vault in which he keeps so much of what goes on in his mind. Stevie Wonder is one of his idols, and Stevie has recorded some of his finest work in New York. 'Ladies and gentlemen, we have commenced our descent to John F. Kennedy Airport. Please remain in your seats and keep your seat-belt fastened.' Stevie. The best. New York City. The best.

It was winter on his last visit, snow everywhere, piled on parked cars and the branches of trees. This year, the snow is actually falling. Michael has rented an apartment on Bleecker Street in Greenwich Village, just west of Broadway and a couple of minutes down from Washington Square. Gurrumul stands on the balcony with his chin raised, letting the snowflakes settle on his face. Later, Michael takes his friend and Bronwyn down to MacDougal Street for a burger.

Electric Ladyland Studios on West 8th, built by Jimmy Hendrix in 1970, is the intended venue for the recording of the new album, but at about the time that Gurrumul and Michael were landing at Kennedy, the mixing board at the studio blew up. A technician from London is flying in to rebuild the board, which is all well and good, but it will take two weeks. As a backup, Michael had asked Avatar Studios, further afield on West 43rd Street, to hold a few days for Gurrumul, and it's in Avatar that Gurrumul prepares to record the first track for what will become *Rrakala*, his second solo album, two days after arriving in Manhattan.

The snowflakes. Gurrumul in the open air on the balcony. Maybe not such a great idea. On the morning of the third day in Manhattan, Gurrumul won't open the door to his room.

'Have to get down to the studio!' Michael calls through the door. But the door remains shut.

'What's wrong?'

Gurrumul won't say. Bronwyn won't say.

'Are you sick, *wäwa?*'

Because he almost certainly is. He's not about to say so; it embarrasses him. Michael can hear him coughing.

'You've got a cold? Is that it? You've got a cold? Got the flu?'

Nothing.

'I'll get you some medicine.'

Nothing. But the offer of medicine was unlikely to be taken up in any case. Gurrumul harbours a deep suspicion of medicines, doctors and hospitals.

Michael can only wait. Gurrumul knows that the bill at the studio has to be paid even when he's in his room dealing with the cold or the flu or whatever he's suffering from, and it distresses him. It is at the foundation of his relationship with Michael that silences like this are accepted as a form of eloquence.

Avatar is prepared to hold Gurrumul's slot in the schedule for a couple of days. The studio has only once before extended this courtesy to an artist, and that was for Mariah Carey.

And two days is enough. Gurrumul emerges from his room maybe a little the worse for wear, but ready to record.

'You okay, *wäwa?*' Michael enquires.

'Yo. Good.'

Recording the first solo album was a delight for Gurrumul in most ways, but a delight mixed with apprehension, at times. He was puzzled. What was he supposed to achieve? He had performed with Yothu Yindi, with Saltwater, but he had never thought of himself as a solo act. Some of Michael's suggestions during that period of recording the first album had struck him (so he later confessed) as insanely over-optimistic. He found it difficult to imagine customers queuing up to purchase a disc in Yolŋu Matha by a musician they'd never heard of. The great success of Gurrumul, artistically and commercially, has altered the way he thinks about himself. Heading into Avatar to record this second album, he is more confident in what can be achieved, more willing to take the initiative. He has come to accept, in a certain way, that he can do things that other people cannot; that his talents single him out. This has sometimes

MEANING OF HOME

No English words are good enough to give a
sense of the links between an Aboriginal group
and its homeland. Our word 'home', warm and
suggestive though it may be, does not match the
Aboriginal word that may mean 'camp', 'hearth',
'country', 'everlasting home', 'totem place',
'life source', 'spirit centre' and much else all in
one. Our word, 'land' is too spare and meagre
… To put our words 'home' and 'land' together
into 'homeland' is a little better but not much.
A different tradition leaves us tongueless and
earless towards this other world of meaning
and significance.

W.E.H. Stanner

Weekends are special times on Elcho Island.
Families go hunting and finish the day
cooking fish or damper on the beach.

GURRUMUL
— R R A K A L A —

The front cover of Gurrumul's second album Rrakala. *This photograph by Adrian Cook captures everything about Gurrumul at that time in his life — the calm and peace that had always been there, now merged with his new-found confidence in his solo career.*

been awkward for him. His culture has only a limited use for celebrity pedestals. It has taken some getting used to, but in the studio, day after day, he demonstrates what might be termed as loyalty to his gift, as if it is as much a part of his identity as his totems. Or almost.

Michael: 'It's a singer–songwriter's album — not intended to be the same as *Gurrumul*. In the making of the first album, he took up every suggestion I made. *Rrakala* is Gurrumul after three years of attracting attention; this is him confident enough to exert more influence on what we did on the album. He was making comments all the way through, like, "Michael, Michael, we need to do this — I want to do this — we should do this traditional thing here".'

Gurrumul and Michael are in the studio for ten days, and over that time, they develop a fine rapport with the engineer, Anthony Ruotolo. Ten days in a studio — any studio – builds an intimacy very like that of a domestic relationship. It takes in the dash and daring of each party (the artist, the producer, the engineer) but also the insecurities, the doubts. Creating the album calls for hundreds of individual judgments. The artist can't get all of those calls right; nor will the producer, nor will the engineer, but between the three of them, something bigger than the sum of the parts is possible. And this is exactly what unfolds at Avatar. Michael and Gurrumul eek out the nuances they're hoping for by trial and error, by intuition. Gurrumul's voice is new to Anthony, but he picks up its potential quickly and offers his enabling suggestions. The recording of the album is regularly set aside for Gurrumul's calls to Elcho, for a cigarette upstairs, a Pepsi, a burger. Song by song, this second album finds its form. And in the background, in the foreground, New York. So strange to think that this blind musician from Elcho Island should respond so sympathetically to a place that stands at the other extreme from the Galiwin'ku backwater. New York. Stevie Wonder. The best.

So what was achieved in *Rrakala*, this album that went on to sell seventy thousand copies in its first year of release, and to attract a great deal of critical acclaim?

Gurrumul's first solo album, *Gurrumul*, was characterised by the poignancy, sweetness and passion of the singing and included as many as five out of twelve songs that could be considered masterpieces. All but a few verses of two songs were rendered in languages native to Gurrumul.

The songs on *Rrakala*, like all but two of those on the first solo album, are also sung entirely in language — once again, a deliberate strategy of drawing closer to the clan origins of Gurrumul's music. The second album, like the first, is determined to provide a largely non-Indigenous audience with the opportunity to embrace the music. This is not the ritual music of the Gumatj, designed to support ceremony and nothing else, but music in the language of ritual, tempered by an emphasis on melody and familiar narrative progression.

Rrakala, like *Gurrumul*, is a collage portrait of ancestors, family, country and ritual, but it provides Gurrumul with a greater opportunity to engage the listener with a sound more typical of unmediated Gumatj voices.

One important innovation on *Rrakala* is the introduction of piano parts. Listeners to the first album wouldn't have known that the piano was one of the instruments within Gurrumul's mastery, although piano was prominent on the exquisite, 'Djilawurr', the first track on the second Saltwater album, *Djarridjarri*. This was the song and setting that announced Gurrumul's individual genius, and both Michael and Gurrumul wanted more piano on *Rrakala*. A grand piano is a huge departure from the vernacular musical traditions of the Gumatj, yet its contributions on the album come across as entirely natural, as if the Indigenous languages in which Gurrumul's songs are rendered and the keyboard of the quintessential Western musical instrument were in perfect sympathy.

The tracks of the album, including the piano parts, were first recorded at Avatar, of course, but back in Australia neither Gurrumul nor Michael was satisfied with the piano's tone and carry. Maybe one listener in ten thousand was likely to notice that the Steinway was fractionally out of tune, but one in ten thousand was too many. For the sake of that one listener in ten thousand, Michael sought out another studio to re-record the piano complement and suggested 301 Studios at Byron Bay, since Gurrumul loved Byron: 'Michael, here, this place, Michael. If we make some money, one day I want to buy a house here.'

Another priority on *Rrakala* was to give Gurrumul's voice its fullest range, or really his voices, plural, because there are a number. He can sing in his 'old man' voice with an edge like bark being torn from a tree trunk; and he can sing with a soft, caressing lilt, like Sam Cooke on 'Soothe Me' or Johnny Mathis on 'When I Fall in Love'; he has another voice full of shadows and mists, reserved for songs of sorrow; another that rings with the liberty of a young man throwing his arms around life, heard on the Saltwater albums; and yet another when he sings of love and longing and finds in his throat varying qualities of poignancy. And more still. These voices aren't produced simply by the modulation of emotion; each is distinctly formed to suit a particular song.

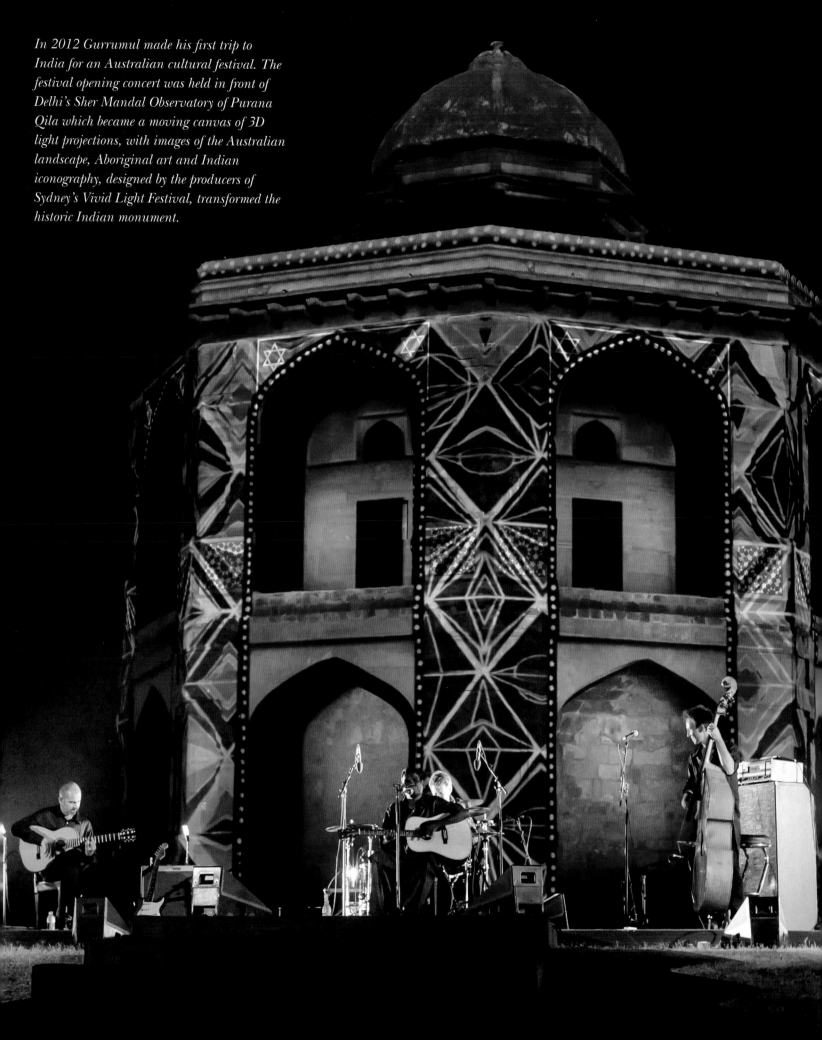

In 2012 Gurrumul made his first trip to India for an Australian cultural festival. The festival opening concert was held in front of Delhi's Sher Mandal Observatory of Purana Qila which became a moving canvas of 3D light projections, with images of the Australian landscape, Aboriginal art and Indian iconography, designed by the producers of Sydney's Vivid Light Festival, transformed the historic Indian monument.

CHAPTER 24

Sight

The eyes are left in darkness not to dramatise
Gurrumul's sightlessness, but to suggest the mystery
of what he sees in his mind's eye.

It's Grand Final day in the Gove Australian Football League: Nguykal Kingfish v. Gopu Stingrays. The match is being played at Gove further down the coast from Elcho, across Buckingham Bay. Ten people have gathered at Galiwin'ku airport to catch a charter flight to the game. The women are dressed in the Top End Indigenous costume of loose top, brightly patterned skirt flowing below knee-level; the men in T-shirts and long, baggy shorts. Gurrumul is amongst the men. This is his treat, the Grand Final outing. He's on his mobile attempting to arrange a second aircraft, since it's strictly five to a plane. He says: 'No way!' Then: 'Gove, yeah.'

The pilot of the waiting plane gives a small sigh and shakes his head. 'Are we good to go?' he asks, not with optimism.

Gurrumul tries another number.

'Grand Final,' he says. 'Gove.'

Two of the kids in the party handball an empty juice pack to each other, pausing to see if there's been some good news. Everything depends on Gurrumul. Sharing is at the foundation of Indigenous culture and it would be unthinkable, on a day like this, if one of the clan, with the money and a mobile, refused to get you to the Granny. The pilot, a white guy, is hunkering down for a protracted period of negotiation, holding his clipboard to his chest and jabbing with the toe of his shoe at the red earth on the side of the runway.

I'm watching. And as far as I can tell, nobody's going to get to the Grand Final at Gove.

Bronwyn has a suggestion to make. No sooner has she spoken than four other women lift their hands and shake their heads. This leads to a fresh colloquy which may or may not have anything to do with aeroplanes and football matches. Gurrumul stands in the middle of the group of women, asking for the hush that will allow him to hear what he's saying. The kids return to handballing the juice container.

All at once there's peace and quiet. Gurrumul pockets his mobile and stands with his

At Gurrumul's first solo concert in Darwin, Skinnyfish brought Sam Karanikos up from Melbourne to photograph him. Sam captured Gurrumul's smile — something that had gone unrecorded all through the Saltwater years. Sam was also responsible for the wonderful image of Gurrumul that appears on the cover of the first album. This image is one of Mark and Michael's favourites, distilling the beautiful, gentle spirit behind the music.

DJOMULA

Ya..a, e..e, ya..a, e..e, e..e wo..o..

Djomula djomula, djomula djomula

Djomula, djomula, djomula, djomula

Nhenydja ŋäthiyana, dhiyakuŋu buluwunuwuŋu

Djalathaŋguŋu, Bärra'wuŋu, ŋäthi nhina luŋgurrmawuŋu

Djomula djomula, djomula djomula

Djomula, djomula, djomula, djomula

Nhumanydja gutha ma<u>n</u>da yarrupthurruna

Märraŋana Gäpirrinha, wiripunydja ŋä<u>n</u>di'nha djukurrnha,

Djukurrwu<u>t</u>i

Ya..a, yi..i,

Nhenydja waku bu<u>n</u>bu<u>n</u>ana, makarrnha balalapu

Namba Mirrinydjuraŋu, Wayŋarrŋarr, Yumayŋa

Yi..i wo..o, yi..i wo..o, yi..i wo..o, yi..i wo..o.

Yapa gay, yapa gay

Yapa gay, yapa gay

Yapa gay, yapa gay

Yapa gay yapa gay

Nhälili nhe ŋarranha ganarrana?

Dhipala djomulalili, wuyupthurruna gu<u>n</u>dalili,

Bakitju Rirralinydhu

Nambalili Bandirriyayu, Guymalamurruyu Gawupuyu

Djomula djomula, djomula djomula

Djomula, djomula, djomula, djomula

Nhenydja ŋäthiyana, dhiyakuŋu buluwunuwuŋu

Djalathaŋguŋu, Bärra'wuŋu, ŋäthi nhina luŋgurrmawuŋu

Ya..a e..e..

Ya..a, e..e, ya..a, e..e, e..e wo..o.. (sound of weeping trees)

Djomula djomula, djomula djomula

Djomula, djomula, djomula, djomula

You weep, from this east (wind)

south (wind), west (wind), weep from the north (wind)

Djomula djomula, djomula djomula

Djomula, djomula, djomula, djomula

You my younger brothers go down

Catch Gäpirri, and also (my) mother Djukurruwu<u>t</u>i

Ya..a, yi..i (sound of weeping beach trees)

My sister's child, you make a beach shelter

The big named place Mirrinydjuraŋu,

Wayŋarrŋarr, Yumayŋa

Yi..i wo..o, (sound of wind in the beach trees)

Dear sister, dear sister

Dear sister, dear sister

Dear sister, dear sister

Dear sister, dear sister

For which place did you leave me?

For these Djomula trees you left the Rock over the horizon

The Rock Bakitju, Rirraliny

The big named places; Bandirriyayu, Guymalamurruyu

Gawupuyu

Djomula djomula, djomula djomula

Djomula, djomula, djomula, djomula

You weep, from this east (wind)

south (wind), west (wind), weep from the north (wind)

Ya..a e..e, (sound of wind in the beach trees)

Saltwater gave 'Djomula' a jaunty keyboard and guitar intro and performed it as if they wanted the audience up on their feet and clapping along. It's actually a song recalling the departed. Djomula is the casuarina tree of the far north. The wind blowing over the needles of the trees recalls kin who have gone into the earth. Gurrumul thinks of times past when those who have departed were still amongst his people, still close to him. 'Djomula' is not a song of grief but, rather, a drama of the mystery of life and death.

head lifted. The women shuffle about with nothing more to say. Somehow, an agreement has been worked out.

I ask, puzzled: 'So, two planes?'

Gurrumul shrugs. The pilot attempts to gather the names of those he'll be flying to Gove on his manifest. Spelling is always a problem. The pilot says to one of the women who's following what's he's attempting to write on his clipboard: 'N, G, A?'

The woman says: 'N, G, G, A.'

'N, G, G, A? Like that?'

'No. N, J, A.'

'N, J, A?'

'Yeah, yeah.'

Gurrumul says: 'One plane.'

So this is the resolution. One plane, five passengers. The five who have priority — starting with Gurrumul and Bronwyn — separate themselves just a little from those who have missed out. It's as if a tribal council has been in progress, and a decision handed down.

The pilot says: 'Okay, let's go. All of those whose names I've got. Okay?'

The group of five shuffles out to the small, white Piper. Those left behind have no complaints; some sort of acceptable clan justice has just gone into this resolution, so it seems.

A white friend of Gurrumul's has been standing outside the group of ten contenders for a Grand Final seat, chuckling to himself as the negotiations unfolded. He's here to wave farewell. He calls out something satirical to Gurrumul, reminding him that he's now one of the wise men of his clan, making decisions like those of Solomon.

Gurrumul calls back with a wave: 'You go home now, long-grass man! You go home!'

A 'long-grass man', in the Indigenous argot of north-east Arnhem land, is a no-hoper, sleeping in the outdoors at all hours with his grog and his grievances.

The Grand Final party clambers aboard. Their movements as they stoop and find their seats are expert: it's Indigenous folk who sustain the entire air charter industry of Northern Australia, hopping from island to island or up to Darwin, fulfilling the obligations of ceremony and ritual, funerals, feasts, weddings.

The single-engine plane runs its prop up to taxiing speed and bumps off down the runway. Even before the plane has left the tarmac, the five would-be passengers left behind are sauntering back towards town in that erect way that Indigenous people carry themselves, a striking blend of languor and verticality.

It's airborne now, the little plane, carrying Gurrumul on his umpteenth flight in aircraft great and small. This is his reward — the liberty to ferry his friends and family anywhere and whenever he wishes. The recognition of his genius is welcome in its way, although it's mostly his family he's pleased for. But this is the real repayment for all the absences from his home on Elcho; for the homesickness; for the long hours in studios laying down tracks: flying off to the Grand Final at Gove with Bronwyn, an auntie, a cousin and a niece.

The Grand Final will be played and won. Gurrumul will return from Gove and within a month or so will be working on a new album, and later still commencing a new tour. The new album, the new tour — both are far from his mind today. He wants to be a face in the crowd down near the goal posts, not singing but cheering as a cousin or a nephew takes a spectacular mark and threads one through from hard up against the boundary. But there is a road ahead for his music. He'll put his foot to it when he's ready.

Who is Gurrumul? He is Geoffrey Gurrumul Yunupiŋu, a troubadour, hailing from the sunshine and shoreline of the island of Elcho in the Arafura Sea. He is Gudjuk, another of his names. He is the beloved child of his clan, the son, the father, the brother, the uncle, the nephew. At a deeper level, he is a figure who emerged from the dreaming of his clan; and he has been here as long as the dreaming, in one form or another. He became Gurrumul and the only person he could ever have become was Gurrumul. He has sung of his identity in 'Gurrumul History', in these words:

I am Batumaŋ
I am Djarrami
I am Djeŋarra'
I am Gurrumulŋa
I am Barrupa
I am Dhukulul
I am Maralitja
I am Ŋunbuŋunbu …

He is his ancestors, his totem, his country, his people.
And he is the songs he sings.

TEAM EUROPE

Gurrumul's international success started with a chance meeting between Mark Grose and the lawyer Robert Horsfall at Midem, the music industry's annual get together in Cannes. Robert negotiated a deal with independent label Dramatico. Robert had already been championing Gurrumul which had resulted in an appearance on the influential BBC TV show *Later With Jools Holland.*

I gathered a team to spread the word across Europe. Firstly support in the UK from BBC Radio 2 who playlisted three songs from Gurrumul's debut album, thank you to Jeff Smith, Gary Bones, Simon Mayo, Jeremy Vine & Johnnie Walker. This lifted Gurrumul's profile considerably and performances on TV programmes *BBC Breakfast* and *The Andrew Marr Show* followed. This early coverage paved the way for Gurrumul's appearance three years later on The Queen's Diamond Jubilee Concert at Buckingham Palace.

The song 'Wiyathul' was sent to Thomas Mueller, a producer at SWR3 one of Germany's most popular and influential radio stations, who immediately programmed the song. Due to Thomas' fast reaction Gurrumul came to the attention of Germany's current affairs TV show *Heute Journal* who ran a story on Gurrumul, resulting in a German Top 10 album chart position. Thank you Thomas.

In France radio support from France Inter and Europe 1 and a heart stopping duet with Sting of 'Every Breath You Take' on the TV show *Taratata* sent the album flying up the charts, thank you Nagui. Gurrumul's mainstream success in France and Germany opened the door for further chart action in Belgium and Switzerland where he also went on to appear on many TV and radio shows. The story continues …

Thank you: Robert Horsfall, Mike Batt, Tim Brown, Chris Carr, Emma Camfield, Stuart Emery, Chris Goodman, Chris Hession, Matt Connolly, Sue Harris, Songlines, Sven Meyer, Bernd Herrmann, Bruno Philippart, Marie-Soleil, Philippe Giard, Boris Vedel, Ramon Rey, Rafaela Spitzli, Thomas Vierstraete, Jo Langela, Sophie Van Der Hoeven, Alice Wilems, Paul Davies & Margaret Maliszewska.

Andrew Bowles — Dramatico

BIBLIOGRAPHY

Books

Birch, Bruce, Girribuk, Rae, Hoeng, Sabine *et al* (2008), *Kindi ngamin nuwung? What do I call you? A Guide to Kinship and Address,* Jabiru, Northern Territory

Brown, Graham (2011), *Wildlife of the Northern Territory,* Vol. 2, Charles Darwin University Press, Darwin

Cawte, John (2010), *Healers of Arnhem Land,* Gecko Books, Marleston, South Australia

Flood, Josephine (2006), *The Original Australians: Story of the Aboriginal People,* Allen and Unwin, Crows Nest, Sydney

Goldenberg, Howard (2009), *Raft,* Hybrid, Melbourne

Kleinart, Sylvia and Neale, Margot (eds) (2000), *Oxford Companion to Aboriginal Art and Culture,* Oxford University Press, Melbourne

Mahood, Kim (2000), *Craft for a Dry Lake,* Anchor, Milsons Point, Sydney

Perkins, Rachel and Langton, Marcia (eds) (2008), *First Australians, An Illustrated History,* Miegunyah Press (Melbourne University Press), Carlton, Melbourne

Reynolds, Henry (1998), *This Whispering in Our Hearts,* Allen and Unwin, Crows Nest, Sydney

Rowlinson, Eric (Introduction) (1981), *Aboriginal Australia,* catalogue, contributors Carol Cooper , Howard Morphy, John Mulvaney, Nicolas Peterson, Australian Gallery Directors Council Ltd, Sydney

Stanner, W. E. H (2009), *The Dreaming and Other Essays,* introduction by Robert Manne, Black Ink Agenda, Collingwood, Melbourne

Turner, Margaret Kemarre (2010), *Iwenhe Tyerrtye: What it means to be an Aboriginal Person,* translation Veronia Perrurle Dobson, IAD Press, Alice Springs

Websites

'Gurrumul — Son of the Rainbow Serpent in Gailwin'ku', ABC TV *Message Stick,* 26 October 2008 (www.abc.net.au/tv/messagestick/stories/s2400713.htm)

www.abc.net.au/indigenous (The ABC Indigenous website)

www.indigenousaustralia.info

www.artgallery.nsw.gov.au

www.acih.anu.edu.au (The Australian Centre of Indigenous Studies at Australian National University)

www.australianmuseum.net.au/indigenousstudies

www.cdu.edu.au (The website of Charles Darwin University)

www.dhimurra.com.au/yolngu-culture (The website of the Dhimurra Aboriginal Corporation)

www.ealta.org/yolngupeople (The website of the East Arnhem Land Tourist Association)

www.indigenous.gov.au (A government website dedicated to information on Indigenous affairs and research material on Indigenous cultures)

www.naa.gov.au (The website of the National Archives)

www.ngv.vic.gov.au (The website of the National Gallery of Victoria, including the collection of the Ian Potter Centre in Federation Square)

www.nma.gov.au (The website of the National Museum of Australia)

www.usq.edu.au/caik (The website of the Centre for Indigenous Knowledges at the University of Southern Queensland)

www.yolngu.net (A site dedicated to the culture of the Yolngu people)

Recordings

Gurrumul, Geoffrey Gurrumul Yunupingu, Skinnyfish Music, 2008

Rrakala, Geoffrey Gurrumul Yunupingu, Skinnyfish Music, 2011

Gurrumul Live in Darwin, Geoffrey Gurrumul Yunupingu, Skinnyfish Music, 2010

Gapu Damurrunj, Saltwater Band, Skinnyfish Music, 1999

Djarridjarri, Saltwater Band, Skinnyfish Music, 2004

Malk, Saltwater Band, Skinnyfish Music, 2009

Charcoal Lane, Archie Roach, Hightone, 1990

Looking For Butterboy, Archie Roach, Mushroom, 1997

Archie Roach The Definitive Collection, Archie Roach, Festival, 2004

Go Bush! , Warumpi Band, Parole, 1987

Big Name, No Blankets, Warumpi Band, Powderworks, 1985

Tribal Voice, Yothu Yindi, Mushroom, 1991

Garma, Yothu Yindi, Mushroom, 2000

PHOTOGRAPHIC CREDITS

The publishers and Skinnyfish Music would like to thank the following individuals and institutions for their help and for their permission to reproduce the following images:

Australian Broadcasting Corporation, Library Sales: Page 18 (bottom left)

Kara Burns: Pages 38–9, 46–7, 88–9, 274–5, 276–7

Glen Campbell: Pages 13, 41 (bottom), 69, 136, 137

Gerard Cashin: Pages 80 (top left), 115

Trevor Collins: Pages 145, 185, 188, 192–3

Jeremy Conlon: Pages 150–1

Adrian Cook Photography: iv, 3, 141, 319

Lauren Denis: Pages 199, 208–9

Dumbo Feather: Page 40

Nicholas Gouldhurst: Pages 222–3

Getty Images: Pages 253 and 257 (top) (photographer Leon Neal), 272–3 (photographer Don Arnold)

Julie Herd: Pages 26–7, 28 (both), 29, 30–1

Cameron Herweynen photographer cameronherweyen.com: Pages 86, 87, 218–9

Sophie Howarth: ii–iii, xx–xxi, 71, 76–7, 84–5, 99, 108–9, 191, 228, 268, 279, 284, 285 (all), 286–7, 288 (all), 289, 290, 291 (bottom), 292–3, endpapers

Alan James and Yothu Yindi: Pages 263, 267

Sam Karanikos: Pages 9, 44, 122–3, 134, 148, 169, 182–3, 294–5, 297, 301, 323

Tony Lewis: Pages 158–9, 160

Anne Mirrmirr McClelland / courtesy Matthew McClelland: Pages 18 (all except bottom left), 19, 25

Matt McHugh: Pages xviii, xxii–1, 10–11, 64–5, 118–9, 231, 306–7

Howard Moffat /AUSPIC: Page 229 (bottom)

Tony Mott: Page 171

National Archives of Australia: Pages 22 (M119, 108), 23 (M119, 22)

National Library of Australia: Pages 54–5 (Map Johnston Special Col./8)

Newspix: Pages 91 (photographer Richard Dobson), 94 (News Ltd), 211 (photographer Adam Ward), 225 (photographer Alex Coppel), 229 (top, photographer Brad Fleet), 271 (top, photographer Anna Rogers; bottom, photographer Robert McKell)

Northern Territory Library: Pages 61 (top) (Colin Gill Collection, PH0236/0055), 107 (Howard Truran Collection, PH0406/0578)

Steven Pam: Page 81

Duane Preston: Pages xiv–xv, 33, 41 (top), 49, 56, 57, 58, 59, 61 (bottom), 62, 66, 78–9, 96–7, 103, 104, 125, 130, 131, 138–9, 164–5, 173, 178–9, 180, 181 (top and bottom), 214–15, 217, 250, 291 (top), 309, 314–15, 326–7, 330–31, reverse front endpaper

Carlos Santone: Pages 260–1

Ted Searly / University of Sydney: 63

Shepherdson College: Pages 236–7

Tasso Taraboulis / Polaris: 153, 170

Simon de Trey-White: Pages 320, 321 (both)

The magazine covers appearing on pages 220–1 are reproduced courtesy of the following people: *Rolling Stone*; *Deadly Vibe*, courtesy of Deadly Vibe, a monthly, national magazine for Aboriginal and Torres Strait Islanders; *Songlines*, Songlines magazine, August/September 2009 (#62) www.songlines.co.uk; *Drum Media*, The Drum Media; *!Roar!* Peter Thornley and Eddy Sara; *Off the Leash*, layout by Amy Brand, photo by Anne Brandt; *Aprap*; *Map Magazine*, 'Review', Newspix, News Ltd; *X-Press Magazine*

 The ABC 'Wave' device is a trademark of the Australian Broadcasting Corporation and is used under licence by HarperCollinsPublishers Australia.

ABC Books

First published in Australia in 2013
by HarperCollins*Publishers* Australia Pty Limited
ABN 36 009 913 517
harpercollins.com.au

Copyright © Skinnyfish Music Pty Ltd 2013

Text by Robert Hillman

HarperCollins*Publishers*
Level 13, 201 Elizabeth Street, Sydney NSW 2000, Australia
31 View Road, Glenfield, Auckland 0627, New Zealand
A 53, Sector 57, Noida, UP, India
77–85 Fulham Palace Road, London W6 8JB, United Kingdom
2 Bloor Street East, 20th floor, Toronto, Ontario M4W 1A8, Canada
10 East 53rd Street, New York NY 10022, USA

9780733331169 (pbk.)
9781743096307 (ebook)

CD remixes produced by Michael Hohnen
Mixed by Matthew Cunliffe
String arrangements by Erkki Veltheim
Recordings by Craig Pilkington, Anthony Ruotolo and Jeremy Conlon

Cover photographs by Adrian Cook Photography
Cover and internal design by Hugh Ford, Matt Lin and HarperCollins Design Studio
Colour reproduction by Graphic Print Group, South Australia
Printed and bound in China by RR Donnelley on 157 gsm Gold Sun matt art paper

The papers used by HarperCollins in the manufacture of this book are a natural, recyclable product made from wood grown in sustainable plantation forests. The fibre source and manufacturing processes meet recognised international environmental standards, and carry certification.

5 4 3 2 1   13 14 15 16

GURRUMUL

HIS LIFE AND MUSIC
Song notes by Michael Hohnen

BÄPA

Gurrumul's homage to his father, with its hymn-like quality, its universal message of pride in a father and the soaring emotion in the lyrics and arrangements, never fails to inspire. We still love playing 'Bäpa' at all our concerts. Audiences all over the world respond to it. In the production of this song we wanted to enhance the mood of contemplation, and it was mixed as if it was being sung in a cathedral or large hall, with the elegance of strings introduced to reinforce this feeling. This version of 'Bäpa' features a string quartet, arranged by Errki Veltheim and solo bowed double bass.

DJILAWURR

Imagine writing a song about an orange-footed scrub fowl. In the middle of the song Gurrumul sings out to the ancestors and at its end he imitates the bird call for the Djilawurr. One of Gurrumul's favourite songs, it originally appeared on the Saltwater Band's *Djarridjarri* album, so it was a must to have. This embellished version again features the string quartet arrangements we use in some live shows, which add interest and depth to the music. It is a beautiful rock ballad, even given its avarian subject matter.

GOPURU

Gurrumul brought this song into the studio with the idea to perform it a cappella. The song worked beautifully in that style, but it also didn't quite fit on an album of other Gurrumul songs. We then put instruments with it, but it was still missing something. So we tried this piano riff after some encouragement, and what you hear on the track is the first melody Gurrumul came up with. So close and complimentary to the lead melody but so 'on its own'. It illustrates Gurrumul's melodic pop writing. His musicianship and natural ability to focus on the melody are always refreshing. The tuna dives in and out of the water and feels the splash of the waves on its face. The mix here is more atmospheric than the original.

DJÄRRIMIRI

With its moving lyric content, strong melody and harmony, many people tell us 'Djärrimiri' is their favourite Gurrumul song. We toured and performed this song across Europe, accompanied by a string quartet. This version features the same quartet parts with two violins, viola and cello. One day Gurrumul would love to do a series of concerts across Australia accompanied by a chamber string group with this as a feature track.

WUKUN

This track is a mix of traditional and contemporary styles. The traditional melody is sung as it has been sung for thousands of years, but with a very simple repetitive chord sequence. Here 'Wukun' is supported, accompanied and embellished by a moving string arrangement and a different mix.

GATHU MAWULA

Mawula Dhurrkay, Gurrumul's relative, cared for him for a period of his life. He wrote this song as a tribute to her and it is something she is very proud of. The first viola riff and quartet, written and played by Erkki Veltheim, is a real bonus to this version of 'Gathu Mawula'.

BAYINI

This is a grand folk hymn about the ancestral female spirit Bayini, who still watches over Bawaka, a region in North-east Arnhem Land. It was written by Gurrumul's relative Raywun Maymurru. It is beautifully composed in every respect, and features Gurrumul on piano playing in his lilting style, and is mixed as you would hear it in a concert hall.

WIRRPANU

Whenever there is a thunderstorm coming, Gurrumul calls out 'Wirrpaṇu'. Musically, the song is referencing the history of the local Methodist church, an influence that has been so present on Elcho Island through a part of the last century. I think there should be more gospel-style songs in Gurrumul's repertoire, but as there are not we have included this one. It is Gurrumul with pathos, singing out to the elements. This version features a piano part, played in an early Saltwater Band recording session.

BÄRU

The saltwater crocodile from Arnhem Land is Gurrumul's dominant totem. When we came to record Gurrumul's debut solo album he chose to do this song in an upbeat style, reminiscent of his Saltwater Band version. That recording showcased him as a drummer and multi-instrumentalist. I personally feel Gurrumul's songs have more emotional impact when played as ballads. So here is 'Bäru' as a ballad. Djirikitj … Wa.

BANBIRRNU

Before I knew what this song was about I turned to Gurrumul one day and said I wanted it to be sung at my funeral. I was also with his brothers that day, and I was surprised that they were upset. Later, when recording the song, I found out its meaning and realised why they were upset. It is a funeral song and they thought I was dying. Written by Johnathon Yunupiṇu, Gurrumul's cousin and co-songwriter, and in many respects an equally emotive singer as Gurrumul, the chord structure of this song always reminds me of those classic, cyclical songs, which is ironic.

GURRUMUL HISTORY

This is one of the few songs Gurrumul performs in English, and is one of the few 'contemporary' style songs. It gives the listener an insight into a little of Gurrumul's personal world, and his feelings, which you wouldn't experience otherwise. We always choose to end his concerts with this song. This version features the string quartet accompanying Gurrumul, the guitars and bass.

WIYATHUL

The humming at the start of this song captivates many people. It was a song I kept being drawn to as an opener for his debut solo CD *Gurrumul*, and I am so glad we decided to do this. 'Wiyathul' captures the essence of the emotion in Gurrumul's songs and what he is singing about. It is a song about longing, about nostalgia, and about connection that Yolŋu still have to place. In this recording the strings add another sonic and textural layer with the string quartet parts written by Erkki Veltheim.

BAKITJU

This song first appeared earlier in Gurrumul's career when he recorded it with the Saltwater Band. It's very much a song of identity, this time about a sacred rock called Bakitju. Gurrumul's family have sung this song hundreds of times, but the traditional version has been told thousands of times. Gurrumul's introduction and his piano on this version, feels alone and unique to me, and the track is mixed more atmospherically than the version on *Rrakala*.

MARRANDIL

A long song, probably seven or eight minutes duration, this song is about a place that is special to Gurrumul's family. I remember the first time we heard this song, Gurrumul played an acoustic version into our laptop, at Point Stuart, with his Uncle Djamina close by, and it sounded as strong and beautiful as it does here. The track has the feel of a lilting waltz, and with the perfect string arrangements by Erkki, it carries the listener across the sea and away to the islands north of Elcho without even realising it. This version, unlike the album version, is so stripped back, it reminds me of the first time I heard it.

WARWU

This is a song about worry, but not about sadness. It is about emotional connection to the spirit of the land. 'Warwu' was the first song of Gurrumul's to make me cry, and it was because of the way he sang his harmonies. The song is an emotional treatise about connection with each other and worrying about each other, which is almost all I hear and feel, without speaking the language fluently. This song is again mixed more ethereally than on *Rrakala*.